D1187377

New Directions in Educational Psychology: 2. Behaviour and Motivation in the Classroom

New Directions in Educational Psychology: 2. Behaviour and Motivation in the Classroom

Edited and
Introduced by

Nigel Hastings and Josh Schwieso
Bulmershe College of Higher Education

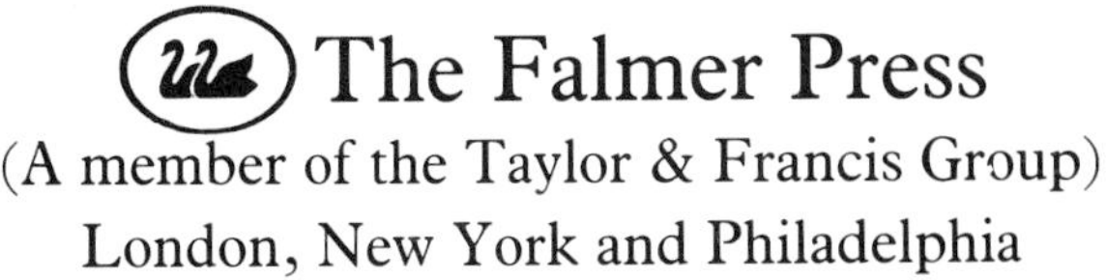

(A member of the Taylor & Francis Group)
London, New York and Philadelphia

UK The Falmer Press, Falmer House, Barcombe, Lewes, East Sussex, BN8 5DL

USA The Falmer Press, Taylor & Francis Inc., 242 Cherry Street, Philadelphia, PA 19106-1906

First published 1987

Library of Congress Cataloguing in Publication Data is available on request

ISBN 1-85000-228-2
ISBN 1-85000-229-0 (pbk.)

Jacket design by Leonard Williams

Typeset in 10½/12 Plantin by
Imago Publishing Ltd, Thame, Oxon

Printed in Great Britain by Taylor & Francis (Printers) Ltd, Basingstoke

Contents

Acknowledgements

The Publishers are grateful to the following for permission to reproduce copyright material.

The editors and publishers of *Educational Psychology* and Dr Ted Glynn for: GLYNN, T. (1985) 'Contexts for independent learning', *Educational Psychology*, 5, 1, pp. 5–15.

The editors are extremely grateful to Dr Frank Merrett for compiling the index.

General Editor's Preface

This is the companion volume to *New Directions in Educational Psychology 1: Learning and Teaching* and, as did its predecessor, it addresses issues which daily confront teachers; issues of behaviour and motivation, order and discipline. In addition, it examines the ways in which teachers give meaning to the life of the classroom; meanings which enable them to develop coping strategies.

All fifteen contributions are original and written by acknowledged authorities. Each provides a valuable conspectus of an issue of concern to the practising teacher and a useful bibliography. In fact, together, the fifteen chapters of the book make both an excellent textbook *and* a work of reference. The credit for accomplishing this twin task so very well must go to the Editors, as must the credit for sensing so well the salient issues which confront teachers in the classroom. The Editors must also be congratulated on demonstrating how much psychology has to offer in the explication of practical educational issues and problems. This has been needed for some time.

Finally, this and its companion volume stand witness to the intellectual understanding available in the service of teaching; understanding which, to paraphrase William James in his classic, *Talks to Teachers on Psychology*, 'May save us from mistakes and put theory into our practice'.

Philip Taylor
Birmingham
June 1987

Introduction: Behaviour and Motivation

Nigel Hastings and Josh Schwieso

Generations of teachers in training have studied aspects of educational psychology as part of their courses. Some have found the subject to be of considerable intellectual interest, but many have felt a degree of frustration at the way a discipline which, on the face of it, ought to have so much to offer teachers, seems to yield few clear cut findings or theories which have obvious and unqualified implications for classroom practice. The study of children's intellectual and social development, of language and thought, of social relationships and personality would seem almost bound to be of direct value to those whose work is, or is to be, teaching. Yet frustration with the lack of apparent utility of what they have learned has been a common outcome for the student.

How can this feeling be explained? How can this apparent failing of educational psychology be accounted for or justified? A full exploration of these questions is more than we can attempt in the space we have available — even supposing that it is within our competence — but there are aspects of these questions which have been of concern to us in compiling this volume. By exploring briefly one or two points which arise from the perhaps unduly pessimistic scenario we have portrayed, we hope to explain the purpose of this collection of recent contributions to educational psychology.

When psychology emerged as a discrete discipline in the last century, high hopes were held of it by many involved in education. If the ways in which children learn could be understood, then teachers could surely tailor their methods to match those ways. If the bases of human motivation could be disclosed, then teachers could surely foster those dispositions that were noble and develop ways of containing or redirecting those that were malevolent or unwholesome. If the factors which enable potential to flourish could be discovered, then teachers could surely employ them. Beliefs of this sort were among those that were held at the time, despite the notes of caution struck by some psychologists, and were often held in vain, then and now.

The generation of such high expectations for educational psychology rests on a belief which is commonly held about the relationship between scientific understanding on the one hand and practice on the other. Expressed succinctly, the belief is that action follows from theoretical understanding. That this is not the case in most aspects of the social sciences is soon discovered by student teachers, but it is not well appreciated that it is not even generally true of the 'harder' sciences either where, for many centuries, machines and techniques ran well ahead of scientific understanding. All sorts of procedures were found to 'work' with only the vaguest idea of how or why. In the case of physics, for instance, it is only relatively recently that knowledge derived from the discipline has been of direct value in informing what we tend to refer to as 'technology' (Fores and Rey, 1979; Hastings and Schwieso, 1981).

The expectation that scientific research will inform practice also presupposes that this is a prime objective of a science. While it may be one aim, or hope, the main purpose of any science is to describe and generate understanding, expressed in the form of theories, of those phenomena with which it is concerned. Similarly, the prime objective of psychology as a science has generally been taken to be to generate understanding, not to change or influence things. This is not to say that understandings or theories about how things happen as they do may not be helpful in generating hunches about what to do in particular circumstances, merely that it is not the central purpose of any science and consequently not the main criterion by which it should be judged.

If this is accepted to be the case for psychology, it might still be argued that educational psychology is different in that its concerns lie within a field of practice. However, a review of the research published over the last fifty years or so in volumes or journals bearing the words 'educational psychology' in their titles would reveal that much of the work has been concerned more with the development of understanding than with informing practice in any direct way; that much of it was not conducted in schools; that the questions to which the research was directed arose not from the concerns of those working in schools so much as from theoretical debates; and that most of it was published in contexts and forms which were far from accessible to the average teacher. This is demonstrated in the approach taken in many of the better known student textbooks on educational psychology over recent decades, which has been first to review psychological research and then to apply it to educational contexts. In short, educational psychology has proceeded on the assumption that practice will be informed by the parent scientific discipline.

In the long run, it may well turn out this way. As with physics and other hard sciences, it may be that as our understanding of things develops and becomes more precise, so it will serve us better in informing decisions about teaching. In the meantime, however, we can discern a noticeable trend in educational psychology. In the relatively recent past, the amount of research conducted in classrooms has increased. The starting point of more research can be seen to lie in the practical concerns of teachers and schools; a more modest approach is evident, attempting to describe carefully what happens in schools before leaping to prescriptions, but with a greater concern for the potential practical implications. Educational psychology has moved closer to the concerns of teachers; it has moved more into their classrooms and it is demonstrating a greater concern with its practical value. Rather than seeking simply to draw upon the concerns and methods of psychology, its parent discipline, educational psychology now derives more of its concerns from those of schools and teachers.

In speaking of practical value, however, we need to be clear what forms this can take. Any belief that empirical research will yield findings from which could be deduced exactly what should be done in any particular context, is fundamentally flawed. For example, even if we knew precisely and irrefutably how children's moral reasoning developed, such knowledge would not prescribe *what* we should teach. At best, it might indicate how we might most effectively teach whatever it is that we decide to teach, but even this would be subject to our judgments about whether these methods were morally acceptable. In other words, while research may inform educational decisions by indicating what is possible and what is more, or less, effective, it cannot, in any circumstances, alone determine what should be done: value judgments are involved.

While factual information is of value and relevance to most decisions about what to do in particular educational contexts, clear and dependable information about what is the case is rarely available from educational research of any type. Research is always conducted in selected contexts and generalizations are made about what would be the case in other, broadly similar contexts. No laws have been discovered which we can trust to be applicable in all contexts. Judgments have to be made about the likelihood of what was found to be the case 'over there' being true 'over here'. If it was found to be so in a number of situations, so our confidence may increase in its being the case 'over here'. In this way, we can see that the value of educational psychology lies not in the disclosure of transportable facts, so much as in the raising of awareness about what *might* be the case in a given situation; about what *might* work here as it did there. In some areas, sound hunches can now be derived from research about what might be helpful. We have in mind particularly work within the areas of applied behaviour analysis and social skills training in education, which is now sufficiently substantial to provide clear indications about how certain sorts of things can be done or achieved. Even here, however, what is to be gained from research findings is not pre-packaged kits for instant use, but empirically justified guidance about how a situation might most profitably be approached.

In summary, it is our view that recent developments in educational psychology have reflected a change in the belief that research designed to generate understanding of psychological processes *per se* will yield findings that can be memorized as 'tips for teachers' and applied without any regard for the details of the particular situation — if this was ever generally believed. Increasingly, educational psychology is concerned with those issues which confront teachers, with investigating them in the contexts in which they arise, and with a view of the potential value of its activities being to inform hypotheses about what might apply in given situations. This does not mean that we think educational psychology has become a service industry and abandoned attempts at generating theories to account for its findings, merely that this has become a less prominent aim.

How does all this relate to the contents of this volume? We think it relates in three ways. Firstly, it has informed the general focus of the book; secondly, it has guided our choice and commissioning of articles, and, thirdly, it has led us to formulate a view about the ways in which we hope you, the reader, will find it both of interest and of value. We will consider each of these in turn.

Words used within psychology often mean something slightly different from what they mean in everyday usage. Behaviour and motivation are two such words. Within psychology, behaviour is usually taken to mean anything that a person does. Thus, saying 'Hello', playing football, passing the salt, waving goodbye, kissing, making a model and turning off the television are all behaviours. What they have in common is the fact that they are observable by another person, whereas imagining, thinking, feeling pain and dreaming are not, and are therefore not described within psychology as behaviours. This is not at all what teachers mean in the staffroom when they refer to children's behaviour. Behaviour in this context, as in most others, refers to conduct. It has to do with compliance with social conventions. Usually, when children's behaviour is discussed it is because it is a matter of some concern; they are not behaving appropriately.

Similarly, the word motivation has a different meaning in the school staffroom from those it has within psychology. For many years, motivation was one of psychology's main concerns. All behaviour was considered to be motivated in that it had direction and energy, and much research energy was directed towards trying to disclose the bases of human motivations within biological needs. Over recent decades, however, the psychologist's conception of motivation has developed in a way that has brought it closer to its everyday meaning. When we ask about someone's motivation for, say, applying for a job, we expect an answer to be expressed in terms of reasons, expectations and consequences. We expect the answer to tell us something about the person's understandings, present situation, his view of himself, ambitions and so on. It is to factors such as these that psychological study of motivation in education has turned.

In the context of school, motivation generally refers to children's attitudes and approaches to school work. When teachers express concern about motivating their pupils, they are considering the ways in which the curriculum and their teaching methods provide interest, worthwhile outcomes, satisfaction and enjoyment. Similarly, when discussing an individual child who 'lacks motivation', concern is being expressed about the way in which the child in question appears to find little of value in school work and possibly more in activities which are incompatible with it.

Children whose behaviour is causing their teachers concern often turn out to be children whose motivation for school work is also causing concern. Indeed, in educational contexts, behaviour and motivation are often considered as two sides of the same coin, or as mutually influential aspects. It is sometimes suggested that pupils are poorly behaved *because* they are poorly motivated or that they are poorly motivated *because* they are poorly behaved. Whether such causal attributions get us very far is another matter; the point is that behaviour and motivation, as the terms are used in school, are seen as related.

In compiling this volume, we have had in mind the school staffroom usage of the terms behaviour and motivation, rather than the meanings they have within psychology. However, although the words have different meanings in the two contexts, they are not entirely unrelated, as is evident in some of the articles that follow.

Children's behaviour and motivation in school are areas of major importance to those involved in education, particularly for teachers, as the opening chapters of this book indicate. Moreover, they are areas of educational psychology in which recent developments hold great promise. However, factors which relate to children's behaviour and motivation in school have been the subject of considerable research activity within education for many years. It has long been known, for instance, that pupil performance and motivation are related to parental interest and various socioeconomic indices. Similarly, conduct, as evidenced in measures of delinquency, for instance, is known to relate to aspects of family and other social relationships. Findings such as these are now part of popular understanding. Unfortunately, one effect of this knowledge has been to suggest that what happens *in* school has little or no effect on children's behaviour or motivation. That this is not true is amply demonstrated by recent studies, but it is still a point which needs to be made. The finding that factors external to schools and classrooms influence children's behaviour and motivation within them, does not mean that factors within schools and classrooms have no, or even little, influence.

This common distinction between *within-school* and *without-school* factors is not merely of value for research purposes. It has important practical value. Schools as institutions and teachers as individuals have potentially much greater influence on what happens within school than they do on what happens within the wider community or within individual children's domestic lives — at least in the short term. For this reason, all of the papers included in this book have the exploration of what happens *within* school and of the ways in which school and classroom organization and interaction relate to behaviour and motivation, as the main focus of their concern. By not including articles which review or report research on factors external to school we are not intending to imply that these issues are of little significance. The decision is based on the pragmatic point that teachers have greater potential control over what happens within schools than without.

Reports of research in educational psychology, as in any discipline, are often fairly technical in nature and are not easy to make sense of without a fairly sophisticated knowledge of research methodology. This made our task difficult, for we have been determined that this collection should be readable by those without detailed knowledge of research procedures. Depressingly little published work in which recent developments in educational psychology are reported or discussed meets this criterion. Consequently, all but one of the articles have been specifically commissioned and written for this collection by people whom we judged to be working in and knowledgeable about the most recent and relevant work in the areas of behaviour and motivation in schools.

We have already discussed the ways in which educational psychology can be of benefit to education. In compiling this collection we have had individual classroom teachers in mind, rather than, say, educational policy makers, and have included articles which we judge to be of potential interest and value to them. The value of these chapters lies in the ways in which their consideration can stimulate informed reflection on, and appraisal of, current practices and in the justification and encouragement they provide for innovation. Together, the contributors amply demonstrate the new directions which educational psychology is taking in addressing, understanding and informing thought and practice in relation to behaviour and motivation in schools.

References

FORES, M. and REY, L. (1979) 'Technik: The relevance of a missing concept', *Higher Education Review*, 11, pp. 43–57.

HASTINGS, N. and SCHWIESO, J. (1981) 'Social technik: Reconstruing the relationship between psychological theory and professional training and practice', *Oxford Review of Education*, 7, 3, pp. 223–9.

1
Teachers' Classroom Concerns

Introduction

In this section we present three papers, all based on empirical research about what problems teachers face in their classrooms. First, Simon Veenman provides an international perspective on what concerns teachers about *teaching*. From a review of ninety-five surveys of the classroom worries of novice teachers, he confirms that classroom discipline and motivation are their most common concerns. Of course, many of the issues that worry beginning teachers give difficulty even to experienced teachers. Nevertheless Veenman suggests that as teachers gain experience the concern with discipline and motivation is supplanted by an emphasis upon relating to children as individuals. That is, teacher priorities move from simply surviving as, and being seen to be, a teacher to being an educator in a more traditional and liberal sense of the word.

The chapter by Ron Dawson shifts the emphasis to a more limited issue, that of the sorts of *pupils* who cause serious concern to teachers. His research in a large conurbation in Northern England suggested that some six per cent of pupils were causing great concern to their teachers. With respect to the problems identified, conduct problems ranked second after learning difficulties, being characteristic of one quarter of the children with problems. Dawson's figures provide both confirmation and disconfirmation of common stereotypes. For example, though most of the children with conduct disorders were boys, secondary school girls were reported more often than boys for both conduct and attendance problems. In passing, it should be said that the fact that Dawson's teachers cited only six per cent of children as causing serious concern does not necessarily conflict with the higher levels of incidence of children with problems or special needs that are often given by authorities such as the Warnock Report. Dawson's emphasis was on *serious* concern at one point in time whereas other estimates typically include any child considered to have some special need at any time in their school career.

Merrett and Wheldall's focus is more precise still, being the specific *classroom behaviours* that concern teachers. They argue that these fall into two categories. In the first there are those rare incidents which excite the popular press, the high intensity, low frequency outrages such as stabbings. The second comprises those ongoing irritations of everyday classroom life, the 'low intensity, high frequency' events such as calling out, looking out of the window and so on. Their paper, based upon recent research, suggests that in both primary and secondary schools the behaviours that are the most troublesome and the most frequently occurring, as far as teachers are concerned, are talking out of turn, hindering other children, not attending and disobedience. These are, of course, of low intensity. Serious, high-intensity misdemeanours such as physical aggression are very rare. From this sort of evidence it would seem that the average teacher is more likely to suffer from exhaustion or frustration at the amount of time wasted on nagging than from physical violence by disaffected or emotionally disturbed pupils.

Problems as Perceived by New Teachers

S.A.M. Veenman
University of Nijmegen

> How to express the quality of his teaching? A thorough mastery of his subjects, an inexhaustible sympathy for the scholastic underdog, a unique ability to make unexpected connexions and to mix in an always fresh and eye-opening way the stuff of lessons with the stuff of life, an effortless humour, a by no means negligible gift for dramatization, a restless and doubting temperament that urged him forward ceaselessly toward self-improvement in the pedagogic craft — these are only parts of the whole. What endures, perhaps, most indelibly in the minds of his ex-students (of whom this present writer counts himself one) was his more-than-human selflessness, a total concern for the world at large which left him, perhaps, too little margin for self-indulgence and satisfied repose. To sit under Mr Caldwell was to lift one's head in aspiration. (John Updike, *The Centaur*)

This picture of Mr Caldwell, as evoked by the prose writer John Updike, may be characterized as an end state in the professional development of becoming a teacher. For many beginning teachers this end state will be a far ideal if they reflect on their first days in the profession. What they dreamed about becoming a teacher paled before the difficulties of adjusting to the role of teacher. Expectations clashed with the hard reality in schools. For most new teachers, the first year is difficult. For some, it is a very traumatic year. The transition from teacher training to the first teaching post is often referred to as the 'reality shock'.

Reality Shock

In general, this concept is used to indicate the collapse of the missionary ideals formed during teacher training by the harsh and rude reality of everyday classroom life.

It has been shown in studies of both primary and secondary teachers in different countries that newly trained teachers experience significant shifts in their attitudes. Students become increasingly idealistic, progressive, or liberal in their attitudes towards education and pupils during their preservice training and then shift to opposing or more traditional, conservative, or custodial views as they move into teaching practice and the first years of teaching (e.g. Dann, Müller-Fohrbrodt and Cloetta, 1981; Hanson and Herrington, 1976; Lacey, 1977; Lagana, 1970; McArthur, 1981; Olgers and Riesenkamp, 1980). In most studies the notion of reality shock is seen as a change in attitudes, as the adoption of the traditional, conservative ways of the schools. The reality shock is rated negatively, because the 'innovative competence' aimed at by the colleges of teacher education is lost in the first year of teaching. However, a more realistic view of the teaching task may be a healthy outcome of the process of confrontation between ideals and reality.

Three remarks must be made about these findings on changes in attitudes. First, liberalization is a general effect of higher education and not particularly an effect of teacher education. If a revision of attitudes takes place it is a general phenomenon at the entry to each career and is not restricted only to teachers.

Second, the change in attitudes does not follow the same pattern for all groups of beginning teachers, but depends in part on personal variables, on preferences for particular subject matter areas, on the quality of teacher training and on situational characteristics of the workplace.

Third, most studies of attitude changes seem to suggest that the impact of teacher education is 'washed out' by everyday experience in the schools. Others, such as Zeichner and Tabachnik (1985), call into question the commonly accepted view of an inevitable loss of idealism during induction into teaching. In a two-year longitudinal study of the development of teaching perspectives by four beginning teachers, they found that a loss of idealism is not an inevitable result of induction into teaching and the efforts of formal teacher preparation programmes are not necessarily in vain. The induction of beginning teachers appeared to be highly context specific, related in each instance to unique interactions of persons (who possess varying levels of skills and capabilities) and school contexts (which differ in the constraints and opportunities for action they present to beginning teachers). Both views, loss or sustaining of idealism, have some credibility.

Ryan (1979) offers the following speculations about the problems of beginning teachers as a group: teachers have difficulty in their first year because they are essentially undertrained for the demands of their work; the absence of clear selection criteria in teacher training; and beginning teachers are not trained for specific jobs in specific schools, they have had a general training. Besides, the beginning teacher is isolated from other teachers. In most schools there is one teacher per classroom. Teachers do not see one another teach. If beginning teachers need immediate help from colleagues or expert teachers, they cannot get it. The cellulár organization of schools (Lortie, 1975) constrains the amount and type of interchange of experience and advice.

The possible causes of reality shock are described here to sketch a frame of reference for the perceived problems of beginning teachers in their first year(s).

Problems of Beginning Teachers

Most research on beginning teachers has been focused on their problems. These problems have been studied since the turn of this century. Research on problems of beginning teachers is based on the assumption that knowledge of the most frequent problems of beginning teachers may provide important information for the improvement and (re)designing of preservice and inservice programmes and for improved supervision and induction practices. No teacher training institution can be indifferent to, or ignorant of, the problems their graduates encounter in their first teaching posts.

Several of these studies on problems of beginning teachers were conducted in the United Kingdom (Bradley and Eggleston, 1978; Clark and Nisbet, 1963; Cornwell, 1965; Cortis and Dean, 1969–70; Hanson and Herrington, 1976; Taylor and Dale, 1971). The latest study was conducted by Her Majesty's Inspectors in 1981. This study tried to assess how well newly trained teachers in general are equipped for the work they are assigned in their first posts and to judge the extent to which support is provided where it is needed (HMI, 1982). These studies are reviewed here in the context of an international perspective.

A total of 86 studies on the problems of beginning teachers were identified, all conducted after 1960. An account of this international literature-search and of the design of the sampling of problems was published in the journal *Review of Educational Research* (Veenman, 1984). (For the purpose of this article the list of 83 studies was extended to 86 studies, three new studies being added: Echternacht (1981), Jordell (1985), Sheridan and Pyra (1975)). Of these 86 studies, 56 were from the United States, 7 from West Germany, 6 from the United Kingdom, 5 from the Netherlands, 4 from Australia, 3 from Canada, 2 from Switzerland, 1 from Finland and 1 from Norway. All studies were based on empirical research.

Most studies in the sample used the questionnaire method, more specifically a rating scale. A minority of the studies used interviews, observations or essays. Studies with notes from diaries from beginning teachers with reflections on their first year(s) of teaching were excluded, although some of them are important because they portray some real life aspects of the young teachers (e.g., Hannam, Smyth and Stephenson, 1976; Ryan, 1970, 1980). A problem was defined as a difficulty that beginning teachers encounter in the performance of their task, which hinders the achievement of intended goals. Beginning teachers were defined as teachers who had not yet completed three years of teaching after qualifying as teachers.

To identify the most serious problems of beginning teachers a list was compiled of the most frequently mentioned problems. From each study the 15 most serious problems were selected and classified according to their importance and rank ordered. In total 68 different problems were identified. The results of this analysis were grouped into three categories to identify differences between school levels: primary education, secondary education and primary and secondary education (if no distinction between school levels was made). Studies that made a distinction between problems of beginning teachers in primary schools and in secondary schools were counted twice, so that the total amount of studies was 95.

The results of these 95 studies are summarized in Table 1. The first three columns refer to all the studies reviewed, the remaining ones of various subsamples of them. The *rank* of a problem is based on the number of times a problem was mentioned in the sampled studies; the raw figures are given in the *frequency* column. Those studies that did mention a problem were scored according to how serious they rated it to be. The *median* gives an indication of how serious the problem was seen to be across these studies that mentioned it. (The median is the number that divides the ranked figures into halves such that half the scores are larger than the median and half are smaller. The original scoring ranged from 15, for the most serious problem, to 1, for the least serious. In Table 1 this scoring has been reversed so that median figures like those of frequency ranking are in descending order of seriousness.)

As shown in Table 1, *classroom discipline* is the most seriously perceived problem area of beginning teachers. Two remarks must be made. First, not all beginning teachers experience problems with classroom discipline. In the sampled studies the percentage of beginning teachers with discipline problems varies from 12 per cent to 83 per cent. But in nearly all studies this problem ranks first. Second, class discipline is not an unambiguous concept. What is called discipline or order by one teacher may be called disorder by another teacher and vice versa. For beginning teachers, experienced teachers, heads of school, administrators, inspectors, parents and pupils the content of this concept may differ. Labels like classroom discipline and classroom management may be regarded as code words for a whole host of specific difficulties and point to kinds of skills that beginning teachers usually lack and to needs they have for assistance (McDonald and Elias, 1983). According to HMI (1982, p. 7) the factors most frequently associated with good classroom management were: 'A crisp, orderly, punctual start to the lesson with any necessary preparations completed before-

Table 1: List of the 24 Most Frequently Cited Problems of Beginning Teachers

Rank Order	Problems	All Studies		Primary School		Secondary School		Prim. and Sec. School	
		Freq.	Med.	Freq.	Med.	Freq.	Med.	Freq.	Med.
1	Classroom discipline	80	3	23	2.5	24	2.5	33	3.5
2	Motivating pupils	49	3	11	4	17	2	21	4
3	Dealing with individual differences	44	3	15	4	13	2	16	4
4.5	Assessing pupils' work	33	6	10	6	8	7	15	5
4.5	Relations with parents	33	7	11	4.5	5	10	17	7
6.5	Organization of class work	27	3.5	10	3.2	2	2.2	15	5
6.5	Insufficient materials and supplies	29	5	9	3	7	6	13	6.5
8	Dealing with problems of individual pupils	27	3.5	7	5	9	3.5	11	3
9	Heavy teaching load resulting in insufficient prep. time	26	4.2	6	3.5	8	7.2	12	4
10	Relations with colleagues	25	8	6	6.7	8	5.5	11	10
11	Planning of lessons and schooldays	24	4.7	7	5	4	3.5	13	5
12	Effective use of different teaching methods	21	4	5	3.5	6	4.5	10	3.7
13	Awareness of school policies and rules	19	5	6	5.5	5	2.5	8	5
14	Determining learning level of pupils	18	4.5	4	2.7	7	6	7	5
16	Knowledge of subject matter	15	5	5	5	5	5	5	7.5
16	Burden of clerical work	15	7	4	5	1	9	10	7
16	Relations with principals/administrators	16	7.2	4	7.5	5	10	7	7
18	Inadequate school equipment	14	5	6	5.5	2	4.7	6	5
19	Dealing with slow learners	13	4	3	5	6	4	4	3
20	Dealing with pupils of different cultures and deprived backgrounds	12	7	3	13	2	7	7	7
21	Effective use of textbooks and curriculum guides	11	7.5	3	9.5	2	2	6	8.2
22	Lack of spare time	11	5	1	11	3	6	7	5
23	Inadequate guidance and support	9	8	2	6.2	1	2	6	8
24	Large class size	8	6.5	3	7	0	—	5	6
Number of studies		N = 95		N = 29		N = 29		N = 37	

Note: This table was adapted from: Veenman, S. (1984) 'Perceived problems of beginning teachers', *Review of Educational Research*, 54, pp. 143–78. For the purpose of this article three additional studies were included.

hand, and a planned and tidy ending, an assured manner, good use of the eye and voice and the giving, where necessary, of clear instructions by the teacher.'

Motivation of pupils is the second highest ranked problem in the view of beginning teachers. Table 1 shows a clear difference between school levels. Beginning secondary teachers report more problems with motivating pupils than beginning primary teachers. The beginning teacher often thinks that pupils are eagerly waiting to be instructed, that they are highly motivated. This image soon appears to be not correct. This misunderstanding can in part be attributed to the training institutions. There is a tendency of teacher educators to describe pupils as they would like them to be rather than as they are. Teacher preparation tends to deal with what ought to be going on in schools rather than what is actually happening (Ryan, 1970). This tension between what should be and what is has to be solved by the beginning teachers. Most of them are forced to reshape their ideals and standards. Studies in attitude change point to a 'curve of disenchantment'. Data on truancy and school absenteeism, dropouts, vandalism, teacher stress and teacher burn-out suggest that motivation is a problem at our schools. It is not easy to be a beginning teacher nowadays. A grim labour market with restricted job possibilities for school leavers, cuts in financial budgets, a greater emphasis on leisure activities, the influence of the mass media and changed family conditions may all contribute to the problem of motivation at school. The beginning teacher may profit from existing (psychological) theories of motivation (for example, attribution theory, achievement motivation, reinforcement theory), but in most instances the problem of motivation can be dealt with only at the level of the school (for example, adaptive education, pupils planning and evaluating their own learning, tutorial guidance, small group instruction, cooperative learning situations).

Dealing with individual differences among pupils is the third most frequently mentioned problem. Again, the difference between ideal education (the continuing development of the learning potential of each pupil) and what goes on in schools (dealing with class diversity so that instruction can be workable) is great. Adapting instruction to individual differences proves to be difficult in a classroom with 25–30 pupils.

Assessing pupils' work and *relations with parents* are the fourth and fifth most frequently mentioned problems. Accumulating reliable information and acting as an evaluator are problematic activities. On the one hand, schools are supposed to stimulate the unique capacities of each pupil to their full potential, on the other hand schools are supposed to socialize pupils and prepare them for roles in the society by processes of selection and role allocation. This discrepancy gives rise to problems. Adapting instruction to individual needs and pupils' assessment are at about the same level of ranked problems.

The problematic relationship with parents has several aspects. Beginning teachers complain about inadequate preparation for establishing and maintaining proper relationships with the pupils' parents. Contacting parents and the organization of parents' nights are difficulties. Furthermore, beginning teachers complain about parents' insufficient support for their ideas and about parents' inadequate interest in the well-being of their children at school. Many complaints are also directed at parents' lack of confidence in the beginning teachers' competence. An observational study by McIntosh suggests that parents placed pressure on beginning elementary teachers through phone calls and comments made during visits to the school. 'The parents tend to emphasize the value of traditional academic work, and to indicate support for quiet and order in the classroom' (McIntosh, 1977, p. 3193).

Because Table 1 is fairly self-explanatory, I will not discuss the remaining problems. In addition to the problems listed in this table, the following were reported in the sampled studies: doubts and worries about own competence, inexperience with audio-visual aids, relationships with pupils, relationships with the school community, insufficient preparation for the job of teaching. All these problems were mentioned frequently.

Another difficulty which surprises many beginning teachers is that teaching is a physically exhausting job. In our research 90 per cent of the beginning teachers felt exhausted. The heavy teaching load caused different physical complaints, among which the abnormal need to sleep was the most prominent one. One beginning teacher stated: '. . . I had to go home at 4 o'clock in the afternoon and go to bed. I slept until 6 o'clock, then I had dinner and went to bed again. Oh, how tired I was! That's indescribable. I've never felt like that before. Once it got so serious that I went to see a doctor. I really began to worry about my health' (Veenman, Berkelaar and Berkelaar, 1983, p. 32).

Ryan (1980, p. 7) offers a suggestion as to why exhaustion of this magnitude is commonly reported. 'One reason is that new teachers are not in a condition for the physical and mental demands of teaching. They are not prepared for the strain of being in command, of being responsible for so many people for so long each day.' After a while, however, teachers become toughened to the routine of school.

A side-effect of the physical strain was that their private relationships suffered. Exhaustion was sometimes accompanied by feelings of failure, insecurity and depression: 'I felt very strongly at the beginning of the school year that it was a disaster for my thirty children that I was their teacher. It was very depressing' (Veenman *et al.*, 1983, p. 32). Teacher training cannot fully prepare students for the exhaustion of the first weeks of teaching.

Views of Heads and Experienced Teachers

In many of the studies reviewed, not only new teachers, but also their heads, expressed their views. In the heads' reports problems of beginning teachers with class discipline get a high priority. Successes in teaching are often seen in terms of discipline. Furthermore, many parents view the head as a person who is primarily responsible for the discipline at school. Besides class discipline, beginning teachers, according to their heads, primarily have problems in dealing with differences between pupils, motivating pupils, teaching slow learners, organizing classes, assessing pupils' progress, and devising schemes of work.

To see the problems of beginning teachers in the right perspective, it must be noted that even experienced teachers have difficulties with several of the identified problem areas. In several studies from different countries (Veenman, 1984) experienced teachers report the following problems: too large classes, lack of interest from parents, discipline problems, extra-school obligations, inadequate teaching materials, overloaded teaching task, too many administrative duties, motivating pupils. These problems are listed here to illustrate that not only beginners experience problems and that these problems are not linked solely with the entrance into the profession. They do not suggest that these problems are unsolvable or that it is not necessary to take formal steps to induct new members into the teaching profession. New teachers experience difficulties and need help in their first years of teaching.

However, one should not conclude from this list of problems that beginning teachers are discontented with their working conditions or that they are dissatified with their jobs. In several studies from different countries about 80 per cent or more of beginning teachers are satisfied with their jobs, see, for example, HMI (1982). This level of satisfaction is, as the inspectorate notes, influenced by the circumstances which surround the first post, including relief at finding a job at all. The support the probationers received from the head and members of staff, the availability of advice from school, the quality of relationships with head and colleagues, all tended to enhance the new teachers' satisfaction with their jobs. There was also an association between the probationers' satisfaction and both the schools' judgment of their effectiveness and HMI's assessment of their mastery of teaching skills: the better equipped teacher was the happier teacher. Both primary and secondary teachers were most satisfied when the school provided conditions which encouraged their full professional development.

Concluding Remarks

The ninety-five studies reviewed in this article, as summarized in Table 1, vary with regard to national and regional school systems, teacher preparation programmes and the working environments of beginning teachers. Despite these differences the problems of beginning teachers in general are similar. This suggests that the problems of new teachers are almost universal. But the apparent universality of the problems also suggests that these problems cannot be attributed solely to personal characteristics of beginning teachers, to situational characteristics of the workplace and to deficiencies in teacher training. Of course, these factors must be acknowledged, but the results also point to factors beyond those of the individual person, school, teacher training programme and workplace. Factors inherently connected with the task of teaching a group of 20–25 pupils, with teaching as a profession and with the influence of that profession upon the person of the teacher, must be considered too, if one looks for solutions for these problems.

According to Lortie (1975, p. 58) the teaching profession has no codified body of knowledge and skills: 'No way has been found to record and crystallize teaching for the benefit of beginners'. The effect is that personal experience, in the form of learning while doing, is seen as the most important source for the acquisition of knowledge and skills. This status of the profession has consequences for teacher education and entrance into the profession. Teacher education is characterized by little competition and selection, and the educational programme, compared with other professions, is not very complex with regard to intellectual demands and organizational features. Entry into the profession is very sudden: from one day to the next the beginning teacher has the same responsibility as a teacher with forty years of service. The beginning teacher is often thrown in at the deep end (the 'sink-or-swim' or Robinson Crusoe approach; Lortie, 1966). This is often reinforced by the cellular organization of the school, so that contacts between beginning teachers and their experienced colleagues are hampered during the school day (Lortie, 1975). When discussing the difficulties of beginning teachers one cannot overlook the status of teaching as an occupation.

The period of transition into teaching is the first stage in the process of becoming a teacher. From a developmental perspective the problems of beginning teachers may be regarded as necessary transitional states along the road to higher levels of performance. The developmental studies of the beginning teacher conducted by Fuller and Bown (1975) posit three distinguishable kinds and stages of concerns that are characteristic of teachers. The first phase involves survival concerns. These are concerns about one's adequacy and survival as a teacher, class control, being liked by pupils, and being evaluated. The second phase includes teaching situation concerns. These are concerns about limitations and frustrations in the teaching situation, methods and materials, and mastery of skills within the teaching-learning situation. The third phase reflects concerns about pupils, their learning, their social and emotional needs, and relating to pupils as individuals. Later concerns cannot emerge until earlier concerns are resolved. The experience of becoming a teacher involves coping with all the three stages. Addressing these concerns during training should increase teachers' feelings of adequacy.

Others factors determining the success of beginning teachers, apart from the quality of initial training, are the appropriateness of their appointment, the nature of the tasks the school has allocated them, the conditions under which they are carrying out those tasks, and the level and quality of support they are receiving from school and local education authority. Underlying all these are the personal qualities that the new teachers bring to their job (HMI, 1982). Taking all these factors into account, HMI rated over half of all newly trained teachers as well or very well equipped for their task and over three-quarters as adequately equipped or better. The heads of the schools considered an even higher proportion to be well prepared for teaching. HMI (1982) considered these findings 'very encouraging'. The findings are also encouraging when compared with those of the studies reviewed here on the problems of beginning teachers. A good initial training and sympathetic and sound support from school or LEA are significant elements in the effectiveness of teachers.

References

BRADLEY, H.W. and EGGLESTON, J.F. (1978) 'An induction year experiment', *Educational Research*, 20, pp. 89–98.

CLARK, R.P. and NISBET, J.D. (1963) *The First Two Years of Teaching*, Aberdeen, Department of Education.

CORNWELL, J. *et al.* (1965) *The Probationary Year*, University of Birmingham, Institute of Education.

CORTIS, G.A. and DEAN, A.J. (1969–1970) 'Teaching skills of probationary teachers', *Educational Research*, 12, pp. 230–4.

DANN, H.D., MÜLLER-FOHRBRODT, G. and CLOETTA, B. (1981) 'Sozialisation junger Lehrer im Buruf: "Praxisschock" drei Jahre später', *Zeitschrift für Entwicklungspsychologie und Pädagogische Psychologie*, 13, pp. 251–62.

ECHTERNACHT, L. (1981) 'Instructional problems of business teachers as perceived by first-year teachers and experienced teachers', *College Student Journal*, 15, pp. 352–8.

FULLER, F.F. and BOWN, O.H. (1975) 'Becoming a teacher', in RYAN, K. (Ed.), *Teacher Education* (Seventy-fourth Yearbook of the National Society for the Study of Education), Chicago, University of Chicago Press.

HMI, (1982) *The New Teacher in School*, London, Her Majesty's Stationery Office.

HANNAM, C., SMYTH, P. and STEPHENSON, N. (1976) *The First Year of Teaching*, Harmondsworth, Penguin Books.

HANSON, D. and HERRINGTON, M. (1976) *From College to Classroom: The Probationary Year*. London, Routledge and Kegan Paul.

JORDELL, K.O. (1985) 'Problems of beginning and more experienced teachers in Norway', *Scandinavian Journal of Educational Research*, 29, pp. 105–21.

LACEY, C. (1977) *The Socialization of Teachers*, London, Methuen.

LAGANA, J.F. (1970) *What Happens to the Attitudes of Beginning Teachers?* Danville, Ill, Interstate Printers.

LORTIE, D.C. (1966) 'Teacher socialization: The Robinson Crusoe Model', in *The Real World of the Beginning Teacher*, Washington, D.C., National Commission on Teacher Education and Professional Standards. (ERIC Document Reproduction Service No. ED 030 616)

LORTIE, D.C. (1975) *Schoolteacher: A Sociological Study*, Chicago, University of Chicago Press.

MCARTHUR, J. (1981) *The First Years of Teaching*, (ERIC Report No. 30). Canberra, Australian Government Publishing Service.

MCDONALD, F.J. and ELIAS, P. (1983) *The Transition into Teaching: The Problems of Beginning Teachers and Programs to Solve Them. Summary Report*. Berkeley, Calif., Educational Testing Service.

MCINTOSH, J.C. (1977) 'The first year of experience: Influence on beginning teachers', (Doctoral dissertation, University of Toronto, 1976), *Dissertation Abstracts International*, 38, pp. 3192–3.

OLGERS, A.J. and RIESENKAMP, J. (1980) *De Onderwijskundige Voorbereiding van Aanstaande Leraren*, (SVO-reeks no. 30). 's-Gravenhage, Staatsuitgeverij.

RYAN, K. (1970) *Don't Smile until Christmas: Accounts of the First Year of Teaching*, Chicago, University of Chicago Press.

RYAN, K. (1979) 'Toward understanding the problem: At the threshold of the profession', in HOWEY, K.R. and BENTS, R.H. (Eds), *Toward Meeting the Needs of the Beginning Teacher*, Lansing, Mich., Midwest Teacher Corps Network. (ERIC Document Reproduction Service No. ED 206 581)

RYAN, K. (Ed.) (1980) *Biting the Apple: Accounts of First Year Teachers*, New York, Longman.

SHERIDAN, D.P. and PYRA, J.F. (1975) 'Problems and self-concepts of beginning teachers', *Saskatchewan Journal of Educational Research and Development*, 5, pp. 30–7.

TAYLOR, J.K. and DALE, I.R. (1971) *A Survey of Teachers in their First Year of Service*, Bristol, University of Bristol, Institute of Education.

UPDIKE, J. (1978) *The Centaur*, Harmondsworth, Penguin Books.

VEENMAN, S. (1984) 'Perceived problems of beginning teachers', *Review of Educational Research*, 54, pp. 143–78.

VEENMAN, S., BERKELAAR, A. and BERKELAAR, J. (1983) 'Problemen van beginnende leraren in het basisonderwijs', *Pedagogische Studiën*, 60, pp. 28–37.

ZEICHNER, K.M. and TABACHNIK, B.R. (1985) 'The development of teacher perspectives: Social strategies and institutional control in the socialization of beginning teachers', *Journal of Education for Teaching*, 11, pp. 1–25.

What Concerns Teachers about their Pupils?

Ron Dawson
General Inspector for Special Needs, Staffordshire

Any attempt to identify what concerns teachers about their pupils from an examination of the daily offerings of the national press or broadcasting networks in this country over the past decade might lead to the conclusion that the total concerns of our teachers were, and perhaps are, focused entirely upon the twin aspects of disruptive and aggressive pupils. The accompaniment to the media 'hype' of these two aspects was the unprecedented upsurge in the number of publications describing, detailing, packaging, and prescribing what teachers have done and/or might do to their disruptive, aggressive, disturbing, violent or hyperactive pupils. These literary acknowledgements were supported and encouraged by a plethora of surveys and research projects, which in turn fed or were fed by the mushroom-like growth throughout the 1970s and early 1980s in the number of special classes and units for disruptive and aggressive pupils (Topping, 1983), collectively known at that time by the derogatory term 'sin-bins', a name now thankfully itself consigned to the waste bin.

Whether this rapid growth of special classes and units reflected a 'real' growth in the incidence of disruptive or aggressive incidents by pupils in schools or the wider society is unclear (see Pearson, 1983, for a good historical account of the societal aspects), but an investigation by the Schools Council Project on Disturbed Pupils into the nature of the problems presented by pupils attending these special classes and units suggested that at least 25 per cent of these pupils were perceived by their teachers as neither disruptive nor aggressive (Dawson, 1980). How far these perceptions of the special class and unit teachers coincided with, or differed from, those of the referring or placement agencies is unknown, but there has been a growing awareness over recent years that the perceptions and ratings by teachers of the difficulties and problems experienced and presented by their pupils can differ quite substantially, not only between teachers but also from 'objective assessments' of these same phenomena by outside or 'disinterested' observers. In their survey of disruptive incidents, Frude and Gault (1984) point out how a whole range of behaviours, together with their associated conveyed attitudes, may remain invisible to the casual observer, even though they are readily perceived and understood by teachers and other pupils, exert a powerful influence on the prevailing classroom atmosphere and play an important part in the 'social reality' of the classroom. Acknowledgement of the need to consider the social relativity, indeed the total context, of the deviant or disturbing characteristics of pupils, in order to help their teachers cope with them, must pay due cognizance to the prime importance of how teachers perceive their pupils and subsequently to the degree to which they become concerned about them.

It was from such a standpoint that, when the author was appointed to direct a research project within the Barnsley LEA (see Dawson, 1981) with a brief to help teachers to cope more effectively with the difficulties they experience, an investigation was carried out to identify what sort of pupil behaviours and difficulties were causing teachers concern.

The Investigation Sample

The investigation was undertaken by means of a survey. A random sample of ten of the Barnsley authority's secondary schools and twenty-three of their feeder primary schools were asked to take part. Of these schools, only one secondary and one primary did not respond and so, with the returns of one secondary school being lost in transit, the overall return for analysis was 91 per cent. The teachers taking part in the survey were asked simply to identify those children who were causing them an 'unusually high degree of concern' and, if possible, to indicate the area or areas in which the concern was rooted. The survey was therefore entirely open-ended, the teachers being allowed complete freedom of response. The difficulties of analysis associated with the use of open-ended questions were known, of course, but it was considered that this method would provide more valid and useful data than would data accrued from preconceived response structures imposed upon the teachers to facilitate easier analysis.

Findings

Responses were returned in reference to an estimated 10,645 pupils (nearly one quarter of the authority's total school population) and of these 649 (6 per cent) were identified as causing a high degree of concern to their teachers. 167 (26 per cent) of those pupils identified were girls. Nearly 40 per cent of the pupils identified (256, 39 per cent) had more than one area of concern specified. The percentage of pupils identified within each of the age bands, and the percentage of pupils in each age band with two or more areas specified, is shown in Figure 1. As can be seen, the two highest

Figure 1: Incidence of Pupils Identified as Causing a High Degree of Concern to their Teachers.

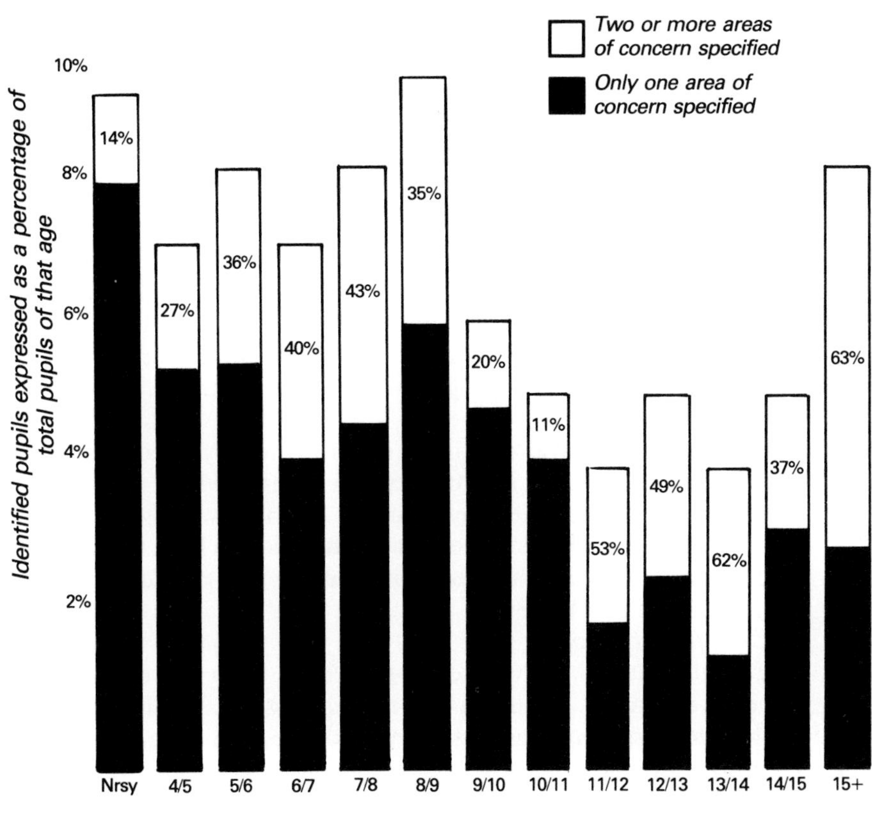

points are at the Nursery level and at the 8/9 age band with another peak following at 15+. It can also be seen that secondary school pupils are more likely to be causing a high degree of concern to their teachers in two or more areas than primary school pupils (53 per cent and 31 per cent respectively, $X^2 < .0001$).

The areas of concern specified were placed into ten basic categories plus a separate category for those responses not adequately described by one of those ten. The categories adopted were evolved both from the responses and from categories developed in other research studies (for example, the Isle of Wight studies (Rutter *et al.*, 1970)) and were as follows:

1 *Conduct Problems.*
This included such responses as 'aggressive behaviour', 'disruptive behaviour', 'lacks self control', 'uncooperative', 'foul-

mouthed'; that is, those responses referring to behaviours which reflect an outward going, acting out attitude.

2 *Neurotic Problems.*
This included responses such as 'withdrawn', 'insecure and miserable' and 'timid'; that is, behaviours which reflect an inward looking, passive attitude.

3 *Mixed Conduct/Neurotic Problems.*
This included those responses which embodied elements of both the conduct and neurotic problem categories. It was included because other researchers have concluded that a substantial percentage of behaviour disordered pupils show elements of both behavioural patterns (for example, in the IOW study 21 per cent were included in the group they termed mixed conduct/neurotic disorders), and a Schools Council Project, (Dawson, 1980) found that teachers in special classes and units for disturbed pupils rated 25 per cent of their pupils to be in this group.

4 *Non-attendance.*
This included those responses referring to any aspect of non-attendance and also included two responses which referred to extremely bad timekeeping. 'School phobia' was also included and, while it could be argued that it should have been recorded in category 9, it was included here because the problem is manifested in non-attendance.

5 *Delinquent Behaviour.*
This includes all of those responses which, at an appropriate age, could constitute a criminal act; this is to say that children below the age of criminal responsibility could be, and were, included.

6 *Learning Problems.*
This included responses such as 'poor attainment in basic subjects', 'low ability', 'poor concentration', 'lazy', and so on.

7 *Home Problems.*
This included responses referring to poor home situations, parental neglect, parental instability, parental imprisonment, absence, etc.

8 *Physical Problems.*
This included those responses referring to a directly physical problem (for example, asthma) and also to those in which a physical problem might be inferred (for example, visual problems, poor coordination, speech problems).

9 *Emotional Difficulties.*
This category was found necessary if the quality of certain responses was not to be lost. It included references to odd, strange or bizarre behaviour, for example, 'lives in a fantasy world', 'high evil resource', 'maladjusted, has attempted suicide,' 'unstable', 'no sense of right or wrong', 'never laughs'.

10 *Attention Seeking.*
This was included because a number of responses were expressed simply as 'attention seeking' with no indication of how this was manifested.

11 *Others.*
This took in all those responses which could not reasonably fit into the other categories, for example, 'victim of a sexual assault', 'unsettled', 'unpopular', 'general welfare'.

The vast majority of responses fitted quite easily into one or more of the categories. The response 'aggressive', for example, was easily counted as a 'conduct problem', and, although the response 'known thief; physically immature; truancy; always appears neglected' appears complex, four areas of concern were easily identified and could be located within the categories adopted. For others, however, it was more difficult to decide into which category they fitted most appropriately. For example, 'nuisance, one minor incident after another', might be considered as a conduct problem or attention seeking, or perhaps neither. In the event, it was classified as a conduct problem. The response 'brother of Wayne (2A)', however, was simply placed in the 'others' category.

Of the categories themselves, some are obviously more difficult to delineate than others; for example, compare 'emotional difficulties' with 'non-attendance'. Some categories have a greater conceptual space than others; that is, many more distinct behaviours might be encompassed by some than others. For example, 'learning problems' is perhaps able to include a much wider range of distinct behaviours than 'non-attendance'. Categorization, however, is necessary if one is to make any sense of a mass of accumulated information and must be utilized, however arbitrarily, at some time in all data analysis. The results should be viewed then with these dangers in mind and an overall 'feel' of the responses sought rather than simply taking the results as precise numerical measures of the types of problems causing Barnsley teachers a high degree of concern.

Before turning to discuss the results shown in Table 1, a brief explanation of how the results are presented is required. The percentages shown are percentages of all nominated children and not percentages of the number of areas of concern specified, or of the total number of children in the sample: they are percentages of the six per cent of children nominated. Consequently, as 39 per cent of the children nominated presented two or more areas of concern, the totals are not 100 per cent. The results are also deliberately presented in a non-ranked way to underline further that ranking on a quantitative basis should only be undertaken cautiously.

The overall pattern of distribution for the specified categories for boys and girls separately was generally similar to that shown in Table 1. There were, however, some exceptions which are of interest. Firstly, while only 9 per cent of all girls nominated in the primary school had conduct problems

Table 1: Percentage of Children Presenting a High Degree of Concern in the Specified Categories.

	Sample Mean Percentage	Primary Sch. Mean Percentage	Sec. Sch. Mean Percentage	Percentage with 2 or more areas specified
Category	(*N*-649)	(*N*-390)	(*N*-259)	
1 Conduct Problems	25	22	31*	62
2 Neurotic Problems	15	12	12	68
3 Mixed Conduct/Neurotic Problems	2	—	—	—
4 Non-attendance	15	3	33***	65
5 Delinquent Behaviour	5	1	11***	94
6 Learning Problems	37	47	26***	46
7 Home Problems	20	19	20	39
8 Physical Problems	16	20	10**	63
9 Emotional Difficulties	9	7	12	52
10 Attention Seeking	2	—	—	71
11 Others	—	—	—	—

* Chi squared probability < .01
** Chi squared probability < .001
*** Chi squared probability < .0001

specified, some 25 per cent of the boys nominated had symptoms falling into this category specified (X^2 $p < .05$). In the secondary schools, however, this situation was somewhat reversed and a greater percentage of nominated girls had symptoms in the conduct problems category specified than was the case for boys (39 per cent and 29 per cent respectively), although the difference between them was not significant.

In relation to non-attendance, the percentage of nominated girls in secondary schools also exceeded that for the boys (46 per cent and 29 per cent respectively, X^2 $p < .02$). Finally, the percentage of nominated secondary school girls having home problems specified (36 per cent) far exceeded that for boys, (14 per cent), (X^2 $p < .0001$). A quite substantial difference between nominated primary school girls and secondary school girls in the areas of conduct problems and non-attendance problems was also found.

Table 2 shows the simultaneous specification of the various categories of concern where it exceeded 10 per cent of the particular category. An example to illustrate this is that of all those children for whom conduct disorder symptoms were mentioned, 20 per cent also had learning problems mentioned.

Discussion

What does all this mean? What does it tell us and how does it fit in with information from other surveys? Firstly, when compared with other sur-

Table 2: The Simultaneous Specification of Categories of Concern

Conduct Problems
- 20 per cent also had learning problems specified
- 14 per cent also had home problems specified
- 13 per cent also had non-attendance problems specified

Neurotic Problems
- 27 per cent also had home problems specified
- 21 per cent also had learning problems specified

*Non-attendance**
- 15 per cent also had learning problems specified
- 13 per cent also had home problems specified

*Delinquent Behaviour**
- 39 per cent also had conduct problems specified
- 29 per cent also had non-attendance problems specified
- 19 per cent also had home problems specified

Learning Problems
- 14 per cent also had conduct problems specified
- 14 per cent also had physical problems specified

Home Problems
- 22 per cent also had conduct problems specified
- 14 per cent also had non-attendance problems specified
- 13 per cent also had learning problems specified
- 12 per cent also had neurotic problems specified

Physical Problems
- 32 per cent also had learning problems specified
- 10 per cent also had home problems specified

* Secondary children only

veys which have identified pupils experiencing difficulties, the figure of 6 per cent of children causing difficulties and concern to teachers is quite small. The Isle of Wight studies, for example, found that 6 per cent needed help because of emotional and behavioural difficulties alone (Rutter *et al.*, 1970). Clark's survey in Scotland (Clark, 1970) found the incidence of reading backwardness among 7-year-olds to be 15 per cent and, more recently, the Warnock Committee (DES, 1978) felt that around 20 per cent of all children have special educational needs but, as less than 2 per cent are placed within special schools, the remaining 18 per cent are provided for within the ordinary school system.

Why is it then that the sampled teachers nominated so few of their pupils as causing them concern? A number of possible explanations immediately spring to mind. Firstly, it may well be that Barnsley schools indeed have fewer children meriting concern than other areas of the country, although in general this would seem to be unlikely. Secondly, the task presented to the teachers was different. They were to identify those children who were causing them 'an unusually high degree of concern', which might exclude those children who need special help or were experiencing difficulties which the teachers might be coping with quite adequately. Some support for this view can be found in the Newsom Report (1963) which also surveyed teacher opinions, although in respect of fourth year secondary pupils only. These teachers were of the opinion that under 5 per cent of their pupils were presenting serious problems of discipline, an incidence rate which compares very favourably with that of this current study.

Further support for this view can also be found in a summary of more recent studies by Griffiths (1983) which suggests that most disruptive behaviour in secondary schools originates from only three per cent of pupils, although their behaviour may be supported by another eight per cent. It might reasonably be anticipated that while all eleven per cent may be a cause of concern to their teachers, it is the three per cent originators who would be most likely to cause their teachers a 'high degree' of concern. Thirdly, the teachers might simply have been reluctant to nominate children in this way or may even have overlooked or missed children who should have been nominated if the significance of certain aspects of their behaviour was appreciated.

Fourthly, it could be reasonably hypothesized that many teachers might be reluctant to nominate too many children in this way as it could be misinterpreted by others as a reflection on their own professional competence. (For a related discussion of this point see Frude and Gault, 1984.) Other explanations abound, but the overall consistency of findings between schools and teachers suggests that they are a valid representation of the concerns of teachers at the time of the survey.

From their response, it was clear that most teachers responded according to some personal internalized classification system. A large proportion of the responses were expressed in one word or short phrases; for example, 'Aggressive', 'Disruptive', 'Reading Difficulties', 'Speech Defect', 'Insecure', 'Unreliable — poor attitude'. Although more than one third of the nominated pupils had two or more areas of concern specified by their teachers, the responses overall suggested that for any child one area of difficulty tended to dominate their teacher's concern. Where more than one area was nominated, they tended to be in conceptually quite discrete and unrelated areas. For example, although the mixed conduct/neurotic category was adopted for analysis, only two per cent of the responses could be included within it. It would seem that teachers prefer the black and white situation of 'he is outgoing' rather than the somewhat greyer situation of 'sometimes he is outgoing and sometimes he is withdrawn and both concern me'.

Overall the impression gained was that teachers' concerns were rooted primarily in 'within the child' variables, including, of course, his home environment. It was the child who 'lacks concentration' (a frequent response, and it was noticeable that the term 'motivation' was not used by any teacher), or had a 'negative attitude to school', or came from 'a poor home background', rather than 'within school' factors, that teachers saw as being at the root of their concern. There were, however, a few responses which suggested that teachers too might have an important or influential contribution to make, for example, 'capable and co-operative with strong teachers'.

The pattern of the percentage of nominations across the age bands is interesting. Overall the highest levels of concern are found within the primary schools and it is only in relation to pupils in their last year of school that the level of concern in the secondary schools exceeds the lowest level in the primary schools. The results also suggest that although the percentage of secondary school pupils causing concern is below that for primary school pupils, secondary school pupils are more likely to be causing concern in more than one area.

Bearing carefully in mind the caveats outlined earlier, it seems, perhaps somewhat expectedly, that for the total sample the most frequently specified area of concern for the nominated pupils is in the area of learning problems or difficulties; over one third of the nominated pupils caused concern to their teacher in this area. In relation to the total number of pupils in the sample, this suggests an incidence rate of only 2 per cent for learning problems — a surprisingly low incidence. In the primary schools, nearly one half of the nominated pupils had learning problems specified compared with one quarter of the secondary schools' pupils. This suggests that learning difficulties are more likely to cause a high degree of concern to primary school teachers than to secondary teachers, although one would, of course, hope that this is an indication of a reduction in the actual incidence of learning problems rather than of differing perceptions by the two groups.

Conduct problems were the next most specified with over one quarter (28 per cent, plus 2 per cent in the mixed category) of all nominated children having a behaviour in this category specified. This suggests a total incidence rate of around one and a half per cent. Here, however, it is secondary school pupils who are most likely to have behaviour in this category specified. Also of interest here is the finding that problems associated with non-attendance and delinquency are almost entirely restricted to the secondary schools. These findings again are probably what one would expect, but this does tend to support the validity of the findings overall. Home problems were specified proportionately the same for primary and secondary pupils, as one would expect, but this was not the case for physical problems which were more frequently specified for primary school pupils. This latter finding may be attributable to the category used which, for example, included speech problems which might be expected to diminish with age or, as one cynic commented, 'the weaker ones die off before secondary age!'. Neurotic problems and emotional difficulties were very similar for the two groups.

Delinquent behaviours were rarely specified without some other category. Well over one third of the pupils with delinquent behaviours specified also had conduct problems specified; just under one-third had non-attendance specified, and around one-fifth had home problems specified. The converse of these relationships was not found, which suggests very clearly that while pupils perceived as delinquent are also generally perceived to have either conduct, non-attendance, or home problems, pupils perceived as experiencing conduct, non-attendance or home problems are not generally perceived as delinquent.

The specification of conduct and neurotic problems was frequently accompanied by both learning and home problems. This association of both with learning problems is somewhat counter to the Isle of Wight studies, which found a strong relationship between learning problems and conduct disorders, but not with neurotic disorders.

As indicated earlier, there is considerable evidence in the data that there is a strong shift in the concerns of primary and secondary school teachers. In the primary school, the management and control of pupils is generally of less concern to teachers than in secondary schools. The concerns of primary school teachers are more likely to be rooted in areas of general pupil development and progress, particularly learning, while these features appear secondary to aspects of management and control in the concerns of secondary teachers. There are several reasons why this may be so. The emphasis on management and control among secondary teachers may in part be a function of the larger and more institutional nature of the schools whose effective operation consequently depends very much upon organizational structures and systems, which in turn depend very much upon more uniformity and conformity among pupils. These increased demands for uniformity and conformity come at a time when many pupils are experiencing the developing and doubtful pressures of puberty and adolescence, and are anxious to test out their growth to adulthood and independence. For some pupils, the ultimate independence from school may be achieved by its rejection and the data show that 45 per cent of the nominations in the final three years of schooling referred to non-attendance. (It should be noted, however, that this only refers to 2.5 per cent of all pupils in that age range.) It would seem natural that, amongst those who remain, there are some who wish to display their growth to adulthood in a more public arena and school is the most readily available. Faced with physically bigger and stronger pupils, the cruder and more simplistic techniques of management and control perhaps open to their primary school counterparts are denied to secondary school teachers. More psychologically based techniques need more careful and refined use when a teacher is faced with more sophisticated and intellectually developed children. Furthermore, the organizational aspects of the school dictate that any one child is likely to meet several different teachers each day, and consequently a consistent approach in meeting a child's difficulties throughout the greater part of the school day lies in the successful co-ordination of a team of teachers rather than in the hands of a single teacher. The management and control of pupils in the secondary school is a much more diffuse and difficult matter than in the primary school, and consequently it might be expected that a greater proportion of the concerns of secondary teachers about their pupils would be in this area.

As mentioned above, the concerns of primary school teachers were very much related to learning difficulties. With reference to the previous discussion regarding secondary schools, it is interesting to note that the highest incidence of concern relating to learning difficulties was for the 10–11 years age band, when 67 per cent of all nominations included reference to this area. This was a leap of 20 per cent over that found for the previous year (i.e. 47 per cent) and some consideration of this finding seems necessary. The explanation may lie in the fact that for most of the schools in the survey this was the final year of primary schooling before transfer to secondary school. It may well be that primary school teachers, whose concerns are more likely to be focused on learning difficulties, are concerned about how their pupils will 'cope' in the secondary school. In the usual first year of secondary schooling the incidence of teacher concern related to learning difficulties falls back to 45 per cent and thereafter progresses steadily downwards to a rate of 19 per cent of all nominations by the final year of secondary school. Perhaps not too unexpectedly, the concerns of teachers regarding pupils in this final year have moved from aspects of learning to those of conduct and attendance problems (50 and 42 per cent of all nominations respectively).

Nearly four times as many boys were nominated as were girls and this sort of ratio accords with numerous other surveys more directly concerned with actual pupil behaviours (for example, the IOW studies; for a wider discussion see also Rutter, 1975). In secondary schools, girls were more likely to be a high cause of concern for their teachers when they displayed conduct, non-attendance or home problems, and, generally, their teachers' concern was more likely to be rooted in more than one area. It would seem that for girls to become a focus of high concern for their teachers they need to display difficulties in more than one area. The quite substantial discrepancy between the two sexes in relation to specification of home difficulties would not seem open to an easy explanation, although some hypothesis related to society's conceptions of the sex roles and associated expectations might merit further investigation.

Conclusion

Perhaps the most simple, and yet perhaps the most significant, conclusion to be drawn from the survey is that teachers are not just highly concerned about their disruptive and aggressive pupils: they are highly concerned about a whole range of difficulties and problems experienced by their pupils. Furthermore, this range of concern generally holds true for teachers across the entire educational age range. Although the results show that as pupils grow older and pass through the educational system, the predominant concerns of their teachers pass from matters related to learning difficulties in the primary school years to matters more related to management and control in the secondary school phase, they also show that teachers are concerned for pupils in other areas too: for example, home difficulties and physical problems feature throughout the age range. This would seem to have important implications in the planning and delivery of inservice training for teachers in schools and in the provision and delivery of the support services to schools, both of which should take account of the wide range of difficulties teachers see as facing them, the wide age range at which they can occur, and about which teachers are experiencing an 'unusually high degree of concern'.

This latter point is important for the task presented to teachers was expressed in these terms: 'an unusually high degree of concern'. Naturally the results must, and were intended to, be expressed in terms of teacher perceptions. But, in so far as these perceptions have reality for the teachers concerned, and although the number of children nominated was relatively small, their effects or consequences for teachers would seem to be substantial. While Galloway's assertion that 'teachers have always expressed concern about a substantial minority of their pupils and probably always will' (Galloway, 1985) may be true, the possible adverse effects or consequences for the teachers themselves of coping day after day with an unusually high degree of concern across a wide range of problem areas cannot, or should not, be dismissed so lightly.

Neither can we dismiss lightly the possibility that many of these teachers' concerns may be expressions of the actual behaviours and difficulties experienced by pupils. Nor can we dismiss the possible effects upon pupils who, day after day, are faced and taught by teachers who are extremely concerned about them in some way. These are all parts of the social reality, the total context, of the classroom referred to earlier and as such may be very real in their consequences.

The responses clearly suggested that the teachers tended to see their pupils as having very particular and specific difficulties which were seen to relate to variables lying within the child or within the home environment, rather than within the classroom or within their teaching. Few of the responses could be interpreted as being expressions of the child's educational need: rather they were expressions of the child's 'problem', often in terms of a category; for example, the child has 'learning difficulties' rather than 'he needs highly structured and systematic teaching'. However, the survey was carried out prior to the implementation of the 1981 Education Act and its hopefully widely disseminated notions of special educational needs, and it is interesting to speculate how teachers would respond to this same task in this new 'era'. Would they respond more in terms of what the child needs, rather than in terms of his 'difficulty' or category of difficulty?

It is also perhaps relevant here to note that all of the responses, without exception, referred to what might commonly or traditionally be regarded as 'difficulties' or 'problems' and none referred to more 'positive' possible causes of concerns, such as 'highly able', 'gifted', or 'his creative talent is not being allowed to flower'.

It should be made quite clear, however, that the teachers' concerns for their pupils were not simply a function of self-interest or personal survival. That would suggest, quite improperly, that they were only concerned about those of their pupils who did not conform to their expectations or who did not learn appropriately in response to their teaching. That this is not so is amply demonstrated in the wide-ranging nature of the teachers' concerns referred to earlier. The teacher, for example, who wrote the following reference to one of her seven-year old pupils: 'He looks extremely neglected, clothes too small and dirty, hair in need of a hot wash and comb. He smells and sometimes has sores on his face', was concerned about something more than just her own survival, as was the teacher who wrote of yet another seven-year old: 'Attendance has been poor — often arrives very late when she attends, looking in need of a wash, food and sleep. Has improved somewhat during the last two weeks. Very shy and timid. Does not mix well, bit of a loner.' These two responses, and there were many others like them, illustrate that many of the teachers' concerns were a direct expression of their caring for their pupils, and of caring for them not as pupils but as children, as fellow human beings with feelings and concerns of their own. It can be all too easy when we talk of teachers and their concerns to overlook the basic caring principles that often lie at the root of those concerns.

One final point: a maxim of the behavioural approach to teaching is to 'start where the students' behaviour is at'. Any training of teachers intended to develop their skills, extend their understanding, modify their attitudes and improve their teaching is most likely to succeed, therefore, if it starts from their perceptions and takes seriously their concerns. This survey has demonstrated that teachers are highly concerned about a substantial minority of their pupils. Their concerns and perceptions in respect of their pupils are undoubtedly real to teachers, and hence may be real in their consequences. While these perceptions and concerns may and should change, they cannot and should not be dismissed lightly by those responsible for the training and professional development of teachers. Rather they should be regarded as the starting point, indeed the vehicle, in any attempt to provide a more beneficial and meaningful educational experience for all our pupils.

References

CENTRAL ADVISORY COUNCIL FOR EDUCATION (1963) *Half Our Future* (The Newsom Report), London, HMSO.

CLARK, M.M. (1970) *Reading Difficulties in Schools*, Penguin Papers in Education, Harmondsworth, Penguin.

DAWSON, R.L. (1980) *Special Provision for Disturbed Pupils*, London and Basingstoke, Macmillan.

DAWSON, R.L. (1981) 'The development of a mechanical psychologist', *Association of Educational Psychologists Journal*, 5, 7, pp. 11–13.

DEPARTMENT OF EDUCATION AND SCIENCE (1978) *Special Educational Needs*, London, HMSO.

FRUDE, N. and GAULT, H. (1984) 'Children's disruption at school — cause for concern', in FRUDE, N. and GAULT, H. (Eds) (1984), *Disruptive Behaviour in Schools*, Chichester, Wiley.

GALLOWAY, D. (1985) *Schools, Pupils and Special Educational Needs*, Beckenham, Croom Helm.

GRIFFITHS, T. (1983) 'Maladjustment in the comprehensive school', *Maladjustment and Therapeutic Education*, 1, 2, pp. 41–5.

PEARSON, G. (1983) *Hooligan, A History of Respectable Fears*, London and Basingstoke, Macmillan.

RUTTER, M. (1975) *Helping Troubled Children*, Harmondsworth, Penguin.

RUTTER, M., TIZARD, J. and WHITMORE, K. (Eds) (1970) *Education, Health and Behaviour*, London, Longmans.

TOPPING, K.J. (1983) *Educational Systems for Disruptive Adolescents*, Beckenham, Croom Helm.

Troublesome Classroom Behaviours

Frank Merrett and Kevin Wheldall
University of Birmingham

Reports from the popular newspapers, television and radio might well lead the man in the street to suppose that the behaviours which trouble teachers most in school are those associated with insubordination and opposition and that many are of a violent nature. The impression we get is that if you are not mugged on your way into school you almost certainly will be on the way out. For example, a recent release from the NAS/UWT following a questionnaire sent to all its members covering the period September 1984 to February 1985 highlights phrases such as 'Pupil violence and serious disorder in schools' and 'Off duty but not out of danger'. It includes an account by a teacher which reminds one of a tale by Gerard Hoffnung, being a veritable catalogue of harassment over a period of some years.

> During the last fourteen years I have been assaulted seven times, once with a knife, once with a stiletto, once with an air rifle (I was shot in the chest), once when a pupil fed gas into my classroom when I was teaching, twice when pupils have attempted to attack me with their fists and once when an ex-pupil tried twice to run me over with a car. (NAS/UWT, 1986, p. 5)

There is no doubt that some teachers are subjected to a great deal of stress and that teaching has become a very much more difficult business over recent years. Nevertheless, it has to be pointed out that the NAS/UWT survey was based on a questionnaire return of 'almost 4000' from a membership of more than 100,000. As they admit, this 'may possibly have produced an unrepresentative sample' (p. 3).

We must not, however, suppose that we are facing a problem that is entirely new. Socrates has been quoted as saying, 'Children now love luxury. They have bad manners and contempt for authority. They show disrespect for their elders and love chatter in place of exercise; children are now tyrants, not the servants of their households'; whilst the words of Peter the Simple (1274) are reported as, 'The world is passing through troubled times. The young people of today think of nothing but themselves. They have no reverence for their parents or for old age. They talk as if they alone know everything and what passes for wisdom with us is foolishness with them. As for the girls, they are foolish and immodest in speech, behaviour and dress.'

Previous Research on the Prevalence of Troublesome Behaviour

Children with behaviour problems are a common type of referral to educational psychologists and teachers frequently cite classroom behaviour problems as one of their major difficulties. However, there is surprisingly little research concerned to identify the behaviours which classroom teachers find most troublesome. Wickman (1928) compared teachers' and mental hygienists' (psychologists') attitudes towards children's behaviour problems and found them to be quite different. Teachers placed the greatest emphasis on children's aggressive, acting out and disobedient behaviours as the most serious problems whilst the mental hygienists rated personality and emotional problems as the most severe. Ziv (1970), using a selection of Wickman's categories, investigated teachers', psychologists' and children's attitudes towards children's behaviour problems in Tel Aviv. The research required each group to rank, in order of seriousness, thirty categories of behaviour. Among those regarded as 'most serious' by both teachers and psychologists were cruelty, dishonesty, aggressiveness, stealing and temper tantrums. Ziv claims that,

> Our research has shown that, in Israel, teachers and psychologists have similar points of view concerning the severity of children's behaviour problems, and children view the problems more like teachers than like psychologists. (p. 878)

In the wider context of children's behaviour problems Whitmore and Bax (1984) studied children from fifteen inner city primary schools in the Paddington district of London. These children were examined on entering school at five and Whitmore and Bax claim that six per cent of these children had 'disturbed' behaviour. By age seven to eight the figure had risen to seven per cent. This included new individuals who had now developed behaviour problems whilst some children included earlier were no longer a problem. Similarly, by the time the children were ten the figure was nine per cent but again the number included some new cases whilst others who were no longer troublesome dropped out of account. Whitmore and Bax also cite Richman, Stevenson and Graham (1982) as claiming that disturbed behaviour is present in 27 per cent of eight year olds transferring from infant to junior schools and Kolvin *et al.* (1981) who identified 25 per cent of seven to eight year olds as 'at risk' and needing treatment for established or imminent abnormality of behaviour, emotional or social relationships.

Laing (1984) found that 144 out of 375 nursery-aged children had behaviour difficulties of varying degrees of severity, mostly in the younger age group. In the group which showed the less severe problems the sexes were equally matched but among those who had severe problems, boys outnumbered girls by four to one. Boys were far more likely to show aggression or overactivity. Earlier studies by Chazan and Jackson (1971, 1974) and Hughes, Pinkerton and Plewis (1979) suggest that generally between 13 and 15 per cent of young children show behaviour difficulties of one sort or another on starting school.

McGee, Sylva and Williams (1984) review previous research which provides estimates of the prevalence of behaviour problems in primary aged children, in the context of reporting their own figures based on research in New Zealand. They cite Davie, Butler and Goldstein (1972) who reported findings from the National Child Development Study which identified 14 per cent of seven year olds as 'maladjusted' and Kastrup (1976) who identified 15 per cent of a random sample of 175 Danish five to six year olds as 'poorly adjusted'. From the Isle of Wight study Rutter, Tizard and Whitmore (1970) found seven per cent of ten and twelve year olds with 'some variety of psychiatric disturbance' and 25.4 per cent in a subsequent study, (Rutter *et al.* 1975) on similar aged children in Inner London. Similarly, Miller *et al.* (1974) classified 19.4 per cent of their sample of Newcastle children as 'maladjusted' with 12 per cent having 'severe and stable' problems and Connell, Irvine and Rodney (1982) estimated that of their sample of ten to eleven year old children from Queensland, 10 per cent of rural, 15 per cent of urban and 18.4 per cent of metropolitan children had psychiatric disorders.

Following their review, McGee *et al.* go on to make the point that the huge variation in prevalence rates (from 6 per cent to 25 per cent) 'probably reflects differences in the ages of the children, differences in the geographical location of the populations and varying techniques for identifying children with problems. Nevertheless, the results suggest that a significant proportion of children suffer from behaviour problems during their early schooling'. Their own study of 951 seven year olds, comprising the Dunedin Multidisciplinary Child Development Study, examined the prevalence of behaviour problems as assessed by reports from parents and teachers. 'About 30 per cent of the sample were identified by the parent and/or teacher as having a high level of problem behaviour' (p. 258). However, 'the parents identified about twice as many children as the teachers' (p. 257). Only about 5 per cent of the sample were identified by *both* parent and teacher as having behaviour problems.

From the above findings it is clear that either behaviour problems fluctuate widely and unpredictably in incidence or, more likely, the definition of 'behaviour problems' varies considerably across studies and also across raters within studies (parents versus teachers). Our own concern is with what teachers regard as troublesome behaviour in the classroom. We are interested to know not only what percentage of primary aged children are behaviourally troublesome to teachers but also just what these troublesome behaviours are. Fields (1986) is one of the few researchers who has attempted to gain information about the extent and nature of the problem behaviours experienced by (primary school) teachers, but his sample is very small.

There are, then, several important aspects of the problem of classroom behaviour that we need to consider. First, there is the question of emphasis. Previous research has tended to be concerned almost exclusively with identifying the incidence of children with behaviour problems. Consequently, the children have been the focus, rather than the behaviour. Those working from a behavioural perspective (see Wheldall and Merrett, this volume) would tend to focus upon the behaviour itself. Secondly, there is the need to define and describe the relevant behaviours which make up the rag bag category of 'troublesome behaviour'. If we use vague, catch-all phrases we must not be surprised if we find variations in incidence. Moreover, what is disturbing to one teacher may be quite acceptable to another, which emphasizes the importance of objective definition of an array of specific behaviours which teachers may find troublesome. Third, there is the question of the *severity* of the problem behaviour as against the *rate* at which it occurs. There is no doubt that an incident of stabbing in the classroom is to be regarded as extremely severe but, thankfully, such events are rare. On the other hand, a relatively trivial offence such as calling out may occur so frequently that the lesson dissolves into total chaos. So it is necessary to consider both degree of troublesomeness and its frequency.

The West Midlands Surveys

We have carried out a number of surveys in the West Midlands in the context of our continuing programme of behaviourally orientated research into classroom management (Merrett and Wheldall, 1986; Wheldall and Merrett, 1986). The behavioural approach is not concerned with global definitions of problems but with specific behaviours which may be objectively defined. Since to have defined specific behaviours would have called for a great number of such definitions it was decided to identify *groups* of behaviours by modifying slightly the categories used by Becker *et al.* (1967). Our enquiries were aimed at gaining the opinions of primary school teachers with particular reference to their own classroom situations.

In our first study (Merrett and Wheldall, 1984) we attempted to determine what teachers themselves believed to be the most frequent and the most troublesome disruptive behaviours occurring in the junior school classroom. An (anonymous) questionnaire, distributed to 29 schools in the West Midlands area, sought information on length of teaching experience,

Table 1: The Eight Categories of Behaviour Used in the First Survey.

- A Orienting behaviours: turning head or body to look at another person, showing objects to another child.
- B Motor behaviours (whilst seated): rocking in chair; moving chair in place; sitting out of position; standing whilst touching chair or desk.
- C Gross motor behaviours (not at desk): getting out of seat; running; jumping; skipping.
- D Disturbing others (including aggression): grabbing objects of work; knocking neighbour's book off desk; destroying another's property; hitting; kicking; shoving; pinching; slapping; striking with object; throwing object at another person; attempting to strike; poking with object; biting; pulling hair.
- E Talking: carrying on a conversation with other children; blurting out answers when not called upon; making comments or remarks.
- F Making a noise: tapping pencil or other objects; clapping; tapping feet; rattling or tearing paper; crying; screaming; laughing out loudly; coughing loudly; singing; whistling or any vocal noise other than in E above.
- G Non-attending and disobeying: doing something other than that which he has been directed to do or is supposed to be doing (includes day-dreaming).
- H Other: please specify, where appropriate.

age of children taught and class size and then proceeded to ask a series of questions related to classroom behaviour problems. The first asked, 'Do you feel that you spend more time dealing with problems of order and control than you ought?' The next three questions were concerned with identifying which of the eight categories of disruptive behaviour (see Table 1) were most frequent and most troublesome. This was first asked in general terms and then with reference to up to six individual children selected by each teacher as being particularly troublesome. Finally they were asked to estimate the number of 'withdrawn' (shy) children in their classes. The questionnaire was briefly piloted in ten schools to check on its acceptability prior to distribution to the larger sample.

As a result of various problems in distribution and cooperation, of the twenty-nine schools approached, only nineteen responded with some completed questionnaires. The rate of response from the schools which did respond was 60 per cent, comprising 119 junior class teachers with an average class size of 30.5 overall. Seventy-three of these teachers (62 per cent) answered 'yes' to the first probe question, 'Do you feel that you spend more time dealing with problems of order and control than you ought?'

In compiling the results, responses were weighted by considering only the first three behaviour categories ranked by each teacher and weighting them 3, 2 and 1 respectively. The results show that categories D (disturbing others, 30.7 per cent) and E (talking, 28.0 per cent) are followed by G (non-attending and disobeying, 14.4 per cent) with regard to troublesomeness. With regard to frequency, category E (42.9 per cent) was followed by G (18.2 per cent). The third question, which directed attention to particular children who were disruptive, showed greatest frequency of occurrence in category E (27.6 per cent), followed by G (16.6 per cent) and then by D (14.5 per cent). Degree of troublesomeness in individuals was reflected by listings of category E (30.9 per cent) followed by D (21.5 per cent) and then G (19.4 per cent).

It can be seen clearly that talking, closely followed by non-attending and disobedience were the behaviours which caused this sample of teachers the greatest concern. These were followed by behaviour which disturbs other children, including aggression. Talking out of turn (TOOT behaviour) appeared to account for about a third of all misbehaviour in primary school classrooms according to this survey of teacher opinion.

An analysis of the children picked out as being especially disruptive showed that the number of boys (281) far exceeded the number of girls (111). Boys also tended to be higher on the lists of disruptive pupils than the girls. The number of children identified as withdrawn was 217, of whom 96 were boys and 121 were girls.

The findings from this study were useful and gave tentative evidence about the degree and type of troublesome classroom behaviours in junior schools. We were not sufficiently convinced, however, of the representativeness of the obtained sample of teachers to place much confidence in the specific findings of our survey, although we certainly believed it to be indicative of general trends. In retrospect, we also felt that the questionnaire could have been more elegantly and economically designed and that some of the behaviour categories (taken from Becker *et al.* 1967) were over-inclusive providing insufficient definition of behaviours. Consequently, it was decided to follow up the original survey with a new one utilizing a modified questionnaire on a larger, more representative sample including teachers of both junior and infant classes. We decided also to find out how many children were typically identified as troublesome by their teachers.

A modified version of our previous category list was tried out with several groups of teachers, the total number of teachers being 57. They were asked to complete the forms and then to suggest amendments and additions to the categories. As a result of this exercise we produced a second and, we think, more suitable list of behaviour categories for teachers to choose from. This is shown in Table 2.

Our second primary survey, using the categories given in Table 2, involved a 25 per cent random sample (32 schools) of the Infant, Junior and Junior/Infant schools in a West Midlands LEA. In this questionnaire teachers were asked to identify the most troublesome (and the next most troublesome) and the most frequent (and the next most frequent) behaviours only. This restricted the number of responses and simplified the analysis. (In the earlier version teachers made as many responses as they wished but only the first three were counted.) Sufficient survey forms were sent to every school in the sample so that each full-time class teacher (excluding nursery classes) could complete the questionnaire. Replies were received from all 32 schools involved, resulting in a very high return of questionnaires (93 per cent overall). Of the 198 teachers replying 73 per cent were women; 22 per cent of the respondents were in their twenties, 40

Table 2: The Categories of Behaviour Used in the Second Survey.

Category	Description
A Eating	Chewing gum, paper or equipment, eating sweets in class.
B Making unnecessary noise (non-verbal)	Banging objects/doors, scraping chairs, moving clumsily.
C Disobedience	Refusing/failing to carry out instructions or to keep class or school rules.
D Talking out of turn	Calling out, making remarks, interrupting and distracting others by talking or chattering.
E Idleness/slowness	Slow to begin or finish work, small amount of work completed.
F Unpunctuality	Late to school/lessons, late in from playtime/break.
G Hindering other children	Distracting others from their work, interfering with their equipment or materials.
H Physical aggression	Poking, pushing, striking others, throwing things.
I Untidiness	In appearance, in written work, in classroom, in desks.
J Out of seat	Getting out of seat without permission, wandering around.

per cent in their thirties, 22 per cent in their forties while 16 per cent were in their fifties. The sample was distributed fairly evenly over the range of ages taught from five to eleven years, with the majority of men teaching the older children.

Half of our sample (51 per cent) responded affirmatively to the question 'Do you think that you spend more time on problems of order and control than you ought?'. The same percentage of men and women responded in this way and there were no major differences between the responses of younger and older teachers or between teachers of younger and older pupils.

The average class size was 27 of whom 4.3 children, on average, were regarded as troublesome by their class teachers and three of these were boys. Asked to pick out the two most troublesome individual children in the classes, boys were picked as the most troublesome by 76 per cent and as the next most troublesome by 77 per cent. This supports the anecdotal view that boys tend to be more troublesome than girls and ties in with our earlier findings.

What was it that these children did that was troublesome? As we said earlier, it was the type and frequency of troublesome behaviours in which we were particularly interested. When asked to pick out the most *troublesome* behaviour 46 per cent of teachers cited 'talking out of turn' (TOOT) and 25 per cent cited 'hindering other children' (HOC). None of the other categories reached over 10 per cent. This was confirmed by the results for the next most troublesome behaviour in which 31 per cent opted for HOC and 17 per cent for TOOT. The findings for the most *frequent* troublesome behaviours gave a very similar picture and when we went on to ask about the troublesome behaviours of individual children, again we got the same response, TOOT followed by HOC. These two categories are not particularly serious misbehaviours. They are hardly crimes, but they are irritating, time-wasting, exhausting and stressful for teachers in that they give rise to a great deal of 'nagging' and to other negative responses. It is interesting to note that these sorts of classroom problem behaviours have been shown to be particularly amenable to resolution by behavioural methods (Merrett and Wheldall, 1986).

McNamara (1985) using a slightly modified version of our first questionnaire and the same behaviour categories (as in Table 1) investigated the nature of the behaviour problems which trouble teachers in *secondary* schools. He asked teachers to complete the questionnaire with reference to a particular class that they teach regularly (the one chosen was that taught just before lunchtime on a Wednesday) and then generally to the whole range of classes taught and to rank order the categories of problem behaviour. The first three choices were taken and assigned scores of 3, 2 or 1. It was then possible to rate the teachers' assessments of different problem behaviours and to compare them. The return rate for the questionnaire was only 56 per cent, however, with two hundred teachers responding. The rate of return was variable from school to school but inspection of the data showed that a similar pattern of responses was obtained from each school irrespective of the rate of return.

McNamara found that inappropriate talking (E) was rated as the most disruptive behaviour by most teachers. This was followed by orienting behaviours (A) and then by non-attending and disobeying (G). Teachers taking part in this study tended not to list the most disruptive categories like motor behaviours out of seat (C) and aggression (D) at all but concentrated on the more mildly disruptive but very frequent behaviours mentioned above. The results obtained from teachers when considering the range of classes they taught during the week gave similar results; inappropriate talking again being rated the most troublesome. Generally, whether the questions related to a particular class or to the range of classes taught, teachers tended to assess talking (E), non-attending (G) and orientating behaviours (A) as the most common and the most disruptive behaviours occurring in the classroom.

We now have the preliminary results of a survey of the opinions of secondary school teachers in the West Midlands carried out with one of our research students (Houghton) using a questionnaire derived from the one used in our second primary survey (see Table 2 above). The survey was based upon a stratified random sample (approximately 30 per cent) of the secondary schools in the same West Midlands LEA as before. Replies were received from all six schools approached yielding a return of 62 per cent. Of Houghton's sample of 251 secondary teachers responding, 55 per cent admitted to spending more time on problems of order and control than they ought, a figure very similar to that found in the survey on primary school teachers. Once again TOOT (50 per cent) and HOC (17 per cent) were readily identified as by far the most frequent and troublesome classroom misbehaviours. The category 'physical aggression' was cited by fewer than one per cent of the teachers as being the most troublesome and came tenth (last) in rank order. As at the primary level, boys were picked as the most troublesome by the majority of teachers; 71 per cent chose boys as the most troublesome and 65 per cent as the next most troublesome. This database has yet to be analyzed in more detail.

Conclusions

What may we conclude from these results? We would appear to be safe in assuming that the classroom behaviour problems experienced by most primary and secondary school teachers are not dissimilar. TOOT and HOC appear to be the two misbehaviours which teachers generally identify as causing them the most trouble and as occurring most often. Additional evidence was produced by Davie (1975) who observed a group of twelve year old girls in their first year in a comprehensive school in Scotland over a period of four weeks. She concluded that, 'Talking, which accounted for almost half of all recorded misbehaviour, was the most chronic form of inappropriate behaviour' (p. 121). This is not to say that serious incidents do not occur occasionally in some schools but they are certainly not as frequent as the media would have us believe. Physical violence appears to be a problem encountered (thankfully) by relatively few teachers but many, if not most, teachers have their job made more stressful by the petty misbehaviours which we have identified and which, as we have said, are readily amenable to amelioration by behavioural methods. Fields (1986), reporting a study involving thirty teachers, agrees with this conclusion:

> The study also supports the view that the great majority of disruptive behaviour in primary classrooms is of a mild nature relating to poor attention, persistent infringement of class rules and procedures and inconsistent on-task behaviour. Extraordinary intervention strategies are not normally required for these behaviours. (p. 56)

Regarding the prevalence of children identified as troublesome, we may relate the figures from our second primary survey to the prevalence rates cited in the literature. On average, 4.3 children per primary class (of average class size 27) were said by teachers to be troublesome (of whom 3 were boys). This yields a prevalence rate of 16 per cent which falls in the middle of the estimates previously referred to but is higher than the rate determined (by teacher ratings only) in the McGee *et al.* study. This figure should be appreciated in the context of the behaviour categories which teachers selected. Even for the most troublesome children the key behaviours identified were not particularly serious or problematic.

The fact that far more boys than girls are regarded as troublesome is supported by casual observation and agreement among teachers generally, but by relatively little empirical evidence, perhaps because it seems so obvious. Hartley (1979) confirms the findings of other researchers (for example, the National Child Development Study) and asserts that, 'teachers rate the classroom behaviour of boys as being less appropriate than that of girls' (p. 188). He also shows that this view is shared by the pupils themselves. Observational data on classroom behaviour differences is sparse but, for example, Wheldall *et al.* (1981) showed in their study on seating arrangements that the on-task behaviour of boys is consistently lower than that of girls irrespective of behavioural interventions. In Fields' (1986) study thirty teachers selected a child in their classes as exhibiting conduct and discipline problems and all thirty were boys.

A behaviour which we have identified from other contexts as being of concern to teachers is that of children needlessly wandering about the classroom. We call this out of seat (OOS) behaviour but it did not figure largely in these results. It may have been obscured by the chosen categories. For example, much of what was being classed as 'disturbing others' would probably have involved the child being out of seat also.

The behaviour problems that teachers encounter vary widely from district to district, school to school and from individual to individual but the results from these studies suggest that there is a consensus of opinion among teachers. The majority are bothered by the behaviour of some of their pupils but the most common and troublesome behaviours are relatively trivial. None of the key troublesome behaviours are serious crimes but they are time-wasting, irritating, stressful and, ultimately, exhausting for teachers. They are the kinds of behaviours which elicit the litany of reprimands and desist commands heard so frequently in classrooms. The good news is that these are the very behaviours which respond well to the simple positive, behavioural methods discussed elsewhere in this volume.

References

BECKER, W.C., MADSEN, C., ARNOLD, C. and THOMAS, C. (1967) 'The contingent use of teacher attention and praise in reducing classroom behaviour problems', *Journal of Special Education*, 1, pp. 287–307.

CHAZAN, M. and JACKSON, S. (1971) 'Behaviour problems in the infant school', *Journal of Child Psychology and Psychiatry*, 12, pp. 191–210.

CHAZAN, M. and JACKSON, S. (1974) 'Behaviour problems in the infant school: Changes over two years', *Journal of Child Psychology and Psychiatry*, 15, pp. 33–46.

CONNELL, H.M., IRVINE, L. and RODNEY, J. (1982) 'The prevalence of psychiatric disorder in rural school children', *The Australia and New Zealand Journal of Psychiatry*, 16, pp. 43–6.

DAVIE, C.A.M. (1975) 'Classroom management: A theoretical and observational study'. Unpublished PhD thesis, University of Dundee.

DAVIE, R., BUTLER, N. and GOLDSTEIN, H. (1972) *From Birth to Seven: A Report from the National Child Development Study*, London, Longman.

FIELDS, B.A. (1986) 'The nature and incidence of classroom behaviour problems and their remediation through preventive management', *Behaviour Change*, 3, pp. 53–7.

HARTLEY, D. (1979) 'Sex differences in classroom behaviour in infant schools: The views of teachers and pupils', *British Journal of Educational Psychology*, 49, pp. 188–93.

HUGHES, M., PINKERTON, G. and PLEWIS, I. (1979) 'Children's difficulties on starting infant school', *Journal of Child Psychology and Psychiatry*, 20, pp. 187–96.

KASTRUP, M. (1976) 'Psychic disorders among pre-school children in a geographically delimited area of Aarhus county, Denmark', *Acta Psychiatrica Scandinavia*, 54, pp. 29–42.

KOLVIN, I., GARSIDE, R.F., NICOL, A.R., MACMILLAN, A., WOLSTENHOLME, F. and LEITCH, I.M. (1981) *Help Starts Here*, London, Tavistock.

LAING, A.F. (1984) 'The extent and nature of behaviour difficulties in young children', *Links*, 10, 1, pp. 21–4.

MCGEE, R., SILVA, P.A. and WILLIAMS, S. (1984) 'Behaviour problems in a population of seven year old children: Prevalence, stability and types of disorder — a research report', *Journal of Child Psychology and Psychiatry*, 25, pp. 251–9.

MCNAMARA, E. (1985) 'Are the techniques of behaviour modification relevant to problems of concern to teachers in secondary schools?' *Behavioural Approaches with Children*, 9, pp. 34–45.

MERRETT, F.E. and WHELDALL, K. (1984) 'Classroom behaviour problems which junior school teachers find most troublesome', *Educational Studies*, 10, pp. 87–92.

MERRETT, F.E. and WHELDALL, K. (1986) 'British teachers and the behavioural approach to teaching', in WHELDALL, K. (Ed.) *The Behaviourist in the Classroom*, (revised, second edition) London, Allen and Unwin in association with Positive Products.

MILLER, F.J.W., COURT, S.D.M., KNOX, E.G. and BRANDON, S. (1974) *The School Years in Newcastle upon Tyne*, London, Oxford University Press.

NAS/UWT (1986) *Pupil Violence and Serious Disorders in Schools*, Rednal, National Association of Schoolmasters and Union of Women Teachers.

RICHMAN, N., STEVENSON, J. and GRAHAM, P.J. (1982) *Preschool to School*, London, Academic Press.

RUTTER, M., TIZARD, J. and WHITMORE, K. (1970) *Education, Health and Behaviour*, London, Longman.

RUTTER, M., COX, A., TUPLING, C., BERGER, M. and YULE, W. (1975) 'Attainment and adjustment in two geographical areas: I. The prevalence of psychiatric disorder', *British Journal of Psychiatry*, 126, pp. 493–509.

WHELDALL, K. and MERRETT, F.E. (1986) 'Training teachers to use the behavioural approach to classroom management: The development of BATPACK', in WHELDALL, K. (Ed.) *The Behaviourist in the Classroom*, (revised, second edition) London, Allen and Unwin in association with Positive Products.

WHELDALL, K., MORRIS, M., VAUGHAN, P. and NG, Y.Y. (1981) 'Rows versus tables: An example of the use of behavioural ecology in two classes of eleven-year-old children', *Educational Psychology*, 1, pp. 171–84.

WHITMORE, K. and BAX, M. (1984) 'Who to treat, who to refer?' *Association for Child Psychology and Psychiatry Newsletter*, 6, 2, pp. 33–4.

WICKMAN, E.K. (1928) 'Teachers' list of undesirable forms of behaviour', in *Children's Behaviour and Teachers' Attitudes*, New York, Commonwealth Fund. (Reprinted in WILLIAMS, P. (1974) (Ed.) *Behaviour Problems in School*, London, University of London Press.)

ZIV, A. (1970) 'Children's behaviour problems as viewed by teachers, psychologists and children', *Child Development*, 41, pp. 871–9. (Reprinted in WILLIAMS, P. (1974) (Ed.) *Behaviour Problems in School*, London, University of London Press.)

2
Achieving Order in the School and Classroom

Introduction

This section is concerned with existing practices and possibilities for dealing with troublesome pupil behaviours in classrooms and schools. In educational research two major approaches to the study of teachers' current classroom practices predominate. The first involves attempting to study them as a totality. The second concentrates on understanding the role and consequences of particular techniques. The first three chapters in this section provide accounts of recent research which have adopted the first of these approaches.

Fry's chapter discusses a series of studies undertaken by herself and her colleagues into changes in pupil-teacher interaction over the course of a school term. This longtitudinal perspective is particularly valuable since most of the other findings in the volume are based upon cross-sectional studies drawing upon the state of the classroom at only one point in the term. Fry showed that, in a number of important ways, the interpersonal climate in the upper junior classes studied changed for the worse over the course of the term from January to April. In particular those children most in need of teacher attention and encouragement received it least. Fry's researches also suggest that different classroom climates, as defined by teachers' attitudes to their students, are related to different outcomes. In particular, children's explanations of their own classroom behaviours varied according to teacher style. All this suggests strong links not just between teacher styles and current pupil behaviour but also between patterns of teacher-pupil interaction and the development of pupil future perspectives regarding academic success.

Doyle and Carter in their chapter look not just at detailed analyses of classroom activity but also at teachers' overall management styles. As with Kounin's pioneering work from 1970 their focus is upon how teachers get things right rather than what happens when things go wrong. Perhaps unsurprisingly, their findings suggest important differences between relatively successful and relatively unsuccessful teachers. Successful teachers, for example, concentrate on work and success rather than idleness and misbehaviour even at the cost of ignoring quite high rates of misbehaviour. Such an approach is particularly interesting since practising teachers often deride the notion of ignoring misbehaviour when it is advocated as part of a behavioural approach to teaching. Indeed many of the practices revealed by Doyle and Carter make good sense from a behavioural perspective.

Lewis and Lovegrove offer a perspective on teachers' classroom style which is, perhaps, too little regarded by educational psychologists: that of the pupils. A number of studies have suggested that pupils clearly prefer teachers who maintain order; rarely, however, do they investigate how teachers are expected to achieve this. Lewis and Lovegrove gathered descriptions of the ideal teacher, the best teachers currently practising and the least acceptable teacher. Their findings are too complex to discuss in detail but a number of interesting points emerge. For example, ideal teachers tell miscreants off in private and do not expose them to public embarrassment. In practice the best teachers inflict public and embarrassing reprimands. A sample of teachers who were interviewed shared students' dislike of public sarcasm and anger but admitted that, when tired, their practice fell short of their principles. Lewis and Lovegrove conclude with the suggestion that teachers need to be provided with alternative models for handling classroom order other than traditional discipline with its ever present threat of confrontation.

The next three chapters move the focus to specific techniques which teachers employ in attempts to control pupils' behaviour in the classroom. In our chapter we look at the ways in which teachers currently use approval and disapproval. Praising pupils for good work has come to be seen as a key feature of good teaching, yet numerous studies of teacher classroom behaviour have suggested that feedback in the average classroom is predominately negative in tone. The most recent work, especially that which takes non-verbal responses into account too, gives a more complex picture. It now appears that approval predominates over disapproval as far as pupils' academic work is concerned whereas the reverse is true where pupils' conduct is the focus of teacher attention. Moreover, pupils' interpretation of teacher praise mediates its effects upon behaviour. Of course, not all praise is intended to serve as a reinforcer. Indeed, we conclude that teachers' untheorized use of praise may be more appropriate than behaviourally oriented researchers have supposed!

Most educators, one suspects, would subscribe to the proposition that education should be a predominantely pleasant experience. As the song has it the teacher should 'accentuate the positive, eliminate the negative'. However, that is not always possible and schools as well as teachers punish deviant pupils. Keith Topping provides a wide ranging review of these sanctions. Some of them, such as time out, might better be seen as alternatives to punishment rather than punishment per se. Topping is particularly concerned that sanctions should be seen as part of the overall school management system. So, for example, loss of privileges needs to be used in a set-up where there are privileges to lose! Despite what some educators, including many users of behavioural approaches, have claimed, punishment can be effective — when used appropriately. Even so, he concludes that teachers would do better to look for ways of avoiding punishment.

The last chapter in this section is more prescriptive than its predecessors, although for the most part it complements or reinforces them. In their second contribution Kevin Wheldall and Frank Merrett examine behavioural approaches in education. Behavioural techniques must count as one of the major contributions made by psychology to educational research and practice. A wide range of techniques have been derived from a set of basic assumptions about human learning. These include reinforcement of appropriate behaviour, ignoring of inappropriate behaviour and the careful preparation of appropriate settings to maximize appropriate behaviour and give minimal opportunity for disruption or inattention. Wheldall and Merrett illustrate these techniques by examples drawn from their own extensive research which show the wide applicability of this approach.

Classroom Environments and their Effects on Problem and Non-Problem Children's Classroom Behaviours and Motivations

P.S. Fry
The University of Calgary, Canada

Most teachers have encountered students whose behaviour in class constitutes a problem. Such children are often thought to constitute problems as a consequence of their personalities, their early home experiences and their relationships outside school. That such factors do affect students' behaviour and motivations in school is not disputed, but what is often not given adequate consideration is the way in which aspects of life within schools and classrooms may contribute to the generation, exacerbation or maintenance of problem behaviour in classrooms.

Over a period of some years, my associates and I have conducted a programme of research designed to explore the possible effects of classroom environments and classroom processes on problem and non-problem children's behaviour and motivations. The general findings of this programme of research on the interactions of teachers, students and classroom social climate have been of considerable educational interest. They have highlighted the variability of interactions and have served to emphasize the fact that, whilst it is possible to talk about classrooms in general, it is important to remember that the nature of classroom life depends upon the particular classroom and the classroom processes involved.

The purpose of this chapter is to present a non-technical account of the major dimensions of student motivations, teacher behaviours, classroom social climate and classroom processes that our research has suggested as being important in relation to the behaviour and motivations of problem and non-problem students. Readers interested in a full report of the technical details of the methodology, reliability and validity of the assessment instruments and the statistical analyses are referred to the individual studies in the programme of research by Fry and associates.

A common hypothesis in the social psychology of education has been that differences in classroom social environment and structure have effects on children's academic motivation and on the social and emotional functioning of students within the classrooms. This hypothesis has been extensively studied in a variety of forms and with an almost equal variety of results. The underlying assumptions of this line of research are: that the environment of the classroom is defined by the shared perceptions of the members of the classroom along a number of environmental dimensions (Trickett and Moos, 1974); that environments exercise important psychological influence over their members (Neilsen and Kirk, 1974); and that these latter psychological influences mediate the academic outcomes and motivations of the members within the environments. Such assessments of relationships between social climates of the classroom and student motivations and academic behaviours are of great interest to the teacher. Not only do they provide feedback to the teacher and students about the characteristics of the classroom milieu, but they also motivate them to change the social milieu in ways that are self-enhancing to their own goals and aspirations (Moos, 1974).

The research suggests that immediate environments of the classroom may also determine young children's locus-of-control beliefs and causal explanations and that differences in causality attributions of success and failure may be closely tied into the differences in the social orientations emphasized in the classroom and in the treatment of students by teachers and counsellors (Cooper, Burger and Good, 1981). The assumption in such literature is that children often become aware of the labels (for example, 'conduct problem', 'withdrawn', 'highly motivated', 'well-behaved', 'bright', 'dull') which are ascribed to them and that these ascriptions influence children's beliefs about the causes of their own and others' successes and failures and their subsequent strivings.

Since problem children as a group are recognized to have somewhat different belief systems from other normal populations of children (see Feshbach, 1969; Galvin and Annesley, 1971; Cromwell, Blashfield and Strauss, 1975; McDermott, 1980; Hale and Landino, 1981), it is assumed that it would be useful for teachers to understand problem and non-problem children's academic motivations and their attributions of success and failure. It is suggested that an understanding of children's attribution systems may permit educators to better assist problem children to develop more productive belief structures and motivations. By training teachers to recognize the impact of the causal attributions that children use to structure their environment, the educational system should be able to foster more appropriate motivations and behaviours in children. Understanding the relationship between school performance and some causes of success and failure more generally used by problem and non-problem children may help the teacher at some point to employ psychological mechanisms (for example, praise, social contact, sustained feedback, encouragement, direct action) to change or modify children's motivations and behaviours.

Recognizing the importance of understanding the academic motivations of students and recognizing also the influence of classroom social climates in enhancing or inhibiting academic motivations, sections of this chapter will be devoted to examining inter-relationships among specific characteristics of the classroom environment and the kinds of academic motivations that may prevail within different social climates.

Interaction among Classroom Processes and Dimensions of Academic Motivation

Although some thought has been given to the large-scale environment of the classroom and to its effects on the performance of students, previous study of the classroom environment has focused on physical aspects (for example, seating, colour and lighting). Of greater interest to the classroom teachers, however, are some of the special and specific psychosocial factors, for example, degree of control maintained by the teacher over classroom activities (Huston-Stein, Friedrich-Cofer and Sussman, 1977), dimensions of classroom climate such as the degree of teachers' involvement, affiliation, task-orientation (Moos and Moos, 1978) and the nature of the influence they have on the academic motivation of students.

Such effects have become a subject of continuing empirical and practical interest to teachers who are beginning to seek explanations for why differences emerge in students' academic motivations in the particular forms in which they do. Why, for example, specifically do certain students become concerned about self-improvement, academic success, and career preparation and why do others have behavioural problems and become passive, anxious and anti-school? Parents, educators, and scientists alike emphasize the impact of classroom interactions with teachers, peers, and the school environment on a child's socioemotional growth and development. Although the influence of teachers in the early elementary school years has received considerable attention from researchers and educators, it has often been without the aid of acceptable process measures for examining teacher interactions and teacher behaviours toward students. Furthermore, only a few studies of classroom processes have been done that examine the fluctuations of process measures over time. In our programme of research, therefore, we focused on classroom processes for a period of four months or more. The study of classroom interactions (Fry, 1983) showed that teachers' behaviour and interactions with their students changed over the period of a term. The general findings were that these unintended changes accompany, and may contribute to, deterioration in the academic motivations and behaviour of students.

In particular three aspects of the data are of continuing interest: Are observation data concerning the effects of teachers' interpersonal style stable (reliable) over time? Do the classroom processes show predictable trends over time? Are these trends similar or different for problem and non-problem children?

In the 1983 study it was hypothesized that unintended changes in teachers' classroom interactions would, over a period of months, influence problem children in a manner quantitatively different from non-problem children. The purpose of this aspect of the research was to elaborate on the process measures themselves so as to identify the significance of some of the high-inference and low-inference teacher behaviours and their differential effects on problem and non-problem children's academic motivations and behaviours.

The main data used were observers' ratings of the verbal contacts between teachers and individual pupils. These contacts were categorized by trained observers who were seated in the classroom where it was possible to hear and overhear conversations. Contacts between the teacher and the student or between student and student were defined as utterances or strings of utterances that were concerned with a single observational category. Each class was observed by trained observers an average of 15 times, for 60 minutes, over a four-month school term (see Fry, 1983, for details of procedure).

Classroom Observation Instrument

This instrument was adapted from Evertson and Veldman (1981). It was used for rating specific dimensions of teacher behaviours with respect to the positive and negative affects that such behaviours are able to generate among students. Also included were other critical dimensions of teacher behaviours, for example, the frequency of teacher-initiated social contacts with students, and the frequency of teacher-initiated problem solving that occurs in the classroom.

The eight teacher behaviours and seven student behaviours that were rated by the observers, described briefly, were:

Teacher Behaviours

1 *Positive affect.* Teacher behaviours that show support or positive regard for students and their behaviour, including such behaviour as smiling, joking, reinforcement and praise.
2 *Negative affect.* Verbal or non-verbal behaviours reflecting hostility or negative feelings of the teacher. This category includes negative teacher evaluation of student behaviour, expressing anger or criticism.
3 *Social contacts.* Contacts that are non-academic in nature but initi-

ated by the teacher as a means of exchanging greetings or conveying some personal message.

4 *Teacher-initiated problem solving.* The degree to which the teacher addresses questions and problems to the individual student. This category includes high level synthesis questions requiring reasoning, interpretation of materials or abstract thinking on the part of the student.
5 *Random, memory or fact questions.* Questions requiring brief factual answers. The student responds from rote memory.
6 *Convergent-evaluative interaction.* Teacher behaviour in this category is directed towards obtaining a correct answer, with little or no attempt to follow up on the contact once the response has been made.
7 *Sustaining feedback.* This category includes several sequences of events in which the teacher provides sustained response opportunity to the student if the first response is not correct, or incomplete or unclear.
8 *Personal questioning* in which students are required to give their personal views and preferences.

Student Behaviours

1 *Level of sustained attention* or absence of attention. This category rates the overall quality of orientation towards the teacher or the task at hand.
2 *Call-outs.* Response opportunities created by students calling out answers to questions without getting teacher's permission.
3 *Mild misbehaviour.* Behaviours judged to be inappropriate but not disruptive; behaviours that involve students talking to or visiting each other.
4 *Serious misbehaviour.* Students' behaviours that are inappropriate and very disruptive to the class.
5 *Student-initiated questions.* Questions that students, rather than teachers, initiate publicly.
6 *Pupil-to-pupil interaction.* Substantive pupil utterances in which one pupil interacts with another pupil, a group of pupils, or responds indirectly only to the teacher.
7 *Passive behaviour.* The extent to which pupils engage in passive, as opposed to active, models of behaviour. Passive behaviours include withdrawal by pupil from engagement, visual wandering, and passive observation.

Teacher behaviours and student behaviours were studied separately for 28 teachers interacting with 200 non-problem children and 200 problem children drawn from 30 elementary classrooms (Grades 5 and 6 students).

Problem and non-problem children observed in the classroom were grouped into these categories by means of teacher ratings on the *Behaviour Problem Checklist* (Quay and Peterson, 1979; revised edition, 1983, is also available now). Although this checklist has several other scales (for example, psychotic behaviour, socialized delinquency, inadequacy/immaturity) for our purposes we were essentially concerned with teacher ratings of students' conduct disorders and personality disorders.

Conduct disorders were assessed by means of teachers' ratings of items suggesting, for example, that the student:

> Seeks attention: 'shows off'; is disruptive: annoys and bothers others, fights, has temper tantrums; is disobedient: difficult to control, uncooperative in group situations; is negative: tends to do the opposite of what is requested; is impertinent: talks back, is irritable, hot-tempered, refuses to take directions, won't do as told; always blames others: denies own mistake; is deliberately cruel to others.

Personality disorders were assessed by means of teachers' ratings on items suggesting that the student shows personality disorder behaviours, for example:

> Repetitive speech: says same thing over and over; incoherent speech, what is said doesn't make sense; expresses strange, far-fetched ideas; expresses beliefs that are clearly untrue (delusions); tells imaginary things as though true; unable to tell real from imagined; repeats what is said to him or her; parrots others' speech.

Students grouped in the non-problem category scored low in all areas of the *Behaviour Problem Checklist* indicating that the teachers viewed them as not displaying behavioural difficulties. Problem and non-problem children were matched also on dimensions of mental ability and socioeconomic status.

The Differential Nature of Teachers' Interactions with Problem and Non-problem Children: A Summary of the Findings

Teacher interactions. An examination of teacher behaviours over the course of four months of observation indicates that problem children

received more negative affect from teachers,

obtained fewer social contacts from them, and

were asked less frequently by their teachers to express their personal views and preferences on academic and class-related issues.

By comparison, non-problem children received from their teachers

- a more positive orientation to their intellectual capabilities. For example, non-problem children were asked more complex higher level cognitive questions by their teachers as compared to problem children who were asked more factual questions involving only rote memory and less reasoning, personal opinion, interpretation or abstract thinking,
- more sustained contact,
- more opportunities for individual interaction, and
- more sustained feedback.

Student interactions. With respect to student behaviours, a comparison of problem and non-problem children showed that problem children

- engaged in greater frequency of serious misbehaviours,
- had fewer instances of sustained attention in the task on hand, and
- showed more passive withdrawal behaviours (for example, preoccupied look; doodling, drowsy; not wide-awake, avoiding eye contact; preferring solitary activity).

Process change over four months. Eight teacher behaviours and seven student behaviours were examined over the months of January, February, March and April. Some significant fluctuations were noted which may have some interesting but serious implications for teachers and pupils. The following trends were noted in teacher responses.

Decline in positive affect. With respect to variations in teacher behaviours, it may be of interest to the classroom teacher to note that the teacher's positive affect *vis-á-vis* students was at its peak in the beginning of the term in January. Positive affect was extended equally to both problem and non-problem children. However, the teachers' expression of positive feelings gradually declined, reaching a significant low in April. Although teachers started out the term showing support or positive regard for a majority of the students, by the end of April their patience was wearing thin, especially with problem children who were being more frequently criticized. Teachers were now observed to be expressing more anger and annoyance toward the problem children.

Decline in social contacts. Similar variations were noted over the four-month period in teachers' convergent-evaluative interactions with their students. As implied in the definition of convergent-evaluative interactions, teachers' interactions with students became more superficial and evaluative than sustaining. In terms of observed teacher behaviours, it was apparent that by the end of the four-month period, there was a gradual decline in the number of social contacts that teachers made with their students and also in the frequency of sustained feedback they provided to students. For example, by the end of the term teachers did not painstakingly point out what was incorrect or incomplete about the students' responses, nor did they elaborate on how a student could improve a given response or assignment.

Decline in sustained feedback. Frequency of sustained feedback behaviours and the number of social contacts that teachers provided were at their highest in January but declined noticeably by April. A substantial amount of this decline in the teachers' sustained feedback was observed *vis-á-vis* problem children, suggesting a sharp increase in teachers' convergent evaluative interactions towards problem children in particular in the month of April compared to the earlier months of January and February. These trends are the most pronounced of any of the changes in teacher behaviours and suggest that, as the winter term drew to a close, teachers' reactions became more negative toward their students. This was especially so toward the problem children in the classroom with whom their interactions became more superficial and evaluative, as opposed to being sustaining and facilitative.

Decline in cognitive activity. Whereas in the beginning of the winter term (January) teachers' behaviours toward both problem and non-problem children were characterized by high cognitive level questioning and complex teacher-initiated intellectual activity, by the end of the term (April) teachers were shifting to more routine types of classroom activity involving more factual and rote-memory activity and less discussion and interpretation. In other words, there was a significant decline in activities requiring students to think and analyze.

The following trends were noted in pupil responses.

Increase in pupil-to-pupil interactions. Whereas in the beginning of the winter term (January) more problem children, compared to non-problem children, had engaged in 'call-outs' and conversation with other pupils independently of the teacher, by the end of the term (April) more non-problem children also had begun to engage in substantive utterances and responses directly with other pupils without obtaining the teacher's consent. These findings suggest inappropriate pupil behaviour that involves pupils socializing with each other without teacher involvement.

Increase in the incidence of serious misbehaviours. Whereas in the beginning of the winter term more problem- than non-problem children were observed to engage in mild misdemeanours (for example, whispering and giggling, visual wandering) by the end of the term there was an increase in the number of mild misbehaviours among both the problem and non-problem children. Problem students' mild misdemeanours, however, became more serious and included disruptive behaviours, such as criticism of peers, negative comments about the teachers, loud chatting and loud noises. These trends were most pronounced for problem children during the months of March and April and suggest that by the end of the term problem children, especially, had become much less sensitive to the teacher's expectations of good behaviour and orderly conduct.

Decline in sustained attention. Sustained attention declined for both problem and non-problem children over the four-month period but the effect was more pronounced during each month for the problem children. It is conceivable that this decline in pupils' sustained attention was an outcome of the decline in sustained feedback and decline in positive interactions on the part of teachers.

Pygmalion in the Classroom: The Phenomenon of Teacher Expectations of Problem and Non-problem Students

Since the publication of Rosenthal and Jacobson's (1968) *Pygmalion in the Classroom*, there have been several studies concerned with the phenomenon of teacher diagnosis, assessment and expectation effects. There are by now convincing data from many additional experiments (for example, Cornbleth, David, and Button, 1974; Rubovits and Maehr, 1971) showing that teachers' positive and negative expectations and labelling of students (such as 'problem' children, 'bright' children, 'dull' children) do indeed affect student behaviour and produce inequalities in teacher-pupil contacts and the quality of intellectual and cognitive interactions. The most reasonable theoretical explanation for the teacher expectation phenomenon has been that teachers, after forming initial assessments about a student's behaviour problems or student's performance transmit their perceptions through a complex series of verbal and nonverbal cues to the student. For instance, Brophy and Good (1970) showed students received differential praise according to their teachers' perceptions, and Rothbart, Dalfren and Barrett (1971) found that teachers gave greater attention to students labelled as 'bright'. Similarly, Garner and Bing (1973) noted that different levels of teacher contacts were received by children assessed as being 'active', 'bright' and 'personable', as opposed to others perceived as being 'dull' or 'misbehaved'. Thus teachers appear to respond differentially to students according to the perceptions they hold of individual students being well behaved or having conduct problems.

In part, at least, the results of the Fry (1983) study are also reminiscent of the Pygmalion effect. This study was concerned with examining how the expectations that a teacher holds about students' behaviours are transmitted over a four-month term and how teacher perceptions or expectations may affect the subsequent behaviours of students. Our results showed that there is a distinct deterioration in teachers' interactions, especially with children whom they had rated as having behavioural problems. Such children received more negative affect and less sustaining feedback from their teachers over the course of four months.

Observations of problem children's behavioural interactions in the classroom also showed an increase in serious misdemeanors, and a corresponding decline in sustained attention presumed to be more closely tied in to differences in treatment by the teachers. One of the possible interpretations of these results, which has serious implications for the classroom teacher, is that teachers become more remiss in their social interactions over the course of a school term and that the deterioration in their social contacts is more pronounced with respect to problem children. This finding supports the earlier findings of Rothbart, Dalfren, and Barrett (1971) who noticed a similar Pygmalion effect: the effect of teacher expectations on the quality of interactions with the students.

While no strong assertions about causality can be made from the Fry (1983) data, the indications are that children's both mild and serious misdemeanors were greater in frequency and that their sustained attention was lower when teachers showed a decline in positive affect, social contact and sustained feedback towards the students. These effects were also much more pronounced towards the problem children. One of the considerations in discussing these results is that of deciding whether the teacher's perception of the child (i.e., having conduct problems or not having problems) determines how he or she will interact with the child or vice versa.

Fry's (1983) data cannot help the teacher resolve this 'chicken and egg' dilemma but certainly it is reasonable for the teacher to assume that the process is interactive. Concerning the question of the teacher as Pygmalion and the counter-responses of problem behaviours by the children, it is clear that there was an interaction phenomenon. It is reasonable to assume that neither the teacher nor the student resembles Pygmalion at all times of the school term. A teacher's impression is formed on the basis of the child's behaviour and then functions as an interpretive framework within which subsequent behaviour of the child is construed, and leads to teacher expectations, which, in turn, help determine the child's subsequent behaviour.

The determinants of disruptive behaviours and problem behaviours in the classroom vary widely and the precipitators of teachers' negative affect in the classroom remain relatively unknown. However, it is important for teachers to recognize that students' disruptive behaviours are mediated more often than we suspect by teachers' expectations and perceptions of their students, and that the attitudes teachers hold towards their students firmly influence the ways in which they interact with their students (Brophy and Good, 1970). Taken together with the results of several previous studies (Evertson and Veldman, 1981; Garner and Bing, 1973; Good and Brophy, 1974), Fry's (1983) study of classroom process measures supports the notion that teachers' expectations about their students may be transmitted to the student and bring about behaviour congruent with those expectations.

Besides the obvious necessity of further teacher effort to guard against some of the teacher expectation effects suggested in the Fry (1983) study, it would seem particularly important to examine problem and non-problem students' perceptions and expectations of teachers jointly with teachers' expectations of problem and non-problem children. It would appear that neither teachers nor students are the sole Pygmalion or Galatea in the classroom. To draw conclusions over time only from the teacher's behaviours or only from the students' behaviours is overly simplistic, given that both teachers and problem and non-problem children bring their own expectations, attitudes and behaviours to what is clearly an undefined and ambiguous social setting of the classroom.

Inequalities in the Quality and Frequency of Teacher Contacts with Problem and Non-problem Children

One point for major consideration concerns the inequalities of contacts. If it is assumed that contacts (other than disciplinary) are beneficial, then many more problem children were being deprived of such benefits, especially in the last few weeks of the term.

The inequality of the teacher contacts with students over the four month period is not surprising. The data on the hourly incidence of teacher-pupil contacts confirm Jackson's observation that, 'In the small but crowded world of the classroom events come and go with astonishing rapidity' (1968, p. 149). The high rate at which contacts occur tends to result in their being of short duration, and it is difficult to see how teachers can become deeply involved in children's problems of understanding when only a minute or so is available for them to make their diagnosis and give their help (Garner and Bing, 1973). In classrooms containing over thirty children more than one child usually requires some kind of social contact at any given interval of a minute or two, and the teacher is faced with a choice between children. The time pressure might account for a choice between a sustained or brief contact.

Given this situation of the rapidity of contacts, the teachers' decline in the frequency of contacts and loss in positive attitude towards students toward the end of the school term is quite understandable (see Evertson and Veldman, 1981). It is a commonsense expectation that teachers get weary by the end of the school term compared to the beginning of the term, and their patience begins to wear thin. However, what is a matter of serious concern is the fact that there is a more significant loss in positive contacts with problem children who at all times are assumed to be in greater need of the teacher's nurturance than are non-problem children generally. It is understandable, therefore, that problem children deprived of teacher attention, as the term progresses, become more misbehaved possibly because of a greater than average need for nurturant contacts with the teacher.

The high levels of teacher-initiated response opportunities and social contacts experienced by non-problem children are easy to explain. It is conceivable that either teachers find contacts with the 'good' non-problem students to be rewarding or that such students initiate their own contacts with the teacher and receive more than average sustained attention. The teacher's sustained attention and feedback to the non-problem children may be attributed partly to the ease with which teachers are able to obtain and hold the attention of these students. Overall, it may be that miscreants become a part of a student group that gets more easily rejected by both teachers and non-problem peers. Composed predominantly of students with poor conduct and work habits, the group pattern invites more of the convergent-evaluative interaction from the teacher, and fewer of the teacher-initiated problem-solving and sustained-feedback interactions.

It may also be that teachers find providing sustained feedback to problem children is a slow and time consuming process. Nevertheless, it is very important that teachers become more aware of their negative interactions with the problem children, especially toward the end of school term when they are prone to be more tired and are concerned simply with keeping control rather than with the well-being of the classroom culture. Teachers should note that problem children in particular appear to be more sensitive to the teachers' aloofness toward them and to declining social contacts. Overall, there seems to be a tendency for problem children to react with more misdemeanors if they feel they are negatively perceived by the teacher or not receiving contacts. In such situations the students may be behaving in ways their teachers may expect them to behave.

Teachers must guard against the possibility that the teacher expecting a problem child holds more negative attitudes (both about the performance and conduct) and behaves somewhat more verbally negatively toward the problem student.

Assessment of Classroom Social Climates

In this section, I will discuss the underlying patterns of social climate in classroom settings, describe the utility of the social climate concept by drawing on examples from my programme of research (Fry and Coe, 1980; Fry and Addington, 1984) and summarize evidence suggesting that the social environments of classroom settings have important relationships with dimensions of academic motivation of problem and non-problem students.

The Classroom Environment Scale (CES) adapted from Trickett and Moos (1974) was used to assess the classroom environment in terms of junior and senior high school students' perceptions of the social climate of the classroom. This scale consists of ninety true-false items which fall into nine different subscales, each of which measures the emphasis on one dimension of classroom climate.

Underlying patterns of the classroom setting according to the CES scale are studied in terms of relationships, personal growth or goal orientation, and system maintenance and system change.

Relationship Dimensions

According to Moos (1979), the relationship dimensions of the CES scale assess the extent to which the teacher and students are involved in the classroom environment, the extent to which teacher and students support and help one another (affiliation), and the extent of spontaneity and free and open expression among them. The three important subscales assessing the relationship dimensions in the Fry and Coe (1980) study provided ratings for

(1) Involvement; (2) Affiliation; (3) Teacher Support

Personal Growth Dimensions

The personal growth or goal orientation dimensions assess the basic directions along which personal development and self-enhancement tend to move in an environment. According to Moos (1979), personal growth dimensions vary somewhat among different environments depending essentially on task orientation (i.e., the extent to which the class activities are centred around specific task objectives), competition for grades and academic honours. The subscales assessing the personal growth or goal orientation of junior and senior high school students in the Fry and Coe (1980) study provide ratings for

(1) Task orientation; (2) Competition

System Maintenance Dimensions

System maintenance and change dimensions assess the extent to which the classroom environment is orderly, the teacher's expectations of classroom conduct are clear and the teacher maintains high control.

Ratings of rule clarity determine the extent to which students know what the consequences will be if they do not follow the rules. Teacher control ratings reflect how strict the teacher is in enforcing the rules and how severe are the consequences for rule infractions. Subscales of the CES employed in the Fry and Coe (1980) study to assess classroom factors look essentially at dimensions of:

(1) Rule Clarity; (2) Teacher Control; (3) Classroom Organization

Assessment of Academic Motivations of Students

The Academic Motivations Inventory (AMI) (Moen and Doyle, 1977; Moen and Doyle, 1978) was used to assess academic motivations of junior and senior high school students in the classroom. This is an 80-item self-report instrument. Each item is cast as a simple declarative sentence on a five-point Likert-type scale: 'Not at all true of me' through to 'Extremely true of me'. The nine factors of the Academic Motivation Scale identified by the authors include:

1 *Desire for Self-Improvement* (15 items): For example,
I hope school will help me become a better person (true).
School will teach me better ways of handling conflicts with people (true).
2 *Anti-School* (17 items): For example,
I dislike most school work (true).
School gives me a feeling of insignificance that I hate (true).
3 *Desire for Esteem* (14 items): For example,
I hope school will make me famous (true).
I hope school will help me to discover my good points (true).
4 *Enjoyment of Learning* (11 items): For example,
I enjoy reading most books and articles teachers assign to me (true).
I just really enjoy learning new things (true).
It is very important that my classes make me use my mind (true).
5 *Enjoyment of Assertive Interactions* (7 items): For example,
I am enthusiastic about school activities providing opportunity to do new things and meet new people (true).
6 *Resentment of Poor Teaching* (3 items): For example,
I dislike teachers who are poor in teaching (true).
Poor teachers make me feel dull and stupid (true).
7 *Academic Success* (4 items): For example,
I try to do my very best on all school work even on things uninteresting (true).
If I get started on something, it is very important for me to complete it (true).
I am enthusiastic about trying to get high grades (true).
8 *Desire For Career Preparation* (4 items): For example,
It is very important that my classes prepare me for a good career (true).
I hope school will teach me better ways of handling career tasks and activities (true).
9 *Enjoyment of Passive Interactions* (5 items): For example,
I enjoy doing things on my own (true).

Major Relationships and Interactions of Classroom Social Climates and Student Academic Motivations

In summary, analyses of classroom social climates in terms of specific characteristics show some significant relationships that are assumed to be of interest and usefulness to the classroom teacher.

Major trends observed in Fry and Coe's (1980) program of research are as follows:

1. Classrooms with a social climate perceived by students to be *affiliation-oriented* (i.e., characterized by emphasis on student-teacher rapport, support and interaction) had a significant number of students reporting a high desire for self-improvement, enjoyment of learning and motivation for academic success.
2. Classrooms with a social climate perceived by students to be *organization- and order-oriented*, had a significant number of students reporting high anti-school feelings and lowered enjoyment of learning.
3. Classrooms with a social climate perceived by students to be *control-oriented* (i.e., in which teacher control is high and the teacher's emphasis is on organization and order) had a significant number of students reporting a significant level of anti-school feeling and a lowered interest in self-improvement.
4. Classrooms with a social climate perceived by students to be *task-oriented* had a significant number of students who perceived themselves to be career-minded and motivated by a desire for career preparation and specific task objectives.
5. Students in classrooms perceived to be *competition-oriented* felt insignificant, disliked school work and felt restricted by the competition for grades.
6. Students in classrooms perceived to be *teacher support-oriented* reported that they enjoyed reading books and felt enthusiastic about grades. They also felt a sense of individual significance and were concerned about becoming better individuals. In other words, they were motivated toward self-improvement and enjoyment of learning.

What Kind of Classroom Social Climates Engender Negative Motivation in Students?

The trends and relationships observed in the Fry and Coe (1980) study confirm that there are distinct relationships between certain social climates of the classroom as perceived by the students and certain dimensions of positive and negative academic motivation. Some of the findings having important implications for the classroom teacher relate to students' feeling of anti-school or negative motivation. The data from Fry and Coe's (1980) study suggest that anti-school feelings predominate in classrooms perceived to have a climate of competition. Thus, the emergent picture of the classroom where high teacher control combines with a competitive climate appears to be linked with student perceptions of limited enjoyment of learning. Although no causal implications can be drawn from the findings, there is the suggestion that classroom climates characterized by competition and restrictive teacher control seem to engender more negative motivation than classroom climates characterized as being interactive and high in teacher support. The question as to whether teachers directly shape negative academic motivation by their 'controlling' style, and should therefore be faulted for their restrictive treatment of students, is indeed difficult to answer because of the complexity of factors involved. An important point to bear in mind is that most teachers do not start out by being controlling or suppressive, but are apt to become this way because of the necessity to deal with students who are poorly motivated and have strong anti-school feelings.

It is to be expected that teachers who continually interact with students who demonstrate a love of learning and have a high motivation for achieving academic success do not need to be 'controlling' or 'punitive' in their relationship with students. In such classrooms teachers have relatively little need to justify their authority (Kaye, Trickett and Quinlan, 1977). By contrast, students with conduct problems, displaying anti-school feelings and little enjoyment for learning or academic success, are often the group of students who subtly coerce teachers toward becoming restrictive and controlling in class, and critical of their students' poor motivations. Indeed, most teachers may not be enduringly controlling by temperament, but may be affected by problem children's negative reactions to become so. Nevertheless, teachers must guard against the tendency to become too controlling with problem children.

Many teachers will want to know how they can affect student motivation and to obtain information which can be used to formulate planned change in the classroom environment so that it becomes compatible with the kinds of strivings or needs that pupils have. It is suggested that data obtained from students' self-reportings on the CES and AMI can be used by the classroom teacher to determine the degree of teacher control, competition, teacher involvement and support that students perceive themselves as needing in order to function effectively in the classroom.

Openness in the Classroom: General Outcomes

Over the past decade a large body of literature (for example, Bennett, 1976; Marshall, 1981; Soloman and Kendall, 1979) has evolved that has considered the positive and negative effects of 'openness' in the social climate of the classroom. Bennett (1976) and Soloman and Kendall (1979) argue that classroom openness does not function as a global construct. Their research recognizes that different components of openness may exist in varying degrees in different classrooms. The concept of openness in the educational environment arose as a counterresponse to the negative effects observed as a result of high teacher control, restrictive discipline and competitiveness seen in the average classroom. As noted by Wright (1975), the implicit assumption is that 'openness' in the social climate of the classroom generates more self-directed learning, stimulates greater creativity and independence, and thus provides the foundation for increased social-cognitive growth and development in children. 'Openness' in the social climate of the classroom is viewed by Walberg and Thomas (1972) as having four important dimensions: openness in provision; open instruction, guidance and extension of learning; humaneness, respect and warmth; assumptions of interest and involvement in children (see Table 1).

Fry and Addington (1984), using the Walberg-Thomas (1972) scale, studied the effects of openness in the classroom social climate on the social problem-solving performance of young children, and on their self-esteem. Five male and five female graduate students trained in observing student-teacher interactional dimensions rated the social climate of 30 classrooms on the following dimensions of openness (see Table 1):

Table 1: Dimensions of Openness Adapted From The Walberg-Thomas (1972) Scale

Dimensions of Openness and Sample Items Representing Dimensions

Openness in Provisioning for Learning (No. of items = 25)
Manipulative materials are supplied in great diversity and range with little replication, that is, not class sets. Children move freely about the room without asking permission. Talking among children is encouraged. The teacher does group children by ability according to tests or norms.[a] Children generally group and regroup themselves through their own choices.

Open Instruction, Guidance and Extension of Learning (No. of items =. 5)
Teacher bases her instruction on each individual child and his or her interaction with materials and equipment. The work children do is divided into subject matter areas.[a] The teacher's lessons and assignments are given to the class as a whole.[a] Teacher bases her instruction on curriculum guides or textbooks for the grade level she teaches.[a] Before suggesting any extension or redirection of activity, teacher gives diagnostic attention to the particular child and his or her particular activity.

Humaneness, Respect, Openness and Warmth (No. of items = 4)
Children use 'books' written by their classmates as part of their reading and reference materials. The environment includes materials developed or supplied by the children. Teacher takes care of dealing with conflicts and disruptive behaviour without involving the group.[a] Children's activities, products, and ideas are reflected abundantly about the classroom.

Assumptions About Children and Learning Process (No. of items = 4)
The emotional climate is warm and accepting. The class operates within clear guidelines made explicit. Academic achievement is the teacher's top priority for the children.[a] Children are deeply involved in what they are doing.

[a] Reverse coding

Influence of Openness on Student Motivations

The results of Fry and Addington's (1984) study showed that students who studied for a two-year period in classrooms characterized by openness achieved enhanced levels of social problem-solving thinking, suggesting that openness in the classroom environment facilitates social problem solving by reinforcing children for self-direction and independent decision-making cognitions. In our study (Fry and Addington, 1984), we speculate that openness in the classroom atmosphere provides students with better opportunities for independent activity, flexible groupings, child-oriented curricula, and informal structure. Other advantages noted by us are that open classrooms include the provision of an emotional climate in which the teacher is warm and accepting, the range of student choices and selection is wide, and teacher guidance and support (as opposed to teacher control and restrictiveness) is available.

In many ways these dimensions of openness observed by Fry and Addington (1984) are reminiscent of our earlier findings (Fry, 1983; Fry and Coe, 1980) which lead us to conclude that student-teacher 'dialoguing' interactions help the teacher to provide students with opportunities for sustained response and sustained feedback. It will be recalled that in all these studies teacher behaviour variables were studied, and the results bear marked similarities in terms of the positive influence of teacher involvement, teacher support and humaneness on the one hand, and the negative influence of teacher control and classroom competitiveness and restrictiveness, on the other hand.

Influence of Openness on Students' Self Esteem

In assessing the effects of openness, our findings (Fry and Addington, 1984) also showed that at the time of follow-up testing, students who had been in open classrooms for a period of two years had higher self-ratings on 'feelings of personal adequacy', 'social interest' and 'involvement' compared to the time of the initial testing. By contrast, students from classrooms not having characteristics of openness obtained higher self-ratings of 'impulsive behaviour' and 'lack of self-confidence' on measures of self-esteem.

The literature to date is most unclear as to the effects of openness in the classroom social climate, and the controversy is far from being over. However, the findings of our two-year longitudinal study (Fry and Addington, 1984) provide for the benefit of the teacher, additional supportive data on the advantages of maintaining an open classroom climate characterized by positive teacher affect, teacher involvement, sustained interest in the student, and low levels of teacher control and restrictiveness. Such data may help to bridge the gap between previous studies that have attempted to assess the effects of teacher discipline, control and competition, on the achievement performance of problem and non-problem children and prospective studies interested in long-term developmental changes in students as a function of continuing and sustained contact, involvement and affiliation with teachers.

The results of the programme of research we have undertaken (Fry and Coe, 1980; Fry, 1983; Fry and Addington, 1984) to study various dimensions of the classroom social climate and similar projected studies may have important implications for teachers who encounter many problem children in their classrooms and who may be concerned about the effects of their classroom environment on the personality development and academic motivations of the children. The results of the studies reported here provide some systematic evidence of classroom social climates that engender positive effects and others that generate negative effects.

Problem and Non-problem Children's Causal Attributions of Success and Failure

The role of causal attributions in determining success and failure motivations of children has been the object of intensive study and valuable results (Fyans and Maehr, 1979). It seems quite clear that causal attributions play a critical role in determining children's perceptions of success and failure and also mediate their responses to these perceived events. Previous research indicates that school children hold different beliefs about personal causation in achievement situations (Crandall, Katkovsky and Crandall, 1965). Some children are likely to believe that success in school is attributable to their efforts and ability, while others are likely to believe that it is simply a matter of luck.

Our examination of children's causal attributions of success and failure (Fry and Grover, 1984) was predicated on the assumption that individual differences in attributional biases are determined by the presence or absence of self-controls and the work habit preferences of problem and non-problem children. Our study was concerned with identifying attributional biases of problem and non-problem children, a facet of attributional style that has been given little attention in the research literature. A nontechnical description of the major findings of this study is presented here. We assume that the results could well have profound significance for teachers in understanding the motivations of problem and non-problem children and for restructuring the environment correspondingly. Readers interested in the details of methodology and procedures for statistical analyses are referred to the Fry and Grover (1984) paper.

Causal beliefs were inferred from elementary school children's responses to stories with achievement and outcome themes. Some distinct differences that emerged in the developmental trends of problem and non-problem children's causal explanations are summarized here.

Non-problem Children
With respect to internal-external locus-of-control variables, internality in causal explanations of success and failures increases with age and grade level.

Self-reliance in belief systems also increases with age and grade level.

Internal factors, such as ability, interest, stable effort and persistence, figure more largely in causal explanations of success and failure with increasing age and grade level.

Problem Children
With respect to internal-external locus-of-control variables, problem children show an increasing reliance on external, unstable and unintentional factors (chance; luck) as causing their success and failures. With increasing age and grade level, problem children manifest increasing anxiety and personal helplessness as inferred from their causal explanations of failure.

External and unstable factors of task difficulty, mood and luck figure more largely in problem children's explanations of success and failure in the classroom task situations.

Overall, it is important for educators and teachers to note that non-problem children report generally stronger effort-outcome covariation in beliefs than problem children, especially for success outcome, whereas problem children have less belief in hard work and persistence determining the outcome of their efforts. Problem children show fewer tendencies toward internality in their self-expectations. Taken together, then, these results from our study suggest that problem children have less mature causal belief structures than their non-problem counterparts and that their locus-of-control beliefs may be affected to a much larger extent by transitory and external process factors in the classroom social environment. One can safely conclude that temporary and unstable features of the classroom social climates and teacher behaviours may mediate problem children's locus-of-control beliefs more strongly than those of non-problem children.

Summary

This chapter has taken its title and contents from a programme of research dealing with the significance of studying classroom social climates and their relationship with problem and non-problem students' academic motivations, classroom behaviours, and causal attributions of success and failure.

The results of this series of studies exhibit close relationships and interaction between classroom social climates and students' positive and negative causal beliefs, academic motivations, and behaviours. Indeed, as far as the educational process is concerned, it is suggested that future research on the classroom culture should focus not singly but simultaneously on several aspects of the classroom environment and their interaction: social climates, teacher processes, student motivations and attributions.

References

BENNETT, N. (1976) *Teaching Styles and Pupil Progress*, Cambridge, Mass., Harvard University Press.

BROPHY, J.E. and GOOD, T.L. (1970) 'Teacher's communication of differential expectations for children's classroom performance: Some behavioral data', *Journal of Educational Psychology*, 61, pp. 365–74.

COOPER, H.M., BURGER, J.M. and GOOD, T.L. (1981) 'Gender differences in academic locus of control beliefs of young children', *Journal of Personality and Social Psychology*, 40, pp. 562–72.

CORNBLETH, C., DAVID, O.L., JR. and BUTTON, C. (1974) 'Expectations for pupil achievement and teacher-pupil interaction', *Social Education*, 38, pp. 54–8.

CRANDALL, V.C., KATKOVSKY, W. and CRANDALL, V.J. (1965) 'Children's beliefs in their own control of reinforcements in intellectual-academic achievement situations', *Child Development*, 36, pp. 91–109.

CROMWELL, R.H., BLASHFIELD, R.K. and STRAUSS, J.S. (1975) 'Criteria for classification systems', in HOBBS, N. (Ed.) *Issues in the Classification of Children Vol. 1*, San Francisco, Jossey Bass.

EVERTSON, C.M. and VELDMAN, D.J. (1981) 'Changes over time in process measures of classroom behaviour', *Journal of Educational Psychology*, 73, pp. 156–63.

FESHBACH, N. (1969) 'Student teacher preferences for elementary school pupils varying in personality characteristics', *Journal of Educational Psychology*, 60, pp. 126–32.

FRY, P.S. (1983) 'Process measures of problem and non-problem children's classroom behaviour: The influence of teacher behaviour variables', *British Journal of Educational Psychology*, 53, pp. 79–88.

FRY, P.S. and ADDINGTON, J. (1984) 'Comparison of social problem solving of children from open and traditional classrooms: A two-year longitudinal study', *Journal of Educational Psychology*, 76, pp. 318–29.

FRY, P.S. and COE, K.J. (1980) 'Interaction among dimensions of academic motivation and classroom social climate: A study of the perceptions of junior high and high school pupils', *British Journal of Educational Psychology*, 50, pp. 33–42.

FRY, P.S. and GROVER, S.C. (1984) 'Problem and non-problem children's causal explanations of success and failure in primary school settings', *British Journal of Social Psychology*, 23, pp. 51–60.

FYANS, L.J. and MAEHR, M.L. (1979) 'Attributional style, task selection, and achievement', *Journal of Educational Psychology*, 71, pp. 499–507.

GALVIN, J.P. and ANNESLEY, F.R. (1971) 'Reading and arithmetic correlates of conduct-problem and withdrawn children', *Journal of Special Education*, 5, pp. 213–19.

GARNER, J. and BING, M. (1973) 'Inequalities of teacher-pupil contacts', *British Journal of Educational Psychology*, 43, pp. 234–43.

GOOD, T.L. and BROPHY, J.E. (1974) 'Changing teacher and student behavior: An empirical investigation', *Journal of Educational Psychology*, 66, pp. 390–401.

HALE, R.L. and LANDINO, S.R. (1981) 'Utility of WISC-R subtest analysis in discriminating among groups of conduct problem and non-problem children', *Journal of Consulting and Clinical Psychology*, 49, pp. 91–5.

HUSTON-STEIN, A., FRIEDRICH-COFER, L. and SUSSMAN, E.J. (1977) 'The relation of classroom structure to social behaviour, imaginative play, and self-regulation of economically disadvantaged children', *Child Development*, 48, pp. 908–16.

JACKSON, P.W. (1968) *Life in Classrooms*, New York, Holt, Rinehart and Winston.

KAYE, S., TRICKETT, E. and QUINLAN, D. (1977) 'Alternative methods for environmental assessment: An example', *American Journal of Community Psychology*, 4, pp. 367–77.

MARSHALL, H.H. (1981) 'Open classrooms: Has the term outlived its usefulness?' *Review of Educational Research*, 51, pp. 181–92.

MCDERMOTT, P.A. (1980) 'Congruence and typology of diagnosis in school psychology: An empirical study', *Psychology in Schools*, 7, pp. 12–24.

MOEN, R. and DOYLE, K.O. (1977) 'Construction and development of the academic motivations inventory', *Educational Psychology Measure*, 13, pp. 509–12.

MOEN, R. and DOYLE, K.O. (1978) 'Measures of academic motivation: A conceptual review', *Research in Higher Education*, 8, pp. 1–23.

MOOS, R.H. (1974) *Evaluating Treatment Environments: A Social Ecological Approach*, New York, Wiley Interscience.

MOOS, R.H. (1979) 'Educational climates', in WALBERG, H.J. (Ed.), *Educational Environments and Effects*, Berkeley, Calif., McCutchan.

MOOS, R.H. and MOOS, B.S. (1978) 'Classroom social climate and student absences and grades', *Journal of Educational Psychology*, 70, pp. 263–9.

NEILSEN, H.D. and KIRK, D. (1974) 'Classroom climates', in WALBERG, H. (Ed.) *Evaluating Educational Performance*, Berkeley, Calif., McCutchan.

QUAY, H.C. and PETERSON, D.R. (1979) *Manual for the Behaviour Problem Checklist*, New Brunswick, NJ, School of Professional Psychology, Busch Campus, Rutgers State University.

ROSENTHAL, R. and JACOBSON, L. (1968) *Pygmalion in the Classroom: Teacher Expectation and Pupils' Intellectual Development*, New York, Holt, Rinehart and Winston.

ROTHBART, M., DALFREN, S. and BARRETT, R. (1971) 'Effects of teacher's expectancy on teacher-student interaction', *Journal of Educational Psychology*, 62, pp. 49–54.

RUBOVITS, P.C. and MAEHR, M.L. (1971) 'Pygmalion analyzed: Toward an explanation of the Rosenthal-Jacobson findings', *Journal of Personality and Social Psychology*, 19, pp. 197–203.

SOLOMAN, D. and KENDALL, A.J. (1979) *Children In Classrooms: An Investigation of Person-Environment Interaction*, New York, Praeger.

TRICKETT, E. and MOOS, R.H. (1974) 'Personal correlates of contrasting environments: Student satisfaction in high school classrooms', *American Journal of Community Psychology*, 2, pp. 1–12.

WALBERG, H. and THOMAS, S.C. (1972) 'Open education: An operational definition and validation in Great Britain and the United States', *American Educational Research Journal*, 9, pp. 197–202.

WRIGHT, R.J. (1975) 'The affective and cognitive consequences of an open education elementary school', *American Educational Research Journal*, 12, pp. 449–68.

How Order is Achieved in Classrooms

Walter Doyle and Kathy Carter
University of Arizona[1]

Studies of effectiveness in classroom management have under-scored the importance of an efficient activity system in establishing and maintaining order in classrooms (see Doyle, 1986; Emmer and Evertson, 1981). This chapter contains a report of research conducted to define more fully the procedural knowledge and the interpretive processes teachers use to manage classrooms successfully. The findings of this research as well as the concepts used to guide the inquiry have considerable practical significance for beginning and experienced teachers.

The chapter begins with an introduction to the key ideas that shaped the research and a brief summary of the methods used to analyze the classroom data. The discussion then turns to the results of two interrelated studies. The first study focused on how teachers achieved and sustained order in their classes throughout the year. For this study, narrative descriptions of class sessions conducted by seven junior high school English teachers were analyzed in an effort to specify more fully what a teacher needs to know in order to manage classrooms. For the second study narrative descriptions of class sessions were used to construct models of how four junior high school English teachers understood the problem of order and its solution in their classrooms. These models of teacher comprehension provide insight into the knowledge structures and cognitive processes that teachers use to interpret classroom scenes and decide how to act to achieve order. In discussing the findings of these studies, particular attention is given to implications for classroom practice.

Introduction

Basic Concepts

The concept of a classroom *activity* was basic to the research presented in this chapter. An activity can be defined as a bounded segment of classroom time characterized by an identifiable arrangement of people and space; a focal content or concern; and a pattern or programme of action for participants (see Gump, 1967; Ross, 1984; Yinger, 1980). Classroom activities are commonly labeled by seating arrangements (for example, seat-work, small-group discussions, whole-class presentations) or by content (for instance, art, spelling, vocabulary, terms which are often associated with particular arrangements of students). Other key dimensions of an activity are duration, the physical space in which work occurs, the type and number of students, the props and resources used, and the expected behaviour of students and the teacher. Activities, in other words, represent the various ways in which groups are structured, information is communicated, and resources are used in classrooms. Successful teaching is grounded in the management of these units of classroom organization.

At the same time, classroom management is fundamentally a cognitive enterprise (see Carter and Doyle, 1986; Doyle, 1986). Managerial skill, in other words, rests on how a teacher interprets classroom events and thinks about the problem of order in classroom situations. Analyses of what teachers know about classroom activities and how their knowledge is organized for use in coping with daily classroom problems is likely, therefore, to be an important ingredient in learning to manage classrooms.

Method

Sample and data. Data for the studies reported in this chapter were selected from a sample of twenty-five English teachers who participated in the Junior High School Classroom Organization Study (JHCOS) conducted at the University of Texas R & D Center for Teacher Education (see Evertson, Emmer and Clements, 1980). The data on each teacher consisted of approximately fourteen detailed narrative records obtained in each of two class periods. Observations were made throughout the school year with a concentration on the first three weeks of school. Observers were instructed to focus on classroom rules and procedures and on how activities were conducted. The narratives were reasonably complete descriptions of classroom scenes, including information about participants, physical arrangements, objects and props, time, and a running account of action.

In addition to the narrative records, teachers were rated on a variety of management scales covering such items as success of students, task orientation of the class, and amounts of inappropriate and disruptive student behaviours. Students' engagement during lessons and their final academic achievement were also measured. These measures of managerial processes and student achievement were used to estimate the teachers' relative effectiveness in management and instruction and to form contrasting cases of teachers who differed on indicators of management success but worked with similar populations of students. By comparing 'successful' and 'unsuccessful' teachers in similar situations, it was possible to untangle the environmental demands teachers face in managing classrooms. Particular attention in the analysis was also placed on management 'mistakes' because they often occasioned a need for a teacher to 'repair' a situation. Attempts to repair order were frequently rich with information about how teachers think about classrooms.

Procedures for analyzing narratives. The central problem of the analysis was to move systematically from the concrete and particularistic details contained in the narrative records to progressively more general propositions about how the teachers managed classroom activities and understood the problem of order in their classes. In travelling this distance, it was also necessary to preserve the dynamic quality of classroom processes by keeping the action moving as more abstract propositions were formulated. These problems were addressed by designing a sequence of four levels — activity description, activity analysis, comparative analysis, and cognitive modeling — each of which involved transforming the record into a more general description of classroom processes and teacher's knowledge; and by maintaining a focus throughout the analysis on the arrangement of events in time (see Burnett, 1973; Erickson and Shultz, 1981).

The first two levels of analysis — activity description and activity analysis — were carried out with data on a single teacher across all observations. The Level 1 analysis involved segmenting each narrative record for a single class session into activity descriptions to obtain the basic unit for all further analyses. A completed activity description contained five components: a general overview of the session; a description of the opening of the session; one or more segment descriptions with transitions between segments; a description of the way the session ended; and comments about the context of the class session and any general themes that were emerging in the analysis.

The Level 2 analysis consisted of a general description of how a teacher accomplished management across class meetings. This analysis provided a history of a particular classroom group for the school year. As in the Level 1 analysis, the basic unit was still the activity, but the focus shifted to more general propositions about the configuration of events across the year. To capture the classroom as a moving system, attention was given to the format and routines, that is, the standard ways of doing things in a class; the teacher's strategies and manoeuvres, that is, what the teacher did to start the activity system and keep it moving in response to changing circumstances; and the misbehaviour patterns of students and the desist style of the teacher.

The comparative analysis at Level 3 was designed to transform Level 2 propositions about how individual teachers solved the problem of order into more general statements about common patterns across teachers in managing the demands of the classroom environment. Because success in management and instruction was a known quality of the teachers in the sample, it was also possible to make statements about the patterns of activity management related to teaching effectiveness.

The results of the first study reported in this chapter were based on a Level 3 analysis. For the second study, a Level 4 analysis was conducted to transform statements about common patterns of activity management into propositions about how teachers think about or understand classroom events and their management (see Carter, 1985, 1986). At this level, attention shifted to the structure of knowledge implied by descriptions of what teachers reacted to or dwelled upon in solving the problem of classroom order. These models were, in turn, viewed as representations of teachers' comprehension of classroom events and their management.

Study One

Sample

Seven junior high school English teachers were analyzed for the first study. These teachers, grouped by contrast cases, can be described as follows:

Contrast 1: Teacher 14 and Teacher 25. Teacher 14 had eleven years of experience and taught two average-ability 7th-grade classes. The residual gain score (a measure of a teacher's instructional effectiveness) for her Period 1 class was ranked 20 out of the 34 classes in the JHCOS study. Gain for her Period 2 class ranked 24 of 34. Both classes were characterized by low task orientation and success and moderate to high levels of inappropriate student behaviour, and these ratings became worse across the year. In addition to relatively low indicators of instructional effectiveness, Teacher 14 received low overall observer ratings of management success.

Teacher 25 had eight years of teaching experience. Her Period 2 class was a low-ability 7th-grade group with the lowest pre-achievement means in the sample. The residual gain score, however, ranked 13 out of 34. The class was characterized by average success, moderate task orientation, and an average level of inappropriate student behaviour. There was a significant negative correlation between entering achievement scores and residual gain, indicating that lower-achieving students did better than their higher-achieving peers in this class. Period 5 for Teacher 25 was an average-ability 7th grade class with a residual gain rank of 26 out of 34. The class was characterized by moderate success and task orientation and an average level of inappropriate student behaviour. In addition to moderate to high indicators of instructional effectiveness, especially with lower-achieving students, Teacher 25 received high overall observer ratings of management success.

Contrast 2: Teachers 22 and 27. Teacher 22 had twenty years of experience and taught two average-ability 8th-grade classes with a residual gain rank of 28 and 23 out of 34 respectively. Both classes were characterized by moderate success and task orientation and moderate levels of inappropriate student behaviour. However, management ratings for her Period 4 class improved across the year, with an especially noticeable reduction in disruptive behaviour. In Period 6 ratings of success increased while inappropriate and disruptive behaviours decreased across the year. Although indicators of instructional effectiveness were only moderate, Teacher 22 was able to improve management conditions during the year and was rated 'average' on management success by observers. Such 'turn-around' cases are rare and, thus, warrant analysis.

Teacher 27 had two years of experience and taught two above-average ability 8th-grade classes. Residual gain for Period 1 ranked 2 out of 34, and Period 4 ranked 19 out of 34. The classes were characterized by high success and task orientation (both of which increased during the year) and low levels of disruptive and inappropriate student behaviours. In addition to relatively high indicators of instructional effectiveness, the teacher received high overall observer ratings of management success.

Contrast 3: Teacher 42 vs. Teacher 2 and Teacher 3. This contrast case was unique in that it involved three teachers: two classes of Teacher 42 compared to a low-achieving class of Teacher 2 and a high-achieving class of Teacher 3. Classes were combined in this way to achieve appropriate ability-level comparisons for Teacher 42. Teacher 42 was unique, also, in that indicators of instructional effectiveness were high but observer ratings of management success were low.

Teacher 42 had eight years of experience. Her Period 2 class was a high-ability 7th-grade group with the highest residual gain score in the sample. The class was characterized by moderate success and task orientation and moderate levels of inappropriate and disruptive student behaviours. Period 4 was a low-ability 7th grade class with a pre-test achievement rank at 33 out of 34. The residual gain score, however, ranked fifth of 34, the highest residual for a low-achieving class in the sample. Despite these very high indicators of instructional effectiveness, the class was characterized by low success and task orientation and high amounts of disruptive and inappropriate behaviours. Moreover, Teacher 42 received low overall observer ratings of management success.

Teacher 3 had seven years of experience. The class used for this analysis was a high-ability 8th-grade group with a pre-test achievement rank of 3 out of 34. The class was characterized by high success and task orientation, low levels of disruptive student behaviour, and a moderate level of inappropriate behaviour. Teacher 3 received high overall observer ratings of management success.

Teacher 2 had eight years of experience. The class used for this analysis was a low-achieving 7th-grade group with a pre-test rank of 30 out of 34. The residual gain score ranked 17 of 34. The class was characterized by moderate amounts of success and task orientation, low levels of disruptive student behaviour, and a moderate level of inappropriate behaviour. Teacher 2 received high overall observer ratings of management success.

Results and Discussion

For economy of presentation, the results of this study are organized around five major themes: the effect of the junior high school class schedule on activity systems; the nature of activities and their contexts; activity boundaries and distinctiveness; processes of getting activities started; and activity management and the curriculum. Individual cases examined in the analysis are used to illuminate these themes.

Activities within sessions. Teachers in this study sometimes had problems of fitting activities into the 55-minute time block of the single class session. The most commonly occurring activities, such as seat-work and whole-class instruction, often ran from 12 to 18 minutes. The rest of the time was filled with opening and closings, transitions, and shorter segments of lecturing or seat-work. In some cases, activities ran short and students had nothing to do during the last few minutes of a session. In other cases, a distinct closing routine was initiated a minute or so before the end of a session, or the bell for the end of the period interrupted the last activity.

The problem of fitting activities into a 55-minute period is related in part to the achievement levels of students. Ends of sessions were often ragged in low-achieving classes. Nevertheless, teachers with high management ratings (but not necessarily high indicators of instructional effectiveness) were consistently able to fit activities to sessions, especially at the beginning of the year. In addition, more effective managers often either let the bell interrupt the last activity (the work was then completed in class the next day or assigned for homework) or clearly marked the closing of a session with a distinct routine for dismissal.

One particularly difficult segmenting problem existed in classes that were interrupted in the middle for lunch. In these instances, activities had to be scheduled to fit two sessions of approximately 25 minutes. In managing such split sessions successful teachers (for example Teachers 2 and 27) tended to schedule an activity to run across the lunch period. That is, they let lunch interrupt an activity that was to be completed when students returned to class. By carrying over an activity, implicit instructions were available to direct student actions for the start of the second half of the period.

These results suggest that in selecting and arranging activities, a teacher must account for the natural rhythms of individual sessions. To do so requires a considerable store of knowledge about how the problem of fitting activities to sessions is solved under different circumstances.

Activity types and their contexts. In the present study different types of activities — lecture, seat-work, recitation, discussion — seldom existed in pure form in classrooms. Although a particular pattern may have dominated, most segments were mixtures: teachers often inserted questions in lectures or made announcements during seat-work. The greatest amount of mixing occurred during whole-class presentations of content and reviews of completed assignments, segments which occurred frequently (see also Stodolosky, Ferguson and Wimpelberg, 1981). Content was typically presented by going over a worksheet or a section of a textbook using a combination of lecture, questions (often related to information learned previously), and oral exercises or examples. Work was most often checked in class by a combination of recitation and lecture in which students supplied answers and the teacher gave answers or expanded on a student's contribution.

In addition to mixing formats within segments, teachers often bound different segments together by a common theme. This happened most often when a whole-class presentation served as an introduction to seat-work, as most whole-class presentations were, in fact, used. In many cases, seat-work was followed, in turn, by a segment in which the assignment was reviewed and graded in a lecture or recitation format. In one of the more elaborated instances of such binding, Teacher 25 began class on the third day of school with an introduction to the dictionary. Students then copied words from an overhead slide and looked them up in their dictionaries. The final segment consisted of a brief game in which the teacher called out a word and the students raced to see who could find it in the dictionary first. In analyzing narratives it often seemed inappropriate to separate segments which were tied together in this manner. There was a clear sense that the different activities did not function independently but worked jointly as a 'lesson' unit. Indeed the lesson often appeared as an intermediate unit between the session and the activity in teacher planning.

Activity boundaries. Teachers differed in the extent to which they clearly marked the boundaries between activities, and this practice seemed to be related to success in achieving order in classrooms. Arlin (1979) raised this issue in his analysis of transitions. He found that teachers who had identifiable transition segments, that is, who clearly marked the endings and beginnings of activities in a sequence, had higher work involvement. The results of the present study confirm Arlin's finding: teachers with high management ratings (but not necessarily high indicators of instructional effectiveness) had distinct patterns for opening and closing sessions and clearly signaled the beginnings and ends of segments. In other words, they actively orchestrated classroom events. Indeed, Teacher 25 was observed to mark transitions clearly even when there was a natural blending created by self-paced segments in which students were to finish one assignment and begin another. This marking was done by interrupting when most students appeared to have finished the first assignment to collect papers and tell the class to move to the second assignment.

In this area it appeared that effective managers had high situational awareness and communicated this awareness by giving a running commentary on events taking place in the room. In addition, mixed-activity types were not typically used. The 'programme of action' within activities was often simple and predictable, and activities were easy to identify and describe. Less successful managers, on the other hand, often used hybrid activities, especially for introducing seat-work, and frequently blended activities together so that it was difficult to segment the behaviour stream. Beginnings of sessions and of activities were often slow, and endings often drifted off into unstructured free time or talking and disruption.

Although students clearly contributed to this effect, the classes of less successful managers were characterized by a general looseness and lack of attention to detail. Teacher 14, for example, was observed to lose worksheets, hand out the wrong assignment, and erase sentences that she had written earlier for an oral exercise. Other less successful managers failed to have something for students to do at the beginning of sessions or at the end of self-paced seat-work segments. There is also some indication in these data that looseness and lack of attention to details of activities was an especially serious problem for beginning teachers.

Getting activities started. Since most of the data used for the present study were gathered during the first three weeks of the school year, they were especially useful for analyzing how teachers established activity systems at the beginning of the year. In classes of low-achieving students and less effective managers, there was a clear escalation of misbehaviour during the first week of the school year. Often the first day went fairly smoothly and students appeared reluctant to participate in class activities. After this initial hesitation, however, there was a rise in the frequency of misbehaviour and an eventual stabilizing at a moderate to high level of occurrence.

This escalation of misbehaviour was less noticeable in average- to high-achieving classes of successful managers. The analysis of narratives suggested that at least two factors contributed to this early stabilization of order in these classes. First, successful managers tended to hover over activities and usher them along during the first weeks of school. This was especially prominent during seat-work segments. Successful managers gave precise instructions for doing the work, often going over the first few items of an exercise during the introduction to the work. They then moved around the room checking to see whether students were doing the exercise properly and urging slower students to get started. Contacts with individual students were very brief as teacher attention was distributed widely across a class. The teachers would even give answers to students who were having trouble completing the assignment. In other words, the teacher's presence was announced continuously, and the emphasis was on getting work done.

After the first month or so of school, this hovering and ushering declined and there was a 'settling in' to work routines. The teachers were then less active as organizers and conductors during seat-work segments and spent more time with individual students. Less successful managers, on the other hand, often made this shift to individualized attention prematurely and had more difficulty sustaining seat-work segments.

Second, successful managers tended to fill communication channels with information about curriculum content and assignments rather than misbehaviour. This was done in part by giving a running commentary about academic work and activities. For example, during seat-work successful managers often gave private, work-related contacts a public character by talking loud enough to be heard by the rest of the class. They also noticed when a student was on the wrong page or was using the wrong book.

Successful managers also blocked any event or incident that might interrupt the flow of an activity or break the rhythm of the class. During public presentations, for example, they tended to defer interruptions caused by students' questions ('We can take care of that later.') or ignore rule violations that did not disrupt the activity (for example, gum chewing) until transitions or seat-work so that disciplinary contacts were less public. Indeed, successful managers seemed very reluctant to have public confrontations over misbehaviour. In classes in which students often tried to misbehave, the more successful managers would often ignore minor inappropriate actions, such as talking or calling out answers, and push on with activities even though some rules were eventually never enforced. Less successful managers, on the other hand, often readily accepted interruptions and frequently attended to rule violations even if such attention stopped the flow of activity.

Teacher 22 provided a particularly interesting case of activity management. In her Period 4 class, there was a small group of boys who frequently initiated misbehaviour and ignored the teacher's reprimands. Moreover, these students joined one another quickly whenever an incident of misbehaviour began. There was, in other words, a rapid 'spread of effect' for inappropriate and disruptive behaviours. The teacher appeared to respond to this situation by pushing ahead with activities, talking continuously about work, and hovering over seat-work segments. In addition, she ignored the misbehaviour of the small core of disruptive students and reprimanded less serious offences by students who were more likely to cooperate. In effect, she focused public attention on activities and protected these activities from misbehaviour by excluding the disruptive students and preventing other students from joining their ranks. And in the long run she was successful: the activity system took hold and began to run smoothly. Moreover, the original core of disruptive students eventually became involved in academic work, and ratings on indicators of management success showed improvement. In the end the teacher was able to turn the situation around — a rare event in teaching — although the process of getting an activity system in place was protracted.

It seems clear from this analysis that successful managers directed public attention in classrooms to activities rather than misbehaviour. They seemed to prefer handling misbehaviour privately in order to maintain the rhythm or flow of class events. When faced with situations which were difficult to manage, they pushed ahead with the activity system and protected it by ignoring misbehaviour and raising their threshold for accepting rule violations. This approach appeared to contribute to achieving and sustaining classroom order.

Pushing the curriculum. Until recently subject-matter has not been a central consideration in research on teaching. Nevertheless, studies have shown that content-related variables, such as opportunity to learn and curriculum pace, are consistently associated with learning gains (see Brophy and Good, 1986). Curriculum became an issue in the present study because Teacher 42 had high achievement and low ratings of order and management success. The analysis of Teacher 42's classes indicated that she used many of the practices of less successful managers. Openings of class sessions were slow and there was a looseness around the edges of activities. Inappropriate behaviour was high and the teacher seldom attended to details. Yet, the teacher appeared to push students through the curriculum. She introduced work and tended to ignore inappropriate behaviour. In addition, she frequently graded assignments in class either by herself or in whole-class checking sessions.

A similar picture of pushing students through the curriculum was apparent in Teacher 2's low-achieving class. The teacher often seemed to tolerate more inappropriate behaviour than she wanted but continued to direct attention to content and held students accountable for work.

This combination of low management success and high achievement gain is probably unusual. Nevertheless, it does call attention to a potentially important connection between management and curriculum. Orderliness does not necessarily mean that students will learn, especially if teachers abandon the curriculum to stop misbehaviour and maintain cooperation in activities.

Conclusion

This analysis of activity management in junior high English classes provides insight into the complex processes of achieving order in a classroom. In particular, the study suggests that successful managers are able to:

1 Construct lessons that fit the externally-paced schedule of the school day.
2 Use activities that have a clear programme of action for participants.
3 Explicitly mark the boundaries of activities and the transitions between activities.
4 Demonstrate situational awareness by attending to details and commenting on events taking place in the room.
5 Protect activities until they are established by actively ushering them along, focusing public attention on work, and ignoring misbehaviour that disrupts the rhythm and flow of classroom events.
6 Push students through the curriculum even when misbehaviour is prevalent in the class.

Study 2

The results of the first study implied that teachers who differed in managerial and instructional success thought about classrooms and the problem of order in very different ways. To explore this possibility, Carter (1985, 1986) analyzed four additional cases of junior high English teachers from this sample in an effort to construct models of teacher comprehension. These comprehension models consisted of knowledge structures and cognitive processes that accounted for how the teachers interpreted classroom scenes and acted to solve the problem of order. The results of these analyses are summarized in this concluding section.

Analyzing Teacher Comprehension

The comprehension models for the second study were constructed from detailed maps of the way teachers achieved order in their classes across the year. These maps were similar to those used in the first study of activity management discussed above. To transform statements about common patterns of activity management into propositions about how the teachers understood classroom events, special attention was given to what a teacher reacted to, talked about, or dwelled upon in solving the problem of class order. In addition, the literature from cognitive psychology was used to guide the formulation of comprehension models.

A central premise of cognitive science is that comprehension is a *constructive* process (see Bransford and Franks, 1976). Meaning does not result from reception or rehearsal of information. Rather, understanding involves an active construction of a cognitive representation of events or concepts and their relationships in a specific context. Schemata play an especially important role in ordering knowledge and accounting for ambiguities in passages or situations (see Rumelhart, 1981; Schank and Abelson, 1977). A schema is an ordered representation of objects, episodes, actions or situations which contains slots or variables into which specific instances of experience in a particular context can be fitted. A schema provides, therefore, a framework for structuring and interpreting experience and for making inferences to complete the picture of association and causality among events or episodes. From this perspective, teachers' knowledge of classrooms consists of schema or scripts that permit them to interpret instances of behaviour and predict the likely configuration of events in a particular classroom.

Sample

The teachers used for this analysis comprehension can be described as follows:

Contrast 1: Teacher 32 and Teacher 18. Teacher 32 had ten years of experience. Her Period 3 class was an average-ability group with a residual gain score that ranked fourth out of 34. The class was characterized by moderate amounts of success, a high level of task orientation, and low levels of disruptive and inappropriate behaviour. Teacher 32's Period 2 was a low-ability class with a residual gain score that ranked 18 out of 34. The class was characterized by moderate amounts of student success, a high level of task orientation, and low amounts of disruptive and inappropriate behaviour. In addition to high indicators of instructional effectiveness, Teacher 32 received high overall observer ratings of management success.

Teacher 18 had four years of experience. Her Period 3 class was a high ability group with a residual gain score that ranked 31 out of 34. The class was characterized by average levels of success, moderate levels of task orientation, and average amounts of disruptive and inappropriate behaviour. Teacher 18's Period 2 was an average ability class with a residual gain score that ranked 32 out of 34. The class was characterized by average levels of success, moderate amounts of task orientation, low to average levels of disruptive behaviour, and average levels of inappropriate behaviour. In addition to low indicators of instructional effectiveness, Teacher 18 received low overall observer ratings of management success.

Contrast 2: Teacher 2 and Teacher 31. Teacher 2 had eight years of experience and taught two low-ability classes. However, the residual gain scores for the classes were high: Period 4 ranked 17 out of 34 and Period 6 ranked eight of 34. Her classes were characterized by moderate to high amounts of success and task orientation and low levels of inappropriate and disruptive student behaviours. In addition to high indicators of instructional effectiveness, Teacher 2 received high overall observer ratings of management success.

Teacher 31 had four years of experience and also taught two low-ability classes. Her Period 4 class ranked 16 out of 34 on residual gain, and her Period 6 class ranked 14 of 34. In contrast to these relatively good indicators of instructional effectiveness, the classes were characterized by low to average amounts of success and task orientation and high levels of inappropriate and disruptive student behaviours. Teacher 31 received low overall observer ratings of management success.

Results and Discussion

The analysis of these cases suggested sharp differences in classroom knowledge and comprehension between more and less successful managers. These differences are summarized below.

Much of what Teacher 32 did to manage her classes successfully can be accounted for by a conception of her role as *a driver navigating a complex route*. She sustained activities, in other words, by steering around obstacles rather than confronting them directly. One day, for instance, Teacher 32 struggled to get a discussion moving. Rather than criticize the students for not participating, she quickly switched the topic to students' preferences for hamburgers. A lively discussion followed during which students practised the routines of hand-raising and turn-taking in class discussion. The teacher then returned to the official curriculum, and the activity flowed smoothly. Because she emphasized movement and navigation, Teacher 32 was reluctant to reprimand individual students when that action might disrupt the flow of activity in the class. She preferred, rather, to incorporate students' comments into the lesson and to speak to misbehaving students privately at the end of class.

Teacher 18's management efforts, in contrast, can be accounted for by a conception of the management role as *a defender of a territory*. This image captures her emphasis on reprimands, authority and supervisory power to control inappropriate and disruptive behaviour. She frequently reprimanded individual students for misbehaviour, as if the problem of order were solved by policing, confronting, and then attempting to 'win out' over students. Indeed, she reacted to nearly all instances of misbehaviour. At times, however, her attempts to defend order stopped the flow of an activity. Thus the flow of activities was quite irregular and order was often in jeopardy.

The second comparison between Teacher 2 and Teacher 31 provides further refinement of our understanding of teacher comprehension.

Teacher 2 moved briskly through activities, set a fast pace for classroom events, and established a regularized and predictable classroom setting. This sense of movement, regulation, and tempo can be accounted for by a conception of the management role as *pathfinder and pacesetter*. The teacher clearly invested her energies in creating an activity system to carry the burden of order in the classes and then monitored and guided that system to ensure that the group functioned efficiently. She resolved tensions between work and order by setting a pace to sustain order, pulling outliers into the group flow, making public the ground that was being covered, and prompting and guiding students through assignments.

Teacher 31, on the other hand, focused on individual students and their maturity rather than the activity system. Her approach can be depicted in an image of the classroom manager as *gentle persuader and arbiter of adult conscience*. She acted as if she needed to convince students of their adult responsibilities by ignoring whenever possible their 'immature' actions and providing them with opportunities to act as adults. As a result, she was especially conciliatory to students who misbehaved the most in order to 'win them over'. This individualistic style often meant that group movement was neglected. As a result, order was often tenuous and most class time was spent showing films or having students or the teacher read the text aloud.

Conclusion

These case analyses indicate clearly that management practices are deeply embedded in the knowledge structures and comprehension processes a teacher uses to interpret classroom scenes. It is how a teacher understands action-situation relationships in classrooms rather than what skills she or he possesses that determines how the problem of order will be solved in a classroom. Indeed, one would expect that the interpretive framework a teacher brings to classrooms would shape what she or he would learn from teacher education experiences. If, for instance, a teacher believes that order rests on the quality of reprimands (as in the case of Teacher 18), then information about monitoring activity systems would likely seem irrelevant to the management task. In learning to teach, then, it is important to examine the preconceptions one has about how classrooms work.

One interesting implication follows from the cases presented here. Successful classroom managers, it would appear, tend to think about classrooms in terms of activities and movement, whereas less successful managers tend to concentrate on individual student contacts. Although more research is needed to verify this conclusion, it is consistent with the analysis in the first study of how order is achieved in classrooms.

General Conclusion

The research reported in this chapter represents an important new direction in understanding the foundations of classroom management. Much previous writing in this area has directed attention to what actions to take after students misbehave. Although such occasions in classrooms highlight the need for teacher intervention to restore order, they do not represent a proper focus for establishing order in the first place. The studies reported here, building on the important research of Kounin (1970) on group management in classrooms, direct teachers' thinking to activities that organize students for working in classrooms. These activity structures ultimately carry the burden of order by defining appropriate actions for both teachers and students in classroom environments. As teachers come to understand these activity systems, they acquire a powerful intellectual resource for creating classroom conditions in which students learn.

Note

The chapter is a revised and expanded version of 'How order is achieved in classrooms: an interim report', which appeared in the *Journal of Curriculum Studies*, 16, pp. 259–77. The research was supported in part by the US National Institute of Education, Contract OB-NIE-G-80-0116, P2, Research on Classroom Learning and Teaching Program, in funds to the Research and Development Center for Teacher Education at the University of Texas at Austin. The opinions expressed here do not necessarily reflect the position or policy of the NIE and no official endorsement by that office should be inferred. Randall Hickman and Margie Gaines provided valuable help in the analysis of narratives.

References

ARLIN, M. (1979) 'Teacher transitions can disrupt time flow in classrooms', *American Educational Research Journal*, 16, pp. 42–56.

BRANSFORD, J.D. and FRANKS, J.J. (1976) 'Toward a framework for understanding learning', in BOWERS, G.H. (Ed.) *The Psychology of Learning and Motivation: Advances in Research and Theory* (Vol. 10), New York, Academic Press.

BROPHY, J.E. and GOOD, T.L. (1986) 'Teacher behavior and student achievement', in WITTROCK, M.C. (Ed.) *Handbook of Research on Teaching*, 3rd ed., New York, Macmillan.

BURNETT, J.H. (1973) 'Event description and analysis in the microethnography of urban classrooms', in IANNI, F.A.J. and STOREY, E. (Eds) *Cultural Relevance and Educational Issues: Readings in Anthropology and Education*, Boston, Massachusetts, Little, Brown.

CARTER, K. (1985) *Teacher Comprehension of Classroom Processes: An Emerging Direction in Classroom Management Research*, paper presented at the annual meeting of the American Educational Research Association, Chicago.

CARTER, K. (1986) *Classroom Management as Cognitive Problem Solving: Toward Teacher Comprehension in Teacher Education*, paper presented at the annual meeting of the American Educational Research Association, San Francisco.

CARTER, K. and DOYLE, W. (1986) 'Teachers' knowledge structures and comprehension processes', in CALDERHEAD, J. (Ed.) *Exploring Teachers' Thinking*, London, Holt, Rinehart and Winston.

DOYLE, W. (1986) 'Classroom organization and management', in WITTROCK, M.C. (Ed.) *Handbook of Research on Teaching*, 3rd ed., New York, Macmillan.

EMMER, E.T. and EVERTSON, C.M. (1981) 'Synthesis of research in classroom management', *Educational Leadership*, 38, pp. 342–7.

ERICKSON, F. and SHULTZ, J. (1981) 'When is a context? Some issues and methods in the analysis of social competence', in GREEN, J.L. and WALLAT, C. (Eds) *Ethnography and Language in Educational Settings*, Norwood, N.J., Ablex.

EVERTSON, C.M., EMMER, E.T. and CLEMENTS, B.S. (1980) *Report of the Methodology, Rationale, and Instrumentation of the Junior High Classroom Organization Study*. Research and Development Center for Teacher Education R & D Report No. 6100, The University of Texas at Austin, ERIC ED 189 076.

GUMP, P.V. (1967) *The Classroom Behaviour Setting: Its Nature and Relation to Student Behavior* (Final Report), Washington, D.C., Office of Education, Bureau of Research. ERIC ED 015 515.

KOUNIN, J.S. (1970) *Discipline and Group Management in Classrooms*, New York, Holt, Rinehart and Winston.

ROSS, R.P. (1984) 'Classroom segments: The structuring of school time', in ANDERSON, L.W. (Ed.) *Time and School Learning: Theory, Research and Practice*, London, Croom Helm.

RUMELHART, D.E. (1981) 'Schemata: The building blocks of cognition', in GUTHRIE, J.T. (Ed.) *Comprehension and Teaching: Research Reviews*, Newark, Del., International Reading Association.

SANFORD, J.P. and EVERTSON, C.M. (1981) 'Classroom management in a low SES junior high: Three case studies', *Journal of Teacher Education*, 32, pp. 34–8.

SCHANK, R.C. and ABELSON, R.P. (1977) *Scripts, Plans, Goals, and Understanding: An Inquiry into Human Kowledge Structures*, Hillsdale, N.J., Lawrence Erlbaum Associates.

STODOLOSKY, S.S., FERGUSON, T.L. and WIMPELBERG, K. (1981) 'The recitation persists, but what does it look like?', *Journal of Curriculum Studies*, 13, pp. 121–30.

YINGER, R.J. (1980) 'A study of teacher planning', *Elementary School Journal*, 80, pp. 107–27.

What Students Think of Teachers' Classroom Control Techniques: Results From Four Studies

Ramon Lewis and Malcolm N. Lovegrove
La Trobe University

Introduction

> Year after year, classroom discipline heads the list of teacher concerns. It produces more stress than any other aspect of teaching, builds high levels of anxiety and frustration that sometimes lead to a sense of helplessness, and consumes monumental amounts of time intended for teaching and learning. All in all it probably contributes more to teacher burnout than any other factor. (Charles, 1981, p. 48)

Two major issues relating to classroom discipline practices can be identified in the above quotation. The first concerns the relationship between student misbehaviour and teacher stress and the second focuses upon the adverse effect that misbehaviour has upon student 'time-on-task' (Charles, 1981; Smyth, 1981; Bloom, 1980; Frederick and Walberg, 1980 and Rosenshine, 1976).

For the last six years our primary interest has been to explore the latter issue both within Australia (Lovegrove and Lewis, 1982; Lewis and Lovegrove, 1983a; Lewis and Lovegrove, 1983b; Lewis and Lovegrove 1984; Lovegrove and Lewis, 1984) and in a comparative context (Lovegrove, Lewis, Oyvind and Stromes, 1983; Lovegrove, Lewis, Fall and Lovegrove, 1985). In this chapter we will examine what we consider to be the most significant findings of our research seen in relation to the problem as it is purported to exist in the classroom. Underlying our interest is the assumption that time-on-task is, amongst other influences, a product of a teacher's control skills and their interaction with students' perceived preferences — an opinion which has been expressed by Smyth (1980). Our belief is that if teachers utilize the sort of control techniques students prefer, then students will, in the course of the school day, be less disruptive and therefore spend more time-on-task. As Charles (1981) has stressed:

> Discipline, class control, classroom management — by whatever name you call it, keeping order in the classroom is a teacher's greatest concern. You may not like the fact; you may wish it weren't true. But it is. That's a given in the daily life of teachers. Discipline is so crucial, so basic to everything else in the classroom, that most educators agree; it is the one thing that makes or breaks teachers .... If students don't stay on task, they don't learn. At least they don't learn what they are supposed to. If they do whatever they want the best plans, activities, and materials don't mean a thing. It needn't be the whole class that misbehaves. Three or four students, even one can so disrupt a class that learning becomes impossible for even the best behaved students. (p. 13)

The issue of student misbehaviour and its control is of considerable interest to parents and teachers. As McDaniel has stated, 'The public puts such emphasis on good school discipline that its absence is cited as the number one problem in America today' (1981, p. 31). To justify his claim, McDaniel references American Gallup polls which indicate that 'for the tenth time in the last eleven years, school discipline is perceived by the public as education's most important problem' (p. 43).

Several arguments have been proposed to show that many teachers find it difficult to manage the behaviour of children in their classes. First, a marked breakdown of student and teacher relationships has occurred in a number of Western countries — a breakdown that reflects the inability of teachers to adapt to the postwar transition from an autocratic to a more democratic society. Secondly, many teachers are unprepared, in terms of skills, for the complex behavioural problems with which they may be confronted in the classroom. This problem is exacerbated when educational economies reduce the range and quality of support services available to teachers. Thirdly, many teenagers perceive the contemporary school and curriculum as 'bankrupt'. The high rate of unemployment among school-leavers encourages such students to believe that schooling can no longer be justified primarily in terms of the school's ability to provide job-related knowledge and skills. Feeling let down, they are not inclined to accommodate to traditional forms of control. Fourthly, the teacher's historic role as a purveyor of knowledge and developer of skills has been eroded by competing forms of 'expertise', namely, the mass media, particularly television. Finally, the factors mentioned above may have interacted in such a way as to mislead teachers into thinking that students, not teachers, have rights in the classroom and that firm control by teachers is no longer acceptable.

The responses of educators to the concern of teachers and parents with classroom management have varied. They range from proposals that teachers become more assertive and adopt a 'take charge approach' (Canter and Canter, 1976) to appeals to teachers to stop 'crippling our children with discipline' and to engage children in power sharing, problem solving, and negotiation (Gordon, 1981).

The Studies

In our work it was inappropriate to replicate the methodology of most of the previous research conducted in the area of classroom control which used observations of teachers and pupils or questioned teachers. This was partly because of methodological difficulties associated with these sources of data. Teachers, apart from being relatively unreliable reporters of their classroom behaviour (Hook and Rosenshine, 1979), were unlikely to provide valid data on their behaviour in an area as sensitive as discipline. Similarly, observation of teachers was likely to influence their classroom control behaviour and thereby make the measure invalid. In addition, student misbehaviour and the teacher's response to it are relatively infrequent occurrences and therefore many lessons would need to be observed to obtain a reliable sample of a teacher's behaviour.

As important as methodological considerations, however, was the fact that the focus of the research was on those control techniques used by teachers which were preferred by students. This clearly required an investigation of the views of students.

We recognize that it is possible to argue that for time-on-task to be maximized, teachers should use techniques least preferred by students. Students will then work hard to avoid being treated in ways they find unpleasant or even offensive. Although there is some appeal to this logic, our extensive, but informal, contact with students has indicated that meeting student preferences in the area of classroom management would not only result in a more pleasant classroom climate but also one which was also more productive. Furthermore, it has been asserted that an essential feature of the learning environment is of an affective nature (Aspey and Roebuck, 1977).

In summary, therefore, one of the ways by which the effectiveness of teachers as disciplinarians, socialization agents and developers of cognitive skills can be assessed is by examining students' reactions to teachers who are perceived to use different types of control techniques.

The primary purpose of this chapter is to provide a synthesis of data from a number of separate studies conducted by the authors. Some of these data have been reported elsewhere (Lewis and Lovegrove, 1983a, 1983b, 1984; Lovegrove *et al.*, 1983). However, most of them are as yet unreported. In addition, at no time have all the data been considered simultaneously with a view to identifying replicated findings which pertain to the degree to which teachers' perceived classroom management behaviour approximates those preferred by students.

During 1980, 1981 and 1982 we undertook a series of studies aimed at exploring students' perception of teachers' control behaviour. To assess the variety of teacher-control behaviour which was relevant to the aims of the studies, we commenced by identifying the approximate range of control behaviours being currently practised in schools. This information was obtained by conducting and analyzing taped interviews with one class of grade nine students in each of five coeducational state schools in metropolitan Melbourne. The schools were selected on the basis of our knowledge of the degree of cooperation we were likely to receive from staff in an area of research often perceived as being threatening and sensitive. Grade nine students (13–14 years of age) were selected rather than grade eight or those in grade ten and beyond, because experienced teachers advised that, on the one hand, grade nine students had, in the main, weathered the transition from primary to secondary school, which occurs at the beginning of grade seven, and in addition their opinions were less likely to be dominated by achievement motives generated by the pressures of external examinations. These factors interacted in such a way as to predispose students at the grade nine level to be more overt in their opinions than those younger or older than themselves.

The interviews referred to above formed the basis of a questionnaire which was compiled using the pupils' own language. The questionnaire was designed to provide information on those teaching characteristics and classroom control practices perceived as typifying both 'good' and 'bad' teachers.

After its reliability was established (Lovegrove and Lewis, 1982) the questionnaire, which included forty-six descriptions of classroom control practices, was administered to 264 grade nine students in eleven state coeducational schools in Melbourne. The students provided indications of the extent to which each of the practices characterized the 'best' and 'worst' teacher they had experienced in the last three years by responding on a 4-point scale ranging from Strongly Agree to Strongly Disagree.

Although students were not asked about the frequency of teachers' use of each of the forty-six classroom control strategies described in the questionnaire, the strategies were taken to be alternative possible responses to a finite number of classroom management situations. Therefore it was assumed that the extent of agreement was generally a rough but approximate measure of the behaviour's occurrence. Even if this were not the case, the degree to which a teacher was perceived as characterized by a behaviour, would have been acceptable as a measure of the extent to which that behaviour would influence a student's generalized response to the teacher. An example will clarify our assumptions. Firstly, if a student strongly agrees that a teacher hits, it is probable that the teacher hits students frequently. Secondly, even if the hitting is infrequent, as long as it is seen as a strong characteristic, we would argue that it will strongly influence a student's response to the teacher, no matter how infrequently the teacher behaves that way.

To obtain some insight into the criteria that students were using to identify 'good' teachers, some additional items were included on the questionnaire. Students combined aspects of teaching skill, the teacher's personality and the quality of the teacher-student relationship in determining which teachers were 'good' (Lewis and Lovegrove, 1983a).

A second study involved 364 grade nine students (attending sixteen classes in nine schools) in describing the classroom control practices of one of their current teachers and providing an indication of the extent to which they liked the teacher. The questionnaire used to gather data for this study was a modified and augmented version of the one used in our earlier work. Thirty-six of the original forty-six classroom control techniques were included in this questionnaire together with a series of statements describing student feelings that might be aroused when teachers attempt to control misbehaviour in their classroom.

Four forms of the questionnaire were produced. In one form students were asked to 'Think of a female teacher who teaches you *one* of the following subjects: Science, Mathematics. DON'T write down her name. *Keep this teacher and only this teacher in mind as you answer the questionnaire*'.

In the second form of the questionnaire the subject grouping was changed to Humanities and comprised History, General Studies and Social Sciences. The third and fourth version of the questionnaire used the same subject groups, but asked for a description of a male teacher.

By systematically administering the four forms of the questionnaire within each classroom visited, it was possible to conclude that between 64 and 364 teachers were being described. The reason individual teachers were not identified was the need to ensure anonymity for teachers and thereby to increase the likelihood of schools' participation in the research. The necessity for anonymity unfortunately attentuates any attempt to generalize from the data as it is possible that all students chose to report on a teacher whom they thought was best (or worst) at controlling classes. However, given the complete lack of guidance in this decision, it is reasonable to assume that useful discussion of the data was not precluded by systematic bias, particularly in view of the fact that we had a further replication in mind.

The third study involved the use of a slightly modified version of the questionnaire used in the second study. This questionnaire was administered, in 1982, to a total of 710 year nine students attending twenty classes in ten state high or technical schools.

Finally, reference will be made below to a further study, this being the one which involved the administration of a culturally modified questionnaire based on that employed in the second study mentioned. It called for students to identify control techniques characteristic of 'good' teachers.

This questionnaire was administered to 408 grade nine pupils in ten high schools in Melbourne, 215 year nine pupils in five junior high schools in Tromsø, Norway, and 532 year nine pupils in five high schools in Buffalo, New York, USA. However, reference in this chapter will be made to the Melbourne data only.

Findings

Good Teachers' Classroom Management

The first step in trying to identify discipline procedures involved consideration of the students' perception of 'good' teachers. The means of the items describing a good teacher's classroom management behaviour were coded either as relevant (R), important (I) or very important (VI) according to the mean score obtained. The key for the coding of items is shown in Table 1. Any item mean within 0.1 of the 'neutral' or 'no opinion' position was labelled as non-significant (NS) in determining the preferences of students because the standard error of each item was approximately 0.08 and was never greater than 0.1. Since it was possible for an item to be significant in that it may be a technique good teachers would use or would avoid, the two need to be distinguished. In the tables which follow, results relating to strategies which good teachers would *avoid* using have been italicized.

Table 1: Coding for Significance of Items Describing a 'Good' Teacher

Coding	*Value of Item Mean*
Not significant (*)	2.4–2.6
Relevant (R)	2.1–2.3 or 2.7–2.9
Important (I)	1.8–2.0 or 3.0–3.2
Very important (VI)	1.0–1.7 or 3.3–4.0

To summarize the data, items were first identified which students saw as significant for the description of good teachers (items classified as at least 'relevant'). These were 41 of the 50 items recorded in Table 2. Of these, 19 described classroom control behaviours good teachers would use and the remaining 22 described behaviours they would avoid. The 41 items will be considered first and the remaining 9 items, for which the student as a group were undecided, will be discussed later.

To facilitate interpretation of these data the 41 significant items reported in Table 2 have been grouped in Table 3 under eight headings.

In summary, one can infer that students appear to desire the teacher to take responsibility for the maintenance of order in the classroom (1, 7, 25, 32, 33) and not involve either parents (18, 42) or other teachers (16, 45). They want clear rules (6), designed in conjunction with students (9)

Table 2: 'Good' Teachers' Management Behaviour

No.	Behaviour	
1	Walk out of class when most of the class misbehave.	*VI*
2	Cane/strap kids.	*VI*
3	Explain that too much noise prevents learning from taking place.	R
4	Punish misbehaving kids rather than the whole class.	VI
5	Keep class in for detention.	*R*
6	Make rules for behaviour very clear.	R
7	Follow up a threat if misbehaviour occurs again.	R
8	Generally treat the same kind of misbehaviour with the same kind of punishment.	R
9	Allow students to work out the rules for behaviour themselves.	*R*
10	Tell off kids in front of the class.	*
11	Explain that he or she is annoyed by misbehaving kids.	R
12	Tell off kids in private.	R
13	Separate kids who misbehave.	R
14	Send misbehaving kids out of class.	R
15	Explain that he or she can't work when kids misbehave.	R
16	Send kids to other teachers for telling off (e.g. Principal).	*R*
17	Explain that the kids in class can't work when other kids misbehave.	R
18	Send note to parents of misbehaving kids.	*R*
19	Keep individual kids in (e.g. detention).	R
20	Keep class in (e.g. detention) because some kids misbehave.	*VI*
21	Have misbehaving kids do yard duty.	*
22	Have misbehaving kids write lines.	*
23	Have kids 'catch up' on work missed due to their misbehaviour.	R
24	Hit kids who misbehave.	*VI*
25	Ignore kids who misbehave.	I
26	Yell at kids who misbehave.	*
27	Give extra work as punishment.	*
28	Remain calm when telling off kids for misbehaving.	I
29	Embarrass kids who misbehave.	*R*
30	Give a warning before moving kids.	I
31	Give a warning before sending kids out of class.	R
32	Stand and wait for misbehaviour to stop.	*R*
33	Let kids off after promising punishment.	*R*
34	Swear at kids.	*VI*
35	Get angry at misbehaving kids.	*VI*
36	Name kids who misbehave.	*
37	Make a loud noise to attract attention.	*R*
38	Stare at kids who misbehave.	*R*
39	Move among kids who misbehave.	*
40	Demand an apology from misbehaving kids.	*
41	Confiscate or destroy objects belonging to misbehaving kids.	*VI*
42	Have interview with parents of kids who misbehave.	*R*
43	Remove privileges from misbehaving kids (e.g. no excursion).	*R*
44	Give reasons why some types of behaviour are not allowed.	R
45	Have misbehaving kids attend a different class.	*R*
46	Reward kids when they don't misbehave.	*R*
47	Praise kids when they behave properly.	R
48	Tell off kids when it's not necessary.	*VI*
49	Tell off the wrong kids.	*VI*
50	Praise the class when everyone is behaving well.	I

Table 3: Classroom Control Techniques Which Should Be Used or Avoided by Good Teachers

	Techniques which should be	
	Used	Avoided
Acceptance of responsibility	7	1 16 18 25 32 33 42 45
Appropriate sanctions	13 14 23	2 24 37 38 41 43
Clear and acceptable rules	3 6 9 11 15 17 44	
Avoidance of danger/embarrassment	12 28	29 34
Selection of miscreant	4 19	5 20 48 49
Warnings	30 31	
Praising acceptable behaviour	47 50	46
Consistency	8	

and based on a number of reasons (44) including the needs of the students (3, 17) and the teacher (11, 15). The use of sanctions should occur after a warning (30, 31), should involve only the miscreant (4, 5, 19, 20, 48, 49) and should be applied in a calm manner (28, 34), minimizing embarrassment to the miscreant (12, 2). The sanctions used should focus on isolating students who misbehave (13, 14, 23) and should not include arbitrary or harsh punishments (2, 24, 37, 38, 41, 43). They should be applied consistently (8). Finally, good teachers should recognize appropriate behaviour, both by individuals (46, 47) and by the class (50).

The Most Acceptable Teachers' Classroom Management

The next stage in the analysis involved a determination of which of the 41 significant descriptions of good teachers' classroom control behaviour were seen occurring in practice. The manner in which this was done was the following. First, all the behaviours were identified which were attributed to the best teachers the grade nine students had been taught by during the past three years (in the 1980 study) and to teachers who were liked a lot (the 1981 and 1982 studies). These data were coded using the same categorization of items as described in Table 1. They are recorded in Table 4.

Since three separate sets of data were being considered, and a generalization was required, an item was accepted as a significant descriptor of the best of the students' current teachers if it was at least 'relevant' in two of the three sets of data.

However, some items were only used in one of the three pieces of research. These items were included as significant if they were classified as 'very important' ($1.5 > \times > 3.5$).

Table 5 records which of the 41 classroom control technques students identified as significant in the description of good teachers were seen as used or avoided by the students' best teachers. Items reported in paren-

Table 4: The Most Acceptable Teachers' Classroom Management Behaviour

	Item Number									
	1	2	3	4	5	6	7	8	9	10
Best (1980)	*VI*	*VI*	R	I	*I*	R	R	R	*R*	R
Liked Alot (1981)	*VI*	NA	NA	R	NA	*	R	NA	*I*	*
Liked Alot (1982)	*VI*	NA	NA	I	NA	NA	*	NA	*I*	I
	11	12	13	14	15	16	17	18	19	20
(1980)	I	*	R	*	R	*VI*	I	I	*R*	*I*
(1981)	I	R	R	*	*	*I*	I	*VI*	*	*I*
(1982)	I	R	R	*	*	*VI*	I	*VI*	*	*VI*
	21	22	23	24	25	26	27	28	29	30
(1980)	*R*	*	R	*VI*	*VI*	I	*R*	I	R	I
(1981)	*VI*	*I*	NA	*VI*	*I*	R	*R*	R	*	NA
(1982)	*VI*	*I*	NA	*VI*	*VI*	R	*I*	I	*	I
	31	32	33	34	35	36	37	38	39	40
(1980)	I	*R*	*I*	*VI*	R	R	*R*	*R*	*	*R*
(1981)	NA	*	NA	*VI*	R	R	NA	NA	NA	*R*
(1982)	*I*	*	NA	*I*	I	R	NA	NA	NA	*I*
	41	42	43	44	45	46	47	48	49	50
(1980)	*I*	*I*	*I*	*I*	*VI*	NA	NA	NA	NA	NA
(1981)	*I*	*I*	*R*	R	NA	NA	NA	*VI*	*R*	NA
(1982)	*I*	*I*	*I*	I	NA	*I*	*R*	*I*	*I*	*

theses in Table 5 are those which are, in general, neither used nor avoided by the best teachers available.

Of the 41 items reported in Table 3, over 60 per cent (26 items) have been classified consistently in Table 5. One may therefore infer that, in general, there is consistency between students' concepts of ideal classroom management and the sort of classroom management provided by the best or most liked of their real teachers. These findings would tend to suggest further support for the preferences attributed earlier to students.

Careful analysis of the 15 classroom control techniques preferred by students which are neither used nor avoided by their best teachers indicates that the gap between the ideal and the real is not large. Firstly with the exception of item 50, all of the items in parentheses in Table 5 are no

Table 5: Good Techniques Which Are Used or Avoided by Best Teachers

	Techniques which should be			
	Used		Avoided	
	Best Teachers Use	Best Teachers Avoid	Best Teachers Use	Best Teachers Avoid
Acceptance of responsibility	7			1 16 18 25 33 42 45 (32)
Appropriate sanctions	13 (14 23)			2 24 41 43 (37 38)
Clear and acceptable rules	9 11 17 44 (3 6 15)			
Avoidance of danger/embarrassment	28	12		34 (29)
Selection of miscreant	4 (19)			20 48 49 (5)
Warnings	30 31			
Praising acceptable behaviour	(47 50)			(46)
Consistency	(8)			

stronger than 'relevant' to the description of an ideal teacher. Secondly 10 of these 15 items show some support for the argument that there is consistency between the ideal and the real teacher behaviour, although the support is insufficient to be classified as significant.

Of the remaining 5 items deemed characteristic of good teachers, ratings on two (14, 50) do not appear to provide any support for the view that the best teachers use them. One could argue that the best teachers have no need to send misbehaving kids out of class (item 14) as they would not allow misbehaviour to go so far as to warrant such extreme measures. However, it is difficult to argue the same case for item 50 — 'praise the class when everyone is behaving well'.

It would appear that even the best teachers available use too little praise. This becomes more evident when item 47 is considered. Once again, students indicate that good teachers should praise kids when they behave properly but in this case the best teachers are actually seen to avoid doing so. One can infer from these findings that in the area of praise there is a clear gap between what students would perceive as good classroom management and the sort they are given by their best teachers.

As indicated at the beginning of these analyses, there were 9 items for which the students as a group were undecided. That is, the behaviours were seen as neither typical nor atypical of good teachers. These were items 10, 21, 22, 26, 27, 35, 36, 39, 40. Analysis of these is very valuable. They can be usefully grouped into the following three categories:

types of sanctions (21, 22, 27, 39)
embarrassing students (10, 36, 40)
anger (26, 35)

These will be considered in turn.

Despite the fact that the best teachers clearly avoid using yard duty, writing lines or extra work as punishment for miscreants, the students are not convinced that good teachers should avoid their use. The same can be said for moving among miscreants (39). It may be argued, as it was earlier, that the best teachers available don't require these techniques but prefer instead to give explanations to miscreants about why they should behave, follow these with warnings about the need to separate them from their friends or to isolate them, and then follow through if necessary (refer Table 3).

The second finding relates to teachers' use of anger. It is perhaps surprising that even the best and most liked of students' current teachers are seen to get angry at misbehaving kids (35) and yell at them (26) (although they don't swear at them (34)).

The fact that students don't see any of these behaviours as relevant to the description of good teachers would appear at first glance to be inconsistent with their desire that the teacher keeps calm when telling kids off. However, subsequent informal interviewing of students and teachers about these findings appeared to indicate that the key factor in making sense of this apparent contradiction is whether the anger is controlled or uncontrolled. Teachers who are, or who appear to be, out of control are one thing, whereas calm, righteous indignation, caused by the miscreant's disregard for reasonable rules, is a different matter. Similarly, shouting to be heard is one thing, whereas yelling because a teacher has 'lost his cool' is another. Although we can interpret the findings, we have yet to gain data on the students' response to the differing forms of anger described above. Despite the slight confusion, students' responses to item 28 (remain calm when telling off kids for misbehaving) are very consistent and strong, and would suggest that even righteous anger would need to manifest itself in calm communications of disapproval.

The final result, regarding teachers' embarrassment of miscreants, is not strong, but tends to indicate that the best teachers available have a tendency to name miscreants (36) and tell them off in front of the class (10) (although they don't demand apologies (40)). These behaviours have been categorized as embarrassing the miscreant because they appear consistent with the students' responses to items 12 and 29. The results of the former indicate that even though good teachers should tell miscreants off in private the best teachers don't. The results of the latter (29), show that even though good teachers shouldn't embarrass miscreants the best teachers were seen to do this in one of the three studies.

Comparison of the Most Acceptable and Least Acceptable Teachers

The next step in our analysis involved consideration of the items which discriminated between best and worst teachers, and between teachers liked a lot and those disliked. The relevance of this analysis was based on an assumption that many of the behaviours above, which characterize good teachers or the best or most liked teachers available, may also be applicable to bad teachers or the worst teachers available. For example, it is conceivable that 'making the rules clear' is as applicable to bad teachers as it is to good. Similarly, as discussed above, getting angry with kids who misbehave may not discriminate due to the ambiguity built into the item.

To consider this question it was first necessary to compute *t*-tests for correlated means for each of the 50 items describing the classroom control behaviours. These analyses allowed a comparison of the best and worst teachers or a comparison of the teachers liked a lot and those disliked, depending on the study. The statistical significance of these differences for each study are reported in Table 6. If the means indicated that the item best described the worst or the disliked teacher, the level of significance was italicized.

Inspection of relevant data in Table 6 indicates that there are 12 items classified as at least relevant ($P < .05$) for which the findings are consistent for the three studies and a further four which were used in only one study and for which the findings are highly significant ($P < .001$). These items can be grouped under four headings, three of which are equivalent to those recorded in Table 3. The first is anger. Students' responses to items 26, 28, 34 and 35 are all very strongly and consistently indicative of a preference for teachers who *remain calm when telling off kids* (28) and who are less likely to get angry at students (35), thereby yelling (26) or swearing at them (34).

The second group of items reflects students' preference for *less mistargetting*. Students strongly prefer teachers who are less likely to tell off kids unnecessarily (48), who choose the correct miscreant (35, 49) and who don't blame the class for the misbehaviour of some of its members 4, 20).

The third factor which strongly distinguishes between teachers is fair warning — teachers who are preferred are more likely to *provide students with warnings before acting against misbehaviour* (30, 31).

The remaining items which discriminate in favour of more preferred teachers are a somewhat miscellaneous collection comprising the provision by teachers of reasons for their reaction to misbehaviour (44) and a lesser likelihood of sending kids to other teachers for telling off (16), demanding an apology from miscreants (40), or walking out of the class when most of the class misbehave (1).

Although a number of other items are possibly relevant to defining students' preferences, in that the findings are consistent and significant for

Table 6: Comparative Use of Different Techniques

	Item Number									
	1	2	3	4	5	6	7	8	9	10
Best/Worst (1980)	*.001*	*.001*	*	.01	*.001*	*	*	.001	*	*.001*
Liked A Lot/Not Liked (1981)	*.001*	NA	NA	.001	NA	.05	*	NA	*	*.05*
Liked A Lot/Not Liked (1982)	*.001*	NA	NA	.001	NA	NA	*	NA	.05	*
	Item Number									
	11	12	13	14	15	16	17	18	19	20
(1980)	*	*	*	*	*	*.001*	*	*.001*	*	*.001*
(1981)	*	*	*	*.05*	*	*.05*	*	*	*.001*	*.001*
(1982)	*	*	*	*.01*	*	*.001*	*.01*	*.01*	*.001*	*.001*
	Item Number									
	21	22	23	24	25	26	27	28	29	30
(1980)	*	*	*	*.001*	*.05*	*.001*	*.001*	.001	*.00*	.001
(1981)	*	*.001*	NA	*	*	*.001*	*	.001	*	NA
(1982)	*	*.001*	NA	*	*	*.001*	*.01*	.001	*	.001
	Item Number									
	31	32	33	34	35	36	37	38	39	40
(1980)	.001	*	*	*.001*	*.001*	*.01*	*.001*	*.001*	*.01*	*.001*
(1981)	NA	*.05*	NA	*.05*	*.001*	*.001*	NA	NA	NA	*.01*
(1982)	.001	*	NA	*.001*	*.001*	*.001*	NA	NA	NA	*.01*
	Item Number									
	41	42	43	44	45	46	47	48	49	50
(1980)	*.001*	*.05*	*.001*	.05	*.05*	NA	NA	NA	NA	NA
(1981)	*.01*	*	*	.01	NA	NA	NA	*.001*	*.001*	NA
(1982)	*.001*	*.001*	*.001*	.001	NA	.001	.001	*.001*	*.001*	.001

two studies while not significant for the third, they will not be included in the discussion but left to the perusal of the careful reader.

Explanations and Implications

The degree to which teachers are actually meeting students' preferences in the areas described above can be inferred by considering the extent to which students' perceptions of teachers' current classroom control practices accord with those they attribute to good teachers.

Teachers are clearly meeting students' preferences in the areas of rule clarity and reasonableness, fairness, the use of appropriate punishment and acceptance of responsibility. In addition, teachers are perceived as using appropriate sanctions, for example, 'punishments' which would be considered as 'logical consequences' of the students' behaviour (Dreikurs and Grey, 1968) and as avoiding other teachers or parents in the control of the miscreant.

It is interesting to contemplate the relative infrequency of what may be viewed as 'arbitrary' discipline behaviours such as strapping, hitting, removing privileges, having lines written, yard duty performed or extra school work completed, when not so long ago the strapping of children was an accepted and frequently used procedure for maintaining school discipline. Similarly, 'punishments' as arbitrary as picking up papers in the school yard, writing lines, digging garden beds, or copying pages from texts were generally recognized as acceptable, even by those 'progressive' teachers who saw themselves as strongly caring for the rights of students, and who stressed the quality of their relationships with students. There was little belief that the imposition of such punishments was at variance with the professional role of a classroom teacher. Clearly, however, many of these sanctions are now only rarely used by teachers. Why?

Two major competing explanations appear plausible. The first is based on an assumption that schools have become places in which the rights of individual students have taken on a new meaning. This recognition of the worth of the individual derives in part from a realization that the school is no longer a place where students are provided mainly with the knowledge and skills necessary to ensure their full and active participation in the world of work. Schools have become institutions with a much broader set of attitudinal aims. They have become entrusted with the development in students of many of the social and leisure skills and attitudes which were once the exclusive domain of parents. Correspondingly, the importance of work-related knowledge appears to have been de-emphasized, with numeracy and literacy being two of the remaining bastions of essential learning.

Within this context, it is not unexpected that teachers should see fit to review their relationships which would facilitate the personal (rather than professional) development of students. Given such a re-evaluation of teacher-student relationships and the 'freeing-up' of the curriculum, it would not be surprising to find teachers wishing to make students more responsible not only for the content and process of their curriculum, but also for their own behaviour. In general, teachers would be seeking to promote a more egalitarian type of school society. They would, therefore, wish to minimize manifesting personalized power by imposing arbitrary sanctions on students as this may inhibit the quality of the relationship that they may establish with them. In contrast, they would view the student as someone with whom to negotiate a solution to any disruptive behaviour and would utilize the power invested in the teaching role to encourage students to engage in negotiation.

Therefore, the first of the potential explanations of the findings of the research suggests that the relative absence of arbitrary punishments is a result of teachers adopting a new 'democratic' view of the role of students, consistent with the increasing emphasis in schools on the personal development of children.

The second possible explanation for teachers' infrequent use of arbitrary punishments is less complimentary. This alternative explanation is based on an assumption that the changes in teachers' behaviour are a result of unthinking reaction. The need for a reaction has arisen as a result of two factors over which teachers have no control. The first of these is a shift in societal values, a movement well described by Balson (1982) who argues:

> The type of society which supported the superior-inferior continuum and the resultant pattern of interpersonal relationships started to change in the late 1950s. Beginning with the Black Power movement, there was a series of similar social revolts including women's liberation, student power movement, and the industrial power movement. All had in common a refusal by a traditional inferior group to accept a position of inferiority. Whites found that they could no longer dominate the coloured people while men, parents, and teachers found a similar resistance whenever they attempted to impose their values on women, children, and students respectively. (p. 3)

The second factor which may have created a need for teachers to appear democratic and resist the temptation to administer arbitrary punishments may be termed the 'bankruptcy' of the curriculum. Today's economic situation is characterized by relatively large numbers of unemployed among the population and more particularly among school leavers. Many students, therefore, have come to believe that schooling can no longer be justified primarily in terms of the school's ability to provide job-related knowledge and skills; skills which used to ensure employability. Thus they will not accept unpleasant teacher behaviour for the sake of their vocational training.

Raffini (1980) appears to be alluding to the implications of the effect of both factors when he discusses students of the past:

> They, unlike the present generation, were goal-oriented; they were willing to subordinate themselves and their identities to the tasks or jobs that had to be done. While they may not have enjoyed studying or doing the work required in schools any more than present-day students, they realized that they must force themselves to do it anyway if they wanted to better themselves in society. The task, job, or goal was the overriding consideration; their identities

> or feelings of satisfaction came second. Glasser believes that children are no longer willing to subordinate themselves, their sense of worth, or their personal identities to the goals of the school. They seek reinforcement as persons, as separate human beings first, before they become involved with goals or tasks. (p. 18)

To determine which of the two competing explanations outlined above pertains most to the teachers referred to in our studies, it is useful to consider an area of management behaviour where students' needs are clearly not being met.

Although, as stated earlier, students perceive as appropriate teacher behaviour in the areas of rule clarity and reasonableness, fairness, the use of appropriate punishment, and acceptance of responsibility, they nevertheless report that, as a group, teachers are apparently engaging in a number of behaviours which are inappropriate, Firstly, they are using public embarrassment of students to control classes and, secondly, they are not remaining calm, but are yelling when admonishing students.

It is interesting to reflect on these additional findings and to reconcile their coexistence with the teachers' use of what appear to be democratic sanctions. In a recent text, Raffini (1980) has blended and augmented the ideas of Thomas Gordon, Rudolf Dreikurs and William Glasser to produce a technique he calls behaviour negotiation. He argues that it is not easy to discriminate between an autocratic and democratic approach to classroom discipline by simply focusing on the type of punishment given. Raffini found that exclusion seemed to be the most widely used logical consequence in the management of classroom disruption, but with some teachers the distinction between using logical consequences and punishment was not always clear (p. 134). He urged that teachers, when using logical consequences, adopt an unemotional tone of voice. 'A simple, matter of fact statement is made in a calm, friendly manner.' Therefore, the key distinction between the democratic and autocratic approaches has as much to do with the medium as the message, and although the messages transmitted by teachers may be democratic in nature, the manner in which they are transmitted is not.

One can conclude, given the prevalence of the perceived use of criticism and the presence of teacher anger in classrooms, that teachers are not acting in accordance with a democratic model, even though they are avoiding the use of obviously 'autocratic' forms of punishment. There are at least two competing explanations for these findings. The first of these is the same as the second of the explanations offered above — teachers may have unthinkingly 'rolled with the punches' and have gone as far as they want to go in reacting to social pressures.

In contrast they may have, as explained earlier, gone through a process of revaluing their relationships with students and would wish neither to scare nor embarrass them. However, they may not be able to operationalize their intentions, and fall back on the use of anger and embarrassment out of frustration, knowing that these techniques, although theoretically undesirable to them, are effective means of correcting unacceptable behaviour.

To gather some information on teachers' responses to these competing explanations, interviews were conducted during 1983 with twenty teachers, two at each of ten state secondary schools in the Northern Region of Victoria. The teachers were recommended by their principals on the basis that they appeared to operate on very different models of classroom control; one teacher reflecting on authority-oriented approach and the other being more humanistic.

The one hour taped interview, conducted by both authors, involved the teacher in trying to define the extent to which non-conforming students had rights. To assist in this process, teachers were provided with six general teacher roles vis-á-vis their response to miscreants. These approaches ranged from one extreme of using whatever techniques were legal, regardless of their psychological impact on the student, through the middle ground of involving any procedure likely to have a negative psychological impact to the other extreme of attempting to deal therapeutically with the miscreant.

With the exception of only two teachers, all interviewees expressed a desire to avoid techniques that may adversely affect miscreants psychologically. The following quotes, each taken from a different interviewee, represent typical responses.

> 'I try not to (make students feel less able or worth less) but at times I'm sure it does.'
>
> 'I try very hard not to use them (anger or belittling of students) because of the effect that it might have.'
>
> 'Well I don't like yelling, because I don't think yelling is very productive and I don't like being yelled at myself . . . and I don't like making any of the kids feel rotten.'
>
> 'I certainly wouldn't want to apply negative psychological impact.'
>
> 'I don't like putting kids, anyone, down. I'm sure I do it sometimes, but it is something that I would try and avoid.'

The two dissenters were of the view that:

> 'If . . . a child's behaviour was affecting the other students, I wouldn't really hesitate to have some sort of negative effect on them, for the benefit of the others, because there are 20 or 21 kids in a class.'

Despite their general desire not to use sarcasm, or display anger towards students, all of the teachers interviewed acknowledged that they did do these things. Two reasons were frequently proferred. The first was as much an attempt at justification of the use of sarcasm and anger as it was an explanation of their use.

Many of the teachers interviewed suggested that although they used sarcasm and anger they were very cautious in its use and only used it on students who required it and who they thought probably wouldn't be affected by its use. Some typical responses were:

> 'I would only occasionally do that (sarcasm) and I would be very careful which kid I chose . . . some kids are just not able to accept it, to take it.'
>
> 'I try to bring a kid down if it's the right kid, to give them a dressing down.'
>
> 'It's only the very timid and shy students that would really shiver at it (anger) I think.'
>
> 'Some of the other well behaved kids you could destroy, but the kids who don't behave I think you'd find it very difficult to have a negative effect on them completely.'

If the teachers were correct in their assumption that the targetted, misbehaving student would withstand the use of sarcasm and anger without it having a very great effect on them, then it remains to be explained why so many students stated a strong preference for teachers to avoid these techniques. We would argue that a 'ripple effect' noted by Kounin (1970) over a decade ago, is in operation. Teachers did not appear to be aware of the possibility that their behaviour towards one student could have an impact on a different 'non-target' student.

The response of one particular interviewee provides a dramatic example. After stating in the early part of the interview that:

> 'I think every kid's different. You've got to really treat each kid differently. There are some kids that are really bad and they seem to go out of their way to annoy the teacher. They are not interested in their work or lessons, their joy in life is to annoy the teacher . . . and I do use sarcasm . . . I use sarcasm to get rid of them, back of the class or even stand them outside the door which you're not supposed to do. But then I can concentrate on the kids that want to learn.'

The teacher later recounted a story of his schooldays in the following terms:

> 'Well, when I was at school I was very, very quiet, I was very, very shy. I still am. I went to the Collingwood Technical School and the teachers there were very tough and if you didn't conform, they really got into you. I remember my mate in my Maths class and the teacher said, I forget his name, come out to the blackboard and

do this equation, and this poor kid couldn't do it, and wow, the teacher bawled him out in front of the class, his mind must have been a blank I suppose and he's doing algebra on the blackboard, and he couldn't do a thing, and this teacher was tearing him to shreds, and I'm thinking oh my God, he's going to ask me next, and I'll die.'

The story is particularly relevant because the teacher suggested that he was a very good student and never misbehaved.

Clearly, in this and no doubt other classroom situations, it wouldn't matter if the target, misbehaving student could handle sarcasm and anger or not, these techniques may still be having desired influences on other 'conforming' students.

The second explanation for the use of sarcasm and anger was common to all teachers and appeared to be the decisive factor. It was a combination of fatigue and concern for survival. In the words of some of the teachers interviewed ...

'... because I've had a very long day.'

'I have the occasional day ... I could just burst into tears and walk out of the room.'

'I know I've snapped because I'm tired ... I suddenly yell or scream.'

All teachers interviewed seem to believe that the use of anger and embarrassment of students would suppress misbehaviour, particularly defiant behaviour. They tended to be unhappy about their use of these techniques but used them when they were tired and/or they didn't know what else to do that would work. The motivation for intervention on these occasions had little to do with the needs of their students but stemmed from the teachers' need to protect their self-esteem. In summary, therefore, of the two competing explanations offered earlier for the use of anger, the latter appears to have the most credibility.

How then can teachers be helped to avoid falling back on the use of anger and embarrassment, techniques which both they and the students would prefer were avoided.[1]

In the first instance it may be necessary to attempt to reduce the degree of stress faced by teachers by considering the four inter-related levels at which stress operates on teachers; namely the individual, the school, the wider education system and society at large. In this context it is important to note that some valuable suggestions for changes at each of three levels have already been offered by Dunham, 1984; Kyriacou and Sutcliffe, 1978; Otto, 1983; Pratt, 1978.

More specifically, teachers firstly need to be formally provided with a number of alternative approaches to classroom management ranging from negotiation through group processes to authority-oriented models (Wolfgang and Glickman, 1980). Secondly, they need to be encouraged to use constructive self-talk to reduce the tension involved in confrontation with miscreants. Many teachers carry unreasonable 'Have to's' with them, for example, 'I *have to* keep the class quiet at all times'. By reducing these 'Have to's' to less imperative 'shoulds', teachers may be able to redirect some of the energies conserved into learning classroom management techniques more compatible with themselves and their students (Bernard *et al.*, 1983).

Note

1 The fact that teachers have a restricted repertoire of techniques is evidenced by the fact that the range of strategies employed by them, as reported by students during interviews, contained no reference to skills such as negotiation, and the use of group processes. Consequently, in our studies to date this has placed constraints upon the extent to which student preferences can be defined. Had we intervened in such a way as to include in our questionnaire reference to techniques such as 'sitting with a student to work out a way for him to behave acceptably' a more comprehensive picture of preferences could well have been obtained. In this connection, it might be of interest to the reader to know that in our latest work we are gathering information on the acceptability to students of a variety of negotiation and group process oriented techniques.

References

ASPEY, D. and ROEBUCK, F. (1977) *Kids Don't Learn from People They Don't Like*, Amherst, Mass., Human Resource Development Press.

BALSON, M. (1982) *Understanding Classroom Behaviour*, New York, Hawthorn, A.C.E.R.

BERNARD, M.E., JOYCE, M.R. and ROSENWARNE, P.M. (1983) 'Helping teachers cope with stress: A rational emotive approach', in ELLIS, E. and BERNARD, M.E. (Eds) *Rational Emotive Approaches to the Problem of Childhood*, New York, Plenum Press.

BLOOM, B.S. (1980) 'The new direction in educational research: Alternative variables', *Phi Delta Kapan*, 61, pp. 382–5.

CANTER, L. and CANTER, M. (1976) *Assertive Discipline: A Take Charge Approach for Today's Educator*, California, Canter and Associates.

CHARLES, C.M. (1981) *Building Classroom Discipline: From Models to Practice*, New York, Longman Inc.

DREIKURS, R. and GREY, L. (1968) *A New Approach to Discipline: Logical Consequences*, New York, Hawthorn Books.

DUNHAM, J. (1984) *Stress in Teaching*, Croom Helm.

FREDERICK, W.G. and WALBERG, H.J. (1980) 'Learning as a function of time', *Journal of Educational Research*, 73, pp. 183–94.

GORDON, T. (1981) 'Crippling our children with discipline', *Journal of Education*, 16, 3, pp. 228–43.

HOOK, C.M. and ROSENSHINE, B.M. (1979) 'Accuracy of teacher reports of their classroom behaviour', *Review of Educational Research*, 9, pp. 1–12.

KOUNIN, J.S. (1970) *Discipline and Group Management in Classrooms*, New York, Holt, Rinehart and Winston.

KYRIACOU, C. and SUTCLIFFE, J. (1978) 'A model of teacher stress', *Educational Studies*, 4, pp. 1–6.

LEWIS, R. and LOVEGROVE, M.N. (1983a) 'Rolling with the punches in modern classrooms', *Journal of Australian Studies*, 13, pp. 32–9.

LEWIS, R. and LOVEGROVE, M.N. (1983b) 'Pupils on punishment', *S.E.T. Research Information for Teachers*, 1, Item 10.

LEWIS, R. and LOVEGROVE, M.N. (1984) 'Teachers' classroom control procedures: Are students' needs being met?', *Journal of Education for Teaching*, 10, pp. 97–105.

LOVEGROVE, M.N. and LEWIS, R. (1982) 'Classroom control procedures used by relationship centred teachers', *Journal of Education for Teaching*, 8, pp. 55–66.

LOVEGROVE, M.N. and LEWIS, R. (1984) 'Students' views of discipline in the classroom', *Education Magazine*, 42, pp. 29–31.

LOVEGROVE, M.N., LEWIS, R., OYVIND, K.J. and STROMES, A.C. (1983) 'The classroom control techniques of "good" teachers: A Norwegian study', *Compare*, 13, pp. 157–65.

LOVEGROVE, M.N., LEWIS, R., FALL, C. and LOVEGROVE, H. (1985) 'Students' preferences for discipline practices in schools', *Teaching and Teacher Education*, 1, pp. 325–33.

MCDANIEL, T.R. (1981) 'Power in the classroom', *The Educational Forum*, Fall, pp. 31–43.

MARTIN, J. (1981) *Models of Classroom Management*, Calgary, Alberta, Detselig for Teachers, Ltd.

OTTO, L.P. (1983) *Structural Sources of Teacher Stress in State High Schools*, Bundoora, Victoria, Department of Sociology, La Trobe University.

PRATT, J. (1978) 'Perceived stress among teachers: The effects of age and background of children taught', *Educational Review*, 30, 1, pp. 3–14.

RAFFINI, J.P. (1980) *Discipline: Negotiating Conflicts with Todays Kids*, Englewood Cliffs, N.J., Prentice-Hall.

ROSENSHINE, B. (1976) 'Recent research on teaching behaviour and student achievement', *Journal of Teacher Education*, 17, pp. 61–4.

SMYTH, W.J. (1980) 'Pupil engaged learning time: Concepts, findings and implications', *Australian Journal of Education*, 25, pp. 238–68.

SMYTH, W.J. (1981) 'Research on classroom management: Studies of pupil-engaged learning as a special but instructive case', *Australian Journal of Education for Teaching*, 7, pp. 127–48.

WOLFGANG, C. and GLICKMAN, C. (1980) *Solving Discipline Problems*, Boston, Allyn and Bacon.

Teachers' Use of Approval

Josh Schwieso and Nigel Hastings
Bulmershe College of Higher Education, Reading

Introduction

All teachers learn that praising pupils' performance is a good thing to do. This is not a new wisdom but it has received additional impetus following the increase of interest, over the last fifteen years or so, in behavioural approaches to teaching and the management of classroom behaviour. It is not uncommon for teachers to give or receive the advice that they should cope with disruptive or poorly motivated pupils by praising them when they are behaving acceptably or working. The fact that teachers can systematically use their own behaviour and responses to pupils in this way with good effect is well established (see Wheldall and Merrett, this volume). In contrast, relatively little is known about the ways in which praise is normally used in classrooms, about the intentions teachers have when expressing approval, about the ways in which such acts are understood and about the variety of effects that praise may have.

In 1981, Brophy published a review of the literature relating to teachers' use of praise. He was concerned with studies which had examined teachers' everyday use of praise, its possible functions and potential effects. Our purpose is similar to Brophy's. Although this chapter will be more modest in length and scope, it will focus more on evidence that has come to light since 1981 and on studies conducted in countries other than USA, as well as considering some of those to which Brophy refers. The central question with which we will be concerned goes something like this. If it is true, and it does seem to be, that teachers can bring about improvements in the behaviour and attainment of some pupils by increasing their use of praise, should all teachers try to increase their normal, everyday rates of praise?

This question itself begs several others which we will need to address. The first of these is to do with the word 'praise' itself. What are we talking about? Studies of teachers' natural, or normal, classroom behaviour often gather data on teachers' praise, approval, positive feedback, positive events or positive affect. Are these equivalent categories? Are they comparable?

In his review, Brophy distinguishes three types of teacher response: feedback, praise and criticism, and non-specific warmth or hostility. Feedback refers to simple statements about the truth, falsity or appropriateness of a pupil's response; it is given without emotion. Praise goes further; it is intended to commend the worth of, or to express admiration for, a specific act. The reverse applies to criticism. Non-specific warmth (or hostility) covers evaluative responses which are not made in relation to any specific act, but which serve to convey the teacher's general feelings of liking for the pupil.

Brophy is primarily concerned with the distinction between the category of simple feedback, or knowledge of results, and that of praise, which conveys both knowledge of results and an expression of the moral worth of the action. This distinction is particularly important for Brophy since he argues that feedback is virtually never harmful whereas praise may be. Some category systems used in studies of teachers' normal classroom practice do not clearly embody this distinction. Those which employ terms such as 'approval' or 'positive events', for instance, include within them both feedback and praise, which are teacher actions which Brophy would regard as discrete.

Conceptually, Brophy's distinction makes sense. In practice, however, it may be difficult to decide, when, for instance, a teacher says 'Correct!', whether this includes an evaluative component or is pure feedback. Moreover, how it is interpreted by the pupil concerned may be different from how the teacher meant it. Observation systems which employ categories such as 'approval', 'positive events' or 'positive feedback' minimize these practical difficulties by including within them all those teacher actions which, on the face of it, seem to include some degree of evaluation.

In this article we shall be concerned with studies which have used all of these terms. Like Brophy, however, we will not be concerned with studies which have recorded non-specific warmth. Nor will we be concerned with the body of literature which has dealt with feedback alone. However, we need to restrict things a little further yet. Not all studies which use the same term mean the same thing by it. In some, 'praise' is restrictively defined, whereas in those employing Flanders' Interaction Analysis Categories (FIAC), for instance, praise, encouragement, joking to relieve tension and utterances such as 'go on' and 'uh-huh' are undifferentiated. We have restricted our concern to include only those studies employing observation categories for teacher responses which entail contingency on pupils' actions, provide feedback and include, or may include, some expression of the teacher's feeling about the worth of the action to which it relates. However, many observation systems meet this criterion. Therefore, when discussing individual research reports, we will use the terms employed by the research concerned, for this helps to highlight the fact that different observation systems were used in otherwise similar studies. In general discussion, however, we will refer to teacher 'approval' and 'disapproval'.

We can now turn to the main issues concerning teachers' normal use of approval and to research which has sought to describe existing practice and to establish the frequency of approval in ordinary classrooms.

Natural Rates of Teacher Approval and Disapproval

We have already suggested that relatively few studies have sought to gather purely descriptive information about the ways in which teachers use approval in the classroom. Most of these have also recorded rates of disapproval, for it is largely through the comparison of these two rates that judgments about the appropriateness of teachers' strategies are made — the assumption generally being that approvals should outnumber disapprovals.

White (1975) reports the results of sixteen separate studies, each of which employed the Teacher Approval and Disapproval Observation Record (TAD) developed by White and her colleagues. This is a schedule in which all instances of teacher verbal approval or disapproval are recorded verbatim, together with the pupil behaviour to which the teachers' remarks were responses. The studies involved one hundred and four teachers who were teaching grades one to twelve in a variety of schools. In summary, the findings were that, with the exception of those teaching children in grades one and two, teachers gave more disapproving than approving comments to their pupils. The studies also showed that, even though disapprovals outnumbered approvals in all but the early years, the overall rates of both teacher approvals and disapprovals declined as the age of children taught increased. Approval rates in excess of one per minute were recorded in some classes of very young children whereas ten approvals per hour was more typical of high school teachers. Disapproval rates fell from around thirty per hour in grade three classes to fifteen to twenty per hour in grade nine classes.

In a separate study, but again using TAD, Heller and White (1975) observed five teachers of mathematics and five social studies teachers teaching pupils in grades seven to nine. Again they found that the mean rate of disapprovals (31.2 per hour) exceeded the mean rate of teacher approvals (17.4 per hour). A similar finding is reported by Thomas *et al.* (1978) who, using a different observation system, studied natural rates of approval and disapproval among ten teachers of grade seven classes in New Zealand. They found the average rates of teacher approvals and disapprovals to be 12.0 and nearly 35 per hour respectively.

The finding that disapproval rates are higher than approval rates, except in the case of teachers working with the youngest classes, is not universal. A series of studies conducted by Brophy and his colleagues, and discussed by Brophy (1981), all found the overall rates of teacher praise to be higher than the overall rates of criticism, and the rates of both to be well below those typical of the other studies so far considered. The differences between this study and those of White and Heller and White may in part be attributable, as already mentioned, to the fact that the Brophy studies were concerned with praise and criticism rather than approval and disapproval. However, the ORACLE study of interaction in 58 top junior British classrooms (Galton, Simon and Croll, 1980) used similarly restrictive definitions of praise and criticism and found average rates of teacher praise to be around half those for statements of critical control, a category which did not include criticism of pupils' work or effort.

These investigations have all been concerned only with what teachers have said. The observation systems were for recording teachers' verbalizations only, but it is clear that approving and disapproving statements are often accompanied by expressions, gestures and possibly physical contact or changes in proximity. Moreover, it is possible to communicate approval and disapproval by non-verbal means alone. A smile, a raised eyebrow or a hand on the shoulder can each inform a pupil what his teacher thinks about his present activity without a word being spoken. Very few studies have employed observation systems which have allowed the recording of such non-verbal manifestations of approval and disapproval. Two which have are reported by Merrett and Wheldall (1986) and by Nafpaktitis *et al.* (1985), though in neither of these does the category system employed allow us to distinguish between verbal and non-verbal responses.

Merrett and Wheldall have developed an observation system (OPTIC) in which teacher approvals, which they term 'positive events', and teacher disapprovals, correspondingly called 'negative events', include both verbal and non-verbal manifestations of approval and disapproval. They report findings from a series of studies involving 128 British primary and middle school teachers in which the mean rate of teacher approvals (69 per hour) was greater than the mean rate of disapprovals (55.8 per hour). Nafpaktitis *et al.* (1985) also found this to be the case in their study of 84 intermediate school classrooms in Los Angeles County which again recorded verbal and non-verbal approvals and disapprovals. They found mean rates of 78 per hour for approvals and 17.4 per hour for disapprovals.

The picture at this stage seems confused. If we consider those investigations which have recorded only what teachers say, it appears that their disapproving statements are more plentiful than their approving statements, at least in classes after the first two years of school, even though the actual rates vary considerably. The exception to this general pattern is the series of studies by Brophy and his colleagues, all of which found praise to be more frequent than criticism, though the rates of both were considerably lower than in other studies. The finding that approvals exceed disapprovals also seems to emerge in research where both verbal and non-verbal approvals and disapprovals are recorded.

A variety of explanations could account for this pattern. It may be that, as children develop, teachers are able to employ a greater proportion of solely non-verbal means of expressing approval and disapproval, but this is no more than an hypothesis as, to the best of our knowledge, no evidence directly bearing on this exists. However, Merrett and Wheldall (1986) comment that, in their experience with their OPTIC observation schedule, solely non-verbal approvals or disapprovals are rare, a hand on the shoulder, for instance, usually being accompanied by a comment. Alternatively, or additionally, it may be that the pattern is a function of the category systems employed. Further possibilities are that the variation between teachers, and between groups of teachers working in differing educational systems and cultural contexts, is so great that wide differences in sample means occur.

What is Approved and Disapproved?

Mean rates of approval and disapproval do indeed conceal a great deal of variation between teachers and beg a whole series of further questions which need to be asked. Important among these is the question of what sort of pupil actions elicit approval and disapproval.

A number of the studies we have already considered recorded the type of pupil activity to which teacher approvals and disapprovals were responses. Typically, the distinction has been made between responses to pupils' work activities and responses to their social conduct or cooperation in routine tasks in the classroom, the distinction being variously described as 'instructional' as against 'managerial', or 'academic' as against 'social'. These appear to be equivalent distinctions and, for the sake of clarity, we will refer to approvals and disapprovals for academic and social behaviour.

In all research which has classified teacher approvals and disapprovals according to whether they were directed towards academic or social behaviours, the finding is the same. Disapprovals are predominantly directed towards social behaviour and approvals are almost exclusively reserved for pupils' academic activities. White (1975) found that approvals for academic activities were more frequent than disapprovals in every grade, while for social behaviour the reverse was the case, with approvals being almost non-existent. Indeed, among the 1105 statements of approval and disapproval recorded by Heller and White (1975), only one was an approval for social behaviour. (This was when a teacher said 'Good' to a child who indicated that he had remembered to bring a pen that day.) Merrett and Wheldall (1986) report that, of the total number of approvals and disapprovals they recorded, fifty per cent were academic approvals, sixteen per cent were academic disapprovals, twenty-eight per cent were social disapprovals and a mere six per cent were social approvals.

This common finding that approval is generally reserved for pupils' work and disapproval for their conduct has been built into the design of some observation schedules. The ORACLE project employed a schedule for recording teacher statements in which one category was used for statements 'which praise pupils' work or effort' and another for statements 'which provide neutral or critical feedback on work or effort'. In the section for recording routine statements was one category for 'critical control' and another for statements which 'provide positive or neutral feedback on routine matters'. Thus, in relation to academic matters, disapprovals were combined with neutral feedback whereas for matters of conduct, approvals were combined with neutral statements. As we noted earlier, the ORACLE project found statements of critical control (relating to classroom behaviour) to be twice as frequent as those of praise (which related to work), though the most frequent of these four types of teacher utterance was 'neutral or critical feedback on work or effort' which accounted for 21.4 per cent of all teacher statements recorded. On the basis of other studies we would suspect that most of these were neutral rather than critical. Similarly, in relation to the 4.5 per cent of statements which were recorded as being 'positive or neutral feedback on routine matters', we would suspect that a minority were positive, but it is impossible to test these speculations in relation to the ORACLE data.

An interesting qualification to the idea that approval is generally used for academic or task related activities, and disapproval for matters of social behaviour, comes from Nafpaktitis *et al.* (1985). They distinguished between appropriate and inappropriate approval. Appropriate approval was defined as approval following pupil on-task behaviour and inappropriate approval as approval following pupil off-task behaviour. Unlikely though this second type of teacher behaviour may at first seem to be, Nafpaktitis *et al.* report that of the mean rate of 78 approvals per hour mentioned above, 24 were inappropriate approvals. This is worth repeating. Nearly one third of the approvals recorded followed inappropriate behaviour by the pupil being observed! The assumption in all the other studies that we have considered has been that approval has been preceded by behaviour of which the teachers concerned approved. This study suggests that some instances of approval, particularly those addressed to a class as a whole or to a group, may follow inappropriate behaviour in the case of some individuals. What the effects of this might be we will consider later. Unfortunately, Nafpaktitis *et al.* did not record inappropriate disapprovals, the existence of which is clearly a logical possibility.

The incidence of misplaced or inappropriate approval has also been examined as part of a study by Strain *et al.* (1983) in which rates of compliance to teachers' requests and teachers' responses to non-compliance were examined in kindergarten to grade three classes. Although we will discuss the details of this study more thoroughly later, for the moment we should simply note that it found that teacher approval following non-compliance with a request was about as common as approval following compliance, though both were relatively infrequent when compared with rates of disapproval following non-compliance. Strain *et al.* did record inappropriate disapprovals and found them to be very rare indeed.

In his review of teacher praise, Brophy (1981) discusses other studies which identified the use of inappropriate praise including one by Anderson *et al.* (1979) in which first-grade teachers were observed to praise about eleven per cent of correct answers and one per cent of incorrect answers. They also found that, when listening to pupils reading, teachers praised those who read with errors as frequently as they praised those who read without errors.

The picture emerging here seems to be fairly clear, if a little puzzling. Disapproval is more commonly related to social behaviour than to academic behaviour, while approval is used almost exclusively for academic behaviour. However, when the conditions under which approval is given are examined more closely, it appears that it is relatively frequently employed in ways which, if it is to function as a reinforcer for desirable behaviour, are inappropriate.

Who is Approved and Disapproved?

We have already noted that White (1975) found that as the age of children increased so the frequency of both approving and disapproving comments decreased. Merrett and Wheldall (1986) report a similar trend in their studies, though the effect was not so marked. Nevertheless, an overall relationship between the use of approvals and disapprovals by teachers and the age of children taught seems to exist, with older classes receiving less of both than younger classes.

Within a single age range or class it is likely that approvals and disapprovals will not be evenly distributed and some research has sought to disclose the basis of distribution. If teachers generally use their approvals in a deliberate way, following the advice of behaviour modifiers, to try to change pupils' academic or social behaviour, then one would expect to find approvals concentrated on lower attaining and disruptive pupils. This is not what is generally found. Heller and White's (1975) study had as its main purpose the examination of rates of teacher approval and disapproval in low ability and high ability classes. They found that teachers' rates of approval did not differ between high and low ability classes, but rates of disapproval were higher in low ability classes. This difference was largely due to the much higher frequency of disapprovals for inappropriate social behaviour in the lower ability group. There is an important methodological point to be noted here. Simple comparison of the rates of approval and disapproval of pupils in two groups could convey a false impression. Brophy (1981) expresses the point well:

> Simple rate measures might reveal, for example, that Mary was praised for good answers ten times and John only five times. However, if it is known that Mary gave 100 good answers during the observation periods, and that John gave only 25, it can be stated that the teacher praised only 10 per cent of Mary's good answers, but 20 per cent of John's. The rate data indicate that Mary was praised more in the absolute sense, but the proportional data reveal that John was praised more in the relative sense (in parallel situations). It is the proportion measures that are most revealing about how teachers use praise in the classroom. (p. 11)

Several studies by Brophy and his colleagues (see Brophy, 1981) produced inconsistent findings concerning the proportional distribution of praise between high and low expectation students, a pattern also detected by Dunkin and Biddle (1974) in their review of research which had generally employed Flanders' observation system.

Proportional measures are often easier to establish for academic than for social behaviours, as units or instances of appropriate social behaviour are rarely easily defined. Strain *et al.* (1983) were able to do this, however, and produced proportional rates. Their study was concerned with teachers' responses, including positive and negative feedback, to compliance and non-compliance with their requests. As we would now expect, disapproval following non-compliance was more common than approval following compliance. But the study also sought to enquire whether this was true for all ability groups. Two groups of pupils were identified on the basis of their teachers' ratings of their ability and their social behaviour. The rates at which teachers made requests or demands of the high and low rated groups did not differ, but their responses to instances of compliance or non-compliance with those requests did. The overall rate of approval following compliance was one in ten. That is, for each ten instances of compliance with a request one would receive teacher approval, but a far higher proportion of the low-rated pupils never received approval following compliance. Indeed, it appears that low-rated pupils were marginally more likely to receive approval when *not* complying than when complying. This extraordinary finding is explained by the authors as being attributable to the fact that low-rated pupils were less likely to comply with general class requests, such as 'Everyone stop talking', which, following compliance by most of the class, received some general statement or non-verbal indication of approval. Low-rated pupils were, however, no more likely to receive teacher disapproval or a further request to comply than were high-rated pupils following non-compliance.

Pupil sex has also been examined in relation to teacher approval and disapproval and the findings are generally that boys receive more approval, disapproval and total teacher attention. Of particular interest in this respect is a study by Dweck *et al.* (1978) which explored rather more finely the distribution of positive and negative feedback given to a sample of fourth and fifth grade girls and boys. In this study, as in most others, boys received considerably more negatives but slightly fewer positives. Teachers' statements of positive and negative feedback were examined in terms of whether they were directed towards work or conduct, but work-oriented comments were further categorized according to whether they were for intellectual qualities or non-intellectual qualities such as neatness. Major differences emerged at this level. As a proportion of the total work-oriented feedback given to each sex, over ninety per cent of the positive feedback received by boys was for the intellectual quality of their work, whereas for girls the figure was eighty-one per cent with nearly twenty per cent being concerned with the form of their work. Differences were more pronounced when negative feedback was examined. For boys, just over half of their teachers' negative comments were concerned with the intellectual quality of their work and just under fifty per cent with its form. For girls, only eleven per cent of the negative feedback they received was for matters such as presentation and eighty-nine per cent related to the intellectual quality of their work. In other words, negative feedback to girls tended to be largely about the intellectual quality of their work whereas for boys it was about as likely to be for presentation as content. In relation to positive feedback the pattern was reversed but with less marked differences. Dweck *et al.* suggest that this pattern may have implications for the ways in which boys and girls come to account for their performances.

A recent study by Irvine (1986) was concerned not only with sex but also with race and age and their relationships to teacher approval and disapproval in sixty-three elementary school classrooms. The only straightforward finding related to pupil sex: boys initiated more contacts with their teachers, through both positive and negative means, and consequently received more of their teachers' attention. Within this study, no clear effects for age or race alone were found, although a puzzling pattern for black girls was suggested. In the upper elementary grades black girls received significantly less total teacher feedback, less positive feedback and fewer public response opportunities than did their counterparts in the lower grades. As Irvine expresses it, 'Black female students present an active, interacting and initiating profile in the early grades but join their white counterparts in the later grades in what appears to be the traditional female sex role behaviours' (1986, p. 20). How the parallel change in teacher behaviour relates to this is a matter for conjecture.

Overall, there is scant evidence on the relationship between pupil race and teacher approval and disapproval patterns. As Irvine (1985, 1986) points out, few of the studies that have been reported have been undertaken in naturalistic settings and those that have produce inconsistent findings. Simpson and Erickson (1983), for instance, found that white teachers gave more negative feedback to black boys than to any other race/sex group, while Byalick and Bersoff (1974) found that both black and white teachers gave more 'positive reinforcement' to boys than girls and to boys of the opposite racial group to themselves.

There is, then, a limited amount of evidence to suggest that age, ability, sex and race of pupils are related to teacher approvals and disapprovals, though the nature of the relationships is not always clear. However, focusing on these fairly gross characteristics of pupils presupposes that teachers respond to pupils significantly in terms of these broad attributes. Alongside this view stands the evidence that it is to individual pupils' characteristic behaviours in class that teachers respond. It may well be that it is not age, sex, ability, race or any other such variable that is itself of major significance, but the behaviours with which these may be associated. In this way we can see that the distinction between 'what' and 'who' is praised, suggested by the titles of this and the previous section, is a little misleading. Teachers' approvals and disapprovals may have some effect on pupils, but they are themselves in part the effects or consequences of pupils' actions: teachers do not approve or disapprove in vacuo. It is a little obvious to say that teaching is an interactive process, but it is a point that is sometimes lost sight of in the quest for patterns and order when researching the complexities of the classroom and seeking potentially causal relationships.

Incidental light is shed on the question of how some pupils come to receive more approvals or disapprovals by the ORACLE research. In addition to monitoring teachers' activities, this project involved the detailed observation of pupils. We have already noted that the observations of the teachers suggested that they made twice as many statements of critical control for behaviour as statements of praise for pupils' work. However, from the pupil observations it appeared that the average child received *ten* times as much criticism for inappropriate social behaviour as praise for good work. These seem to be incompatible findings: teachers criticized twice as much as they praised yet pupils were criticized ten times as much as they were praised. How can this be? The answer must lie in statements of praise being more often given privately or being directed to one or two pupils, while statements of criticism were more often directed at the whole class or at a group of pupils. In this way, one statement of critical control by the teacher would, in effect, be received by each member of the class. However, while the average pupil received ten times as many statements of criticism as praise from his teacher, there was very considerable variation around this mean. Some insight into this variation may be gained from examining the pupil types identified.

Four pupil types were identified and, on the basis of their patterns of behaviour and interaction in the classroom, were labelled attention seekers, intermittent workers, solitary workers and quiet collaborators. Of particular interest for this discussion are the attention seekers who received three times as much praise and twice as much criticism as the average pupil. So, within the ORACLE study at least, it is not that one type of pupil gets more praise and another more criticism, but one type gets more of both. The explanation for this may lie in the name given to the group, for the attention seekers sought their teachers' attention more than any of the other three types. Unfortunately, no details of the sex composition of the four pupil types is given, though a high proportion of boys might be predicted among the attention seekers.

In light of this finding, it may well be that the question with which we began this section, 'Who is approved and disapproved?' is better replaced by one which asks who is it who initiates contact with their teachers and fishes for attention. The fact that children can elicit teachers' attention is well supported by Stokes *et al.* (1978) who taught pre-school children to elicit their teachers' praise for their work.

The issue of pupils actively seeking teacher attention was also examined in a study by Brophy *et al.* (1976) and discussed by Brophy (1981). This found that, for pupil-initiated contacts which were approval-seeking, approval was most likely to be given to pupils who were high achieving and confident. Praise following pupil initiated work-contacts was more likely to be given to pupils who lacked self-confidence and were rated as immature and teacher-dependent. On the basis of proportional measures, praise in public and private contexts combined was also most likely to go to this type of pupil who tended to be not particularly well liked by teachers.

The Brophy *et al.* study also examined teachers' use of praise in relation to troublesome pupils. Overall, troublesome pupils received as much praise as conforming and successful pupils. However, the study revealed two types of troublesome pupil. Those whose behaviour in class was non-threatening and who were unhappy or passive received considerably more praise than did those whose behaviour was threatening and sullen or defiant. Praise following acceptable social behaviour, though relatively rare, did not tend to go to either of these groups, however, but to high achieving, quiet and diligent pupils — those apparently least in need of reinforcement for their conduct.

Although not employing an observational system specifically designed to record teacher approvals and disapprovals, a study by Fry (1983), which is described and discussed more fully in her contribution to this volume, found that problem children received less positive affect and more negative affect from their teachers than did non-problem children. Moreover, the relative differences between the two groups increased over the period of a term.

Approval: How Much, For What, To Whom?

What are we to make of all this? Having examined some of the evidence about teachers' use and distribution of approval, and having noted the possible implications of differences in research methodologies, is it possible to produce an empirically justified picture of the use of approval and disapproval in classrooms? A qualified 'yes' seems appropriate, as some general patterns and relationships do seem to emerge from the evidence.

1 Verbal disapproval is more common than approval except in the youngest classes, where the reverse is the case. The reverse is also the case across all age ranges when non-verbal expressions of approval and disapproval are included, though the number of studies of this type is limited.
2 Approvals are generally given in relation to children's work or effort rather than for their social behaviour, while disapprovals are more frequent for social than academic behaviours. However, a substantial proportion of approvals are given following inappropriate behaviour for some pupils.
3 The frequency of both approving and disapproving comments tends to fall as the age of children taught increases.
4 Approval is not generally distributed in relation to pupil ability. Lower ability groups are inclined to receive more disapprovals, though whether this is true when proportional measures are used is less clear.
5 Boys tend to receive more approval and disapproval from their teachers than do girls. Girls may receive proportionally more approval for the form of their work and more disapproval for its content, than do boys.
6 No clear pattern of approval and disapproval in relation to pupil race has been established.
7 Teachers' approving and disapproving comments are often actively elicited by particular pupils, boys especially, who tend in consequence to receive more teacher attention of all types.
8 Troublesome or problem pupils do not receive more teacher approvals than non-problem pupils and may receive fewer, but they tend to receive considerably more disapproval, even on the basis of proportional measures.

In considering this summary, a further methodological point needs to be noted. All of the studies with which we have been concerned have been essentially correlational in nature. As a consequence, not one is in a position to claim to have disclosed or demonstrated causal relationships. The task at present is simply to describe and to discover associations, some of which may be causal.

Limited and qualified though this picture is, one thing emerges fairly clearly. Teachers do not generally direct their approval particularly towards lower attaining or troublesome pupils. In other words, teachers do not seem to be employing their approval strategies in ways that we would expect if they were following a reinforcement model in order to improve the work and behaviour of those about whom they are most likely to be concerned.

What Are the Consequences of Teacher Approval?

If it is the case that increasing approval for desirable behaviour can reduce the frequency of an incompatible and less desirable behaviour, then it might follow that teachers who generally approve more, in the normal course of events, would have more successful pupil outcomes. In order to see whether there is evidence to support this we will consider three types of study, those that have been concerned with comparing *schools*, those that have compared *classes* and those that have compared individual *pupils*.

If approval can have the effect of increasing the prevalence of the activities which are approved, we might expect to find that schools in which it is abundant would have better outcomes than those in which it is less common. Studies which have examined differences in rates of praise between schools are rare, but Rutter *et al.*'s (1979) study of twelve London secondary schools yields some relevant data. As part of the investigation, which is more fully discussed by Keith Topping elsewhere in this volume, the frequency of teacher praise for pupils' work was recorded. The absolute rates were rather low, usually only three or four instances per lesson, but schools in which praise in lessons was more frequent tended to be schools in which better behaviour and lower delinquency rates were found. Interestingly, rates of praise did not correlate with the measure of academic outcome. Other forms of approval were also recorded, for instance the percentage of pupils who had been commended in assembly, and this was also found to be positively related to measures of behaviour within the schools. Again we need to note the correlational nature of this study, but it, together no doubt with other indirect evidence, may well lie behind a statement in *Better Schools* which the Secretaries of State for England and Wales presented to Parliament.

> ... too few schools ... have a wide enough range of ways to acknowledge, encourage and reward high standards of conduct. In the Government's view many schools could do more to emphasise these positive aspects and so reduce their reliance on disciplinary sanctions. (DES, 1985, p. 57)

Studies which have sought to compare the outcomes of classes taught by teachers who demonstrated differing rates of approval are more plentiful and are of several types. Among those which we have already considered are some which recorded not only rates of approval and disapproval but also the level of task-engagement in classes. Correlations between rates of approval and class levels of on-task behaviour tend to be positive and low. Thomas *et al.* (1978) found the correlation to be 0.40 and Merrett and Wheldall (1986) found correlations between their on-task measure and academic approvals and social approvals to be 0.15 and 0.16 respectively. Nafpaktitis *et al.* (1985) recorded off-task rather than on-task behaviour and found the correlation with appropriate approval to be −0.21, and a corresponding figure for inappropriate approval of 0.40. This study also took a measure of disruption, not all off-task behaviour being disruptive, and found this to correlate with inappropriate approval (0.52). These studies also report correlations between teacher disapproval and their measures of task engagement. For Thomas *et al.* the figure was −0.48, while Merrett and Wheldall report a correlation between academic disapproval and on-task behaviour of −0.31. Nafpaktitis *et al.* found a correlation of 0.54 between teacher disapproval and off-task behaviour.

Using task engagement as the criterion, the evidence of these studies does not appear to lend strong support to the idea that teachers who approve more have classes which spend more time actively engaged with their work. Even if it did, an inference about causation would not be justified. What is minimally necessary for this is information about the relative gains made by classes receiving differing rates of approval over a period of time. Such information is limited, as longitudinal observational studies are necessarily expensive. The ORACLE project (Galton and Simon, 1980) again provides some incidental information on this. The results indicated that the pupils taught by the two teacher-types with the highest rates of approval had the highest and the lowest gains over the year. The case that praise is associated with gains is certainly not well supported by this finding. In his review of the topic, Brophy (1981) suggests that teacher praise only correlates with pupil gains with the youngest classes of lower achieving and/or lower SES pupils, and even here the correlations are unimpressive.

The problem with these naturalistic, longitudinal, correlational studies is that many aspects of what goes on in classrooms correlate with the gains that are made, and any, none or all of these may be important in contributing to those gains. Evidence that higher rates of approval can result in greater gains comes from the many experimental or quasi-experimental studies in which teachers have deliberately altered their rates of approval for work and/or appropriate social conduct. (See, for example, O'Leary and O'Leary, 1977; Merrett, 1985.) Again, a note of caution is necessary. The fact that increasing rates or praise *can* produce changes in classes is not evidence that praise always functions as a contributory factor in class learning or social behaviour. These intervention studies tend to be conducted over relatively short time periods and the long term effects of raising approval levels are unknown. It may well be that the contrast with the previously normal rate needs to be recent. Certainly the rate of improvement cannot continue indefinitely; some ceiling must surely be reached. But whether improvements are even maintained beyond the relatively short term is generally not explored.

The third way in which the relationship between teacher approval and pupil outcomes might be investigated entails an examination of what happens within individual classes. The question here is whether those pupils within a class who receive more than the normal amount of teacher approval have better than average outcomes. The outcomes with which we need to be concerned are again those that relate to progress or gain, rather than to levels of attainment, conduct or task engagement at one point in time. Unfortunately, the same story has to be told; evidence of this type is scant. To the best of our knowledge, no classroom studies specifically designed to explore this hypothesis have been conducted in recent years. Fry's (1983) study, which we have already mentioned and the by now familiar ORACLE research programme do, however, yield information which is relevant to the question.

Fry's study was concerned with pupils' social behaviour in the classroom and found that, over the period of a term, pupils who were previously identified as presenting problems received proportionally fewer and fewer expressions of positive affect from their teachers. In parallel with this, there was a progressive worsening of their behaviour in class. The ORACLE research was concerned more with changes in pupils' academic competencies and found that those pupils who received the greatest rates of praise from their teachers, the ones designated 'attention seekers', in fact made marginally less progress over the year than the other three pupil groups, even when differences in teacher style had been taken into account.

Whether the rates of teacher approval in either of these studies was causally related to the pupil outcomes cannot be determined as the problem pupils and attention seekers differed from their comparison groups in the interaction they enjoyed with their teachers in more ways than approval rates. Experimental studies, which can more clearly identify causal relationships, are, however, relatively plentiful. These usually involve the teacher deciding to try to improve the behaviour or academic learning of a pupil or group of pupils within a class. Typically, in these studies, teachers increase their rates of approval for work engagement or instances of acceptable behaviour, and the abundance of such studies clearly demonstrates that this approach can produce impressive changes in the pupils concerned. (See Merrett (1981) for a review of British studies and Wheldall and Merrett in this volume.) But there is also evidence that the use of approval without disapproval of any inappropriate activities may be less effective than using the two, at least in the case of pupils identified as presenting behaviour problems (Pfiffner *et al.*, 1985). We should note, however, that in the majority of these studies the comparison is made not with other pupils but with the same pupils over the immediately preceding period. The fact that they were selected in the first place is generally taken as evidence that their work or behaviour was poorer than that of their peers.

To summarize this section, it appears that at the school level there is evidence which is at least consistent with the claim that better outcomes are associated with greater frequencies of approval, and there is no evidence that these higher rates are associated with worse outcomes. Naturalistic studies involving the comparison of classes which receive different rates of teacher approval suggest that rates of approval correlate only slightly with measures of task engagement and barely, if at all, with pupils' academic gains. Naturalistic studies in which the rates of approval received by individual pupils are examined and related to their gains yield an uncertain picture. In each of these cases, however, the number of studies available is very limited. Only from experimental studies, in which the rates of teacher approval have been deliberately changed, is the quantity of evidence substantial. Interventions at both the class and individual level demonstrate that changes in rates of teacher approval, which may be accompanied by other changes in strategy, can be followed by desirable changes in pupil outcomes.

Approval As Reinforcement?

As we indicated at the beginning of this article, the rationale for examining teacher approval is that it is often suggested that it functions as a reinforcer for the behaviour on which it is contingent. Whether it does or does not is, of course, an empirical question. However, the evidence we have considered so far suggests that, by and large, teachers do not seem to be trying to employ their approval as a strategy to effect change in their pupils, or that, if they are trying to do this, they are doing it rather badly! However, this line of reasoning, which is not unusual, presupposes that reinforcement is the only function which teachers might have in mind, or at the back of their minds, when engaging in some form of approval. Is it possible that comments such as 'Well done', 'That's terrific', 'I really like that', 'This table has been tidied up very well' and their non-verbal equivalents or counterparts are intended *only* as reinforcement for the behaviours at which they are directed? May teachers sometimes have some other purposes in mind? May such comments also fulfil other functions? May they be understood in differing ways? In short, may teachers tacitly know something about the functions of approval in the classroom which has yet to come under the scrutiny of research?

Brophy (1981) suspects that the answer to these questions is affirmative, and we are inclined to agree with his view that teachers approve for a variety of purposes. Sometimes, of course, expressions of delight with pupils' work or behaviour are not planned or in any sense strategic; they are spontaneous and genuinely felt reactions of surprise and delight. Such comments may have reinforcing effects even though they were not intended as such. Some instances of teacher approval, however, may be attempts to influence the behaviour of pupils other than those to whom the comment was overtly directed. Praise to a whole class for the way in which it is working may be intended to affect the two or three pupils who are currently chattering, rather than to reinforce the behaviour of the remainder of the class. Such a practice might be perceived by an observer as 'inappropriate approval' for those two or three, but it might be effective in establishing an appropriate model. On other occasions teachers may offer approving comments by way of encouragement to a pupil who is finding some aspect of work rather difficult. A further possibility is that approving comment is used to indicate the closing of one activity and the beginning of another (Kounin, 1970; Hargreaves *et al.*, 1975; Doyle, 1984). 'That's good, now we're going to . . .' may be used more as a form of punctuation and as a way of marking the boundaries between activities than as an intended reinforcer. Brophy offers a more extensive list of possibilities, but the point which these raise is that the conceptualization of approval solely in terms of reinforcement may be much too limited. Many purposes may lay behind those acts which research has categorized and studied as one phenomenon. If this is so, finding that approval does not function well as a reinforcer when it is not intended as such, should not come as much of a surprise.

Pupils' Interpretation of Their Teachers' Approvals

Having raised the issue of what teachers intend by their approving utterances and gestures, the question of what pupils understand by these messages immediately arises. For whether the intended effects of teachers' actions are realized will depend, at least in part, on what pupils understand by those acts. What a pupil makes of his teacher saying 'Well done' will depend on a whole range of factors including the teacher's normal pattern of saying such things, his view of the work on which he is being commended, how much effort he put into it, the difficulty of the task, and so on. Suppose, for instance, that you were to be congratulated on having read this sentence accurately. What would you make of such a commendation? It was not particularly difficult; anyone else reading this chapter would be unlikely to have found it difficult; it took little effort. Why should somebody praise you for having read it accurately? The only possible explanation seems to be that they must think that you are not generally capable of such things, that you are rather poor at reading but tried particularly hard on this occasion. Whatever their intentions, the effect is to inform you of their view of your ability. Such an outcome would be consistent with the findings of Meyer *et al.* (1979) who found that adults and high school pupils expect praise for completing tasks, other than those which are intrinsically very difficult, to go only to those of lower (perceived) ability. They also found that if a person was criticized for not successfully completing a task they were judged to be of high ability. Although not conducted in classroom contexts, the results of this research caution against the use of approval without regard to how it is understood. Rather than encourage or reinforce, it may have detrimental consequences for how pupils come to understand their teachers' views of their ability. This, in turn, could have consequences for pupils' own views of their ability, which is precisely what Dweck *et al.* (1978) suggest following their findings of teachers' differing patterns of approval and disapproval for the work of boys and girls. (Colin Rogers offers a fuller discussion of this issue in his chapter in this volume.)

Meyer *et al.*'s finding did not hold for children in the earlier years of school. Young children felt that if a person is praised for something it must be because they did it well. The fact that older children and adults do not interpret praise for performance at a task quite so straightforwardly may relate to Nicholls and Miller's (1983) observation that young children do not distinguish between ability and task difficulty. 'Hard' and 'hard for me' are equivalent for them. What is particularly interesting about this change in children's understanding of task difficulty and the change in understanding of praise, is that they occur at around the age when some of the studies we discussed earlier found that the rate of teachers' verbal approvals began to fall below the rate of disapprovals. Teachers seem to change their strategies of verbal approval and disapproval as children begin to develop a more differentiated basis for interpreting approvals and disapprovals and for accounting for their own performance. When children begin to believe that being praised for doing something that others can do means you are of limited ability, it may be prudent to begin to praise less. Similarly, when they begin to believe that criticism following failure is an indication of high ability, a change of strategy seems appropriate.

In addition to providing information about performance, effort and ability, approval and disapproval can each have consequences for pupils' perceptions of their teachers. An experimental study by Worrall *et al.* (1983) investigated the effects of praise, no feedback and criticism for work on pupils' perceptions of their teacher's regard for them, their regard for the teacher and their self-regard. The results suggested that these nine and ten year olds interpreted praise in ways which slightly enhanced their view of their teacher's view of them and their self regard, but interpreted criticism in ways which substantially affected what they thought of their teacher and what they thought their teacher thought of them. Their self-regard was not at all affected by criticism. We should note, however, that this was an experimental study and was conducted with a strange teacher over a limited period. What it does emphasize, though, is the fact that praise and criticism are not interpreted as equal and opposite and that, like many of us, these children were inclined to accept approval but to displace disapproval by devaluing its source.

Should Teachers' Rates of Approval be Approved?

It is time to try to begin to pull together some of these separate strands of research and ideas. We began this article by suggesting that there is a general belief that teachers do not approve enough. This view is echoed in the remarks of many of the researchers whose work we have reviewed, who often conclude with the prescription that natural rates of approval should be increased. Teachers, however, do not seem to have acted on this advice, and we have begun to suspect that they may have some basis for not doing so. There do seem to be grounds for questioning whether it is sound advice.

The issues and research considered in the last two sections suggest two important points, each of which has suffered from neglect. Firstly, teachers may approve for a whole variety of purposes, reinforcement being just one of them, even though many approvals may be spontaneous and not in any way strategic. Secondly, pupils interpret their teachers' evaluative comments and acts within frameworks which are in part a function of their age, but also of their experience and their perceptions of the specific situation. Research in each of these two areas is limited, but study of the relationship between the two is non-existent. In this relationship lies an interesting possibility which is rarely entertained in discussions of rates of teacher approval. Could it be that teachers' use of approval embodies a far greater tacit understanding of its effects, as mediated by pupils' understanding, than much of the advice stemming from the 'approval as reinforcement' view has generally assumed? We have already noted, for instance, the intriguing parallels in time of changes in teachers' use of approval and disapproval, in children's differentiation of effort, ability and task difficulty, and in their interpretation of praise. May it also be that the overall reduction in rates of approval and disapproval with the increasing age of pupils is appropriate to pupils' changing understandings? Research is mute on this possibility at the present time.

In brief, the possibility being raised is that teachers may, through often long and bitter experience, evolve rates and ways of approving and disapproving which are quite well adapted to their purposes and to the pupils with whom they are working. This is not to suggest that all teachers have evolved such optimal rates and ways. Nor is it to suggest that contingent and highly specific approval for children whose working patterns, achievement or conduct is below what can reasonably be expected, may not be appropriate and effective as a reinforcer when it has previously been pretty scarce. What it is to suggest is three things. Firstly, teachers approve for a variety of purposes and these different purposes need to be examined and accommodated within research on teacher approval. Secondly, pupils interpret their teachers' approvals in ways that are more complex than are commonly supposed, and in ways which may not always reflect their teachers' intentions: these interpretations will necessarily mediate their responses to approval. Thirdly, and as a consequence of these two points, blanket advice that teachers should increase their normal rates of approval is at best premature, and may even be misguided. What has been treated as one phenomenon may, in fact, be many.

Throughout this discussion we have referred to Brophy's review of 'teacher praise'. Though more modest in scope, this discussion has drawn on work published since 1981 and on research conducted outside the United States. Our conclusions, however, are much the same as Brophy's:

> ... teacher praise may have a variety of intended and actual functions in addition to reinforcement of student conduct or academic performance. Classroom research on praise seems unlikely to reveal much unless these different types and meanings of praise are built into the coding systems. In any case, it seems clear that praise cannot simply be equated with reinforcement. Pending such improvements in research methodology, the data suggest qualification in our enthusiasm in recommending praise to teachers (who, in any case, seem to be intuitively aware of its limitations). (1981, p. 27)

References

ANDERSON, L., EVERTSON, C. and BROPHY, J. (1979) 'An experimental study of effective teaching in first grade reading groups', *Elementary School Journal*, 79, pp. 193–223.

BROPHY, J. (1981) 'Teacher praise: A functional analysis', *Review of Educational Research*, 51, 1, pp. 5–32.

BROPHY, J., EVERTSON, C., ANDERSON, L., BAUM, M. and CRAWFORD, J. (1976) *Student Personality and Teaching: Final Report of the Student Attribute Study*, Educational Resources Information Center. (ERIC Document Reproduction Service No. ED 121 799).

BYALICK, R. and BERSOFF, D.N. (1974) 'Reinforcement practices of black and white teachers in an integrated classroom', *Journal of Educational Psychology*, 66, pp. 473–80.

DES (1985) *Better Schools*, Cmnd 9469, HMSO.

DOYLE, W. (1984) 'How order is achieved in classrooms: An interim report', *Journal of Curriculum Studies*, 16, 3, pp. 259–79.

DUNKIN, M. and BIDDLE, B. (1974) *The Study of Teaching*, New York, Holt, Rinehart and Winston.

DWECK, C.S., DAVIDSON, W., NELSON, S. and ENNA, B. (1978) 'Sex differences in learned helpnessness: II The contingencies of evaluative feedback in the classroom and III An experimental analysis', *Developmental Psychology*, 14, 3, pp. 268–76.

FRY, P.S. (1983) 'Process measures of problem and non-problem children's classroom behaviour: The influence of teacher behaviour variables', *British Journal of Educational Psychology*, 53, pp. 79–88.

GALTON, M. and SIMON, B. (1980) *Progress and Performance in the Primary Classroom*, London, Routledge and Kegan Paul.

GALTON, M., SIMON, B. and CROLL, P. (1980) *Inside the Primary Classroom*, London, Routledge and Kegan Paul.

HARGREAVES, D.H., HESTOR, S. and MELLOR, F.S. (1975) *Deviance in Classrooms*, London, Routledge and Kegan Paul.

HELLER, M. and WHITE, M. (1975) 'Rates of teacher verbal approval and disapproval to higher and lower ability classes', *Journal of Educational Psychology*, 67, pp. 796–800.

IRVINE, J.J. (1985) 'Teacher communication patterns as related to the race and sex of the student', *Journal of Educational Research*, 78, 6, pp. 338–45.

IRVINE, J.J. (1986) 'Teacher-student interactions: Effects of student race, sex and grade level', *Journal of Educational Psychology*, 78, 1, pp. 14–21.

KOUNIN, J.S. (1970) *Discipline and Group Management in Classrooms*, New York, Holt, Rinehart and Winston.

MERRETT, F. (1981) 'Studies in behaviour modification in British educational settings', *Educational Psychology*, 1, 1, pp. 13–38.

MERRETT, F. (1985) *Encouragement Works Better than Punishment*, Birmingham, Positive Products.

MERRETT, F. and WHELDALL, K. (1986) 'Natural rates of teacher approval and disapproval in British primary and middle school classrooms', *British Journal of Educational Psychology*.

MEYER, W., BACHMAN, M., BIERMANN, U., HEMPLEMANN, M., PLÖGER, F. and SPILLER, H. (1979) 'The informational value of evaluative behaviour: The influence of praise and blame on perceptions of ability', *Journal of Educational Psychology*, 71, 2, pp. 259–68.

NAFPAKTITIS, M., MAYER, G.R. and BUTTERWORTH, T. (1985) 'Natural rates of teacher approval and disapproval and their relation to student behaviour in intermediate school classrooms', *Journal of Educational Psychology*, 77, 3, pp. 362–7.

NICHOLLS, J.G. and MILLER, A.T. (1983) 'The differentiation of the concepts of difficulty and ability', *Child Development*, 54, pp. 951–9.

O'LEARY, K.D. and O'LEARY, S.G. (1977) *Classroom Management: The Successful Use of Behaviour Management* (Second Edition), New York, Pergamon.

PFIFFNER, L.J., ROSÉN, L.L. and O'LEARY, S.G. (1985) 'The efficacy of an all-positive approach to classroom management', *Journal of Applied Behaviour Analysis*, 18, pp. 257–61.

RUTTER, M., MAUGHAM, B., MORTIMORE, P. and OUSTON, J. (1979) *Fifteen Thousand Hours: Secondary Schools and Their Effects on Children*, London, Open Books.

SIMPSON, A.W. and ERICKSON, M.T. (1983) 'Teachers' verbal and non-verbal communication patterns as a function of teacher race, student gender and student race', *American Educational Research Journal*, 20, pp. 183–98.

STOKES, T., FOWLER, S. and BAER, D. (1978) 'Training preschool children to recruit natural communities of reinforcement', *Journal of Applied Behaviour Analysis*, 11, pp. 285–303.

STRAIN, P.S., LAMBERT, D.L., KERR, M.M., STAGG, V. and LENKER, D.A. (1983) 'Naturalistic assessment of children's compliance to teachers' requests and consequences for compliance', *Journal of Applied Behaviour Analysis*, 16, pp. 243–9.

THOMAS, J., PRESLAND, I., GRANT, M. and GLYNN, T. (1978) 'Natural rates of teacher approval and disapproval in Grade 7 classrooms', *Journal of Applied Behaviour Analysis*, 11, pp. 91–4.

WHITE, M.A. (1975) 'Natural rates of teacher approval and disapproval in the classroom', *Journal of Applied Behaviour Analysis*, 8, pp. 367–72.
WORRALL, C., WORRALL, N. and MELDRUM, C. (1983) 'The consequences of teacher praise', *Educational Psychology*, 3, 2, pp. 268–76.

School Sanction Systems: Myth and Reality

Keith Topping
Kirklees Psychological Service, Huddersfield

> The great enemy of truth is very often not the lie — deliberate, contrived and dishonest — but the myth — persistent, persuasive and unrealistic. (J.F. Kennedy, 1962)

Teaching is the third oldest profession. Professional practice is pervaded with traditional assumptions and automatized responses which are often of doubtful validity and effectiveness, serving mainly to give teachers a sense of belonging. While in some respects teachers operate alone within the confines of their classrooms or teaching areas, the great majority work within an institution which has its own character and procedures. At the start of a teaching career, it is usual to assume that all pupils will be as motivated by the subject matter as you are. Relatively brief experience usually serves to dispel this view and teachers, particularly those working in secondary or high schools, find themselves turning to the institutional procedures for coping with inappropriate behaviour.

Traditionally, certain teacher responses to problematic behaviour are labelled as 'punishment'. However, a proper and precise definition of punishment carries the implication of effectiveness — punishment is a consequence of a behaviour which reduces the frequency of that behaviour. In the sense in which the word punishment is loosely used in schools, it is clear that what is prescribed as punishment may often not prove to be punishing. Thus, it has been demonstrated experimentally that the more teachers said 'sit down', the more children stood up. Other studies have demonstrated that increases in so-called 'punishment' can actually produce increased disruptive behaviour. While large institutions are of necessity organized on assumptions of homogeneity, pupils tend to be inconveniently individual.

The natural inclination of many teachers is to externalize the problem presented by difficult pupil behaviour, i.e. to blame it on someone or something else. It is certainly true that constitutional factors and the home environment are major influences in child development, but there is equally no doubt that within-school factors can make a profound difference. Reynolds and his co-workers (1975, 1976, 1980, 1981) found that high schools with comparable intakes varied considerably in the amount of non-attendance they experienced. High truancy schools typically had high levels of control coupled with harsh and strict rule enforcement, while low truancy schools showed higher levels of pupil involvement and closer parent-school relationships. Power *et al.* (1967) presented data on juveniles appearing before the courts in a London Borough demonstrating that schools with comparable catchment areas differed markedly in the delinquency rates of their male pupils.

The classic work of Rutter *et al.* (1979) lent further weight to the proposition that within-school factors may be important influences in pupils' behaviour. This study found that schools in which better behaviour was recorded were schools in which teachers concentrated on the topic of the lesson, interacted more with the class or groups rather than concentrating on individuals, started and finished lessons on time and required their classes to spend time working silently. Schools in which there were frequent interruptions or reprimands by teachers and in which there was a high rate of use of unofficial punishment tended to have worse behaviour. The overall picture for rewards provided a sharp contrast with the results on punishment. The more immediate forms of positive feedback showed the strongest association with good outcomes. This contrast in relative effectiveness between reward and punishment becomes even more striking when it is considered that, in all the schools studied, punishments tended to be used more frequently than praise — in the ratio of two or three to one.

Awareness of this research has led a number of British schools to develop 'incentive' systems, including commendations, merit certificates, house points and prizes. Various research studies have shown the effectiveness of more concrete rewards, such as prizes, free time and other privileges (see Page and Edwards, 1978, for a useful review). Milburn (1980) describes a 'Merit System of Rewards' in practical detail. In this system, although both merit and de-merit marks can be given by teachers, all teachers are aware that the ratio of the former to the latter must be high. Merit marks can be given for good work output, high levels of participation in class, sustained effort and concentration, attendance and punctuality. Individuals are rewarded and class performance is also noted with repsect to tidiness of classrooms, orderliness of entry to and departure from lessons, and so on. A tutorial period at the end of the week is devoted to 'reward activities' suggested by the children. The performances of individuals and class groups are publicly displayed. Milburn notes that this system can be easily adapted to suit the particular needs of any school, and that its implementation is quick and inexpensive.

The application of a consistent system throughout the school is likely to enhance the effectiveness of the rewards, since as Rotter (1966) points out, the effectiveness of a reward may also depend on the extend to which the pupil sees its acquisition as dependent on personal skill and effort rather than sheer luck or chance. Sharpley and Sharpley (1981) also emphasize the need for rewards to be delivered promptly and contingently in order to be effective, and Milburn's merit system at least lends itself to prompt delivery of the token, even if a delay is organizationally necessary before the delivery of the associated tangible reward. Milburn's system incorporates a degree of democratic pupil involvement, but research demonstrates that this can be taken considerably further, at least to the point where children take control of dispensing rewards to themselves. It is perfectly possible for children to set their own academic goals, monitor their own performances and reward themselves for achieving their objectives.

Despite the evidence and these promising developments, in many schools the predominant mode of attempting to control pupil behaviour is still punitive in intent: sanctions are imposed when pupils behave unacceptably rather than rewards being given for acceptable or improved behaviour. It is to the issue of punishments in schools that we now turn. However, punishment is a complex concept, with different semantic and emotional overtones for different users of the word. It entails issues of justice, desert, deterrence and rehabilitative effect. Within this chapter the focus will be mainly on the *effectiveness* of punishments deployed in schools, but this is not to suggest that ethical, legal, religious, social, emotional and pragmatic considerations should not enter into decisions about the application of school-based sanctions.

Traditional Punishment

> Many punishments discredit a prince, as many funerals a physician. (Ben Jonson, 1640)
> Punishment hardens and numbs, it sharpens the consciousness of alienation, it strengthens the power of resistance. (Nietzsche, 1887)

Just as teacher rewarding behaviour is governed by tradition, teacher personality and conditioning of the teacher by the child, so certain features of the child have an impact on the kind of punishment prescribed by teachers. For example, Wooldridge and Richman (1985) report that white female teachers in the Southern USA recommend more severe punishment for males than for females and for white males than for black males, irrespective of the teacher's age, experience and training.

As with reward, false assumptions are often made about punishment. Both teacher and pupil need to be clear about the precise behaviour to be punished, and the punishment should be delivered systematically and predictably. The effectiveness of the 'punishment' must subsequently be evaluated. If a reduction in problem behaviour ensues, the use of the punishment may be continued, but if this does not occur, it is not necessary to graduate automatically to a 'harsher' punishment — it may merely be necessary to find a different one which actually is effective in the individual case in question. What constitutes an effective punishment will, of course, vary from one pupil to another. Again, a combination of consultation with pupils and experimentation and observation of results is necessary.

Other guidelines for the effective use of punishment in general can be drawn from research studies. An explanation of the nature of the offence and the relatedness of the prescribed punishment tends to improve the effectiveness of the punishment. Thus, an explanation and a mild sanction can have the same effect as a severe sanction. Furthermore, the more immediate the punishment, the more effective it is likely to be, so that an immediate sanction may be effective without an explanation, while a delayed sanction will undoubtedly require a rationale. Punishment from a teacher with whom the pupil has a good relationship is likely to be considerably more effective than punishment from a teacher whom the child dislikes. Hoghughi (1983) proposes other conditions for effective punishment, but it is not clear to what extent these are based on empirical research. He suggests that the better established the behaviour pattern is, the less effective punishment will be in suppressing it. This is also likely to apply to a behaviour in some way involved with a state of high arousal such as anger or hunger. The inhibitory effect of punishment is considered likely to be greater where the problem behaviour possesses some 'discriminative stimuli' linkable with other signs to warn of impending punishment. Hoghughi also warns that while punishment must last long enough to register as unpleasant, it must not last so long that it becomes a feature of life to which adaptation becomes both necessary and probable. He also calls to our attention the effect of novelty — the more familiar the punishment the less powerful will be its effects.

The biggest drawback to punishment, apart from the difficulty of establishing that it is really punishing, is that it often has side effects. Although it often suppresses problem behaviour, it may do so only temporarily, but this short-term effect can reinforce teachers into using more and more aversive punishment, with less and less effect. Punishment may also produce escape behaviour (running away or non-attendance), extreme emotional reactions, the suppression of desired behaviours in addition, developing tolerance, and the undesirability of teacher demonstration of the use of aversive consequences — thereby serving as a model for other pupils, who may subsequently adopt similar techniques. Most crucially, punishment merely suppresses undesired behaviour, it does not teach new behaviour. Punishment is only likely to be effective where the situation provides clearly discriminable alternatives for the children. Where children are confused about what they have done wrong and what they should be doing instead, more intense punishment may serve only to confuse and disturb them further. Consistency of application of punishment is a particular problem in secondary schools, where children are exposed to a large number of different teachers with different expectations and management styles, and it is also worth noting that disruptive pupils have often been subject to inconsistent social training and management at home. In some cases, disruptive behaviour at school may be positively approved of out of school, and there is considerable evidence that the association of both reward and punishment with the same behaviour renders the behaviour much more resistant to extinction. Presland (1980) also suggests that punishment may inhibit all kinds of behaviour (good or bad), alarm well-behaved pupils of a timid nature, lower the self-esteem of children (which can have adverse effects on their behaviour), generate hostility which makes the establishment of positive relationships more difficult, and can generate revenge motivation.

Newsome *et al.* (1983) provide a useful review of the 'side effects' of punishment. The authors note that using punishment for behavioural difficulties is not unlike using surgery for medical disorders: both succeed or fail rather quickly, but each should be chosen carefully and with due deliberation of the possible side effects. Newsome *et al.* note that punishment can generate aggression, both imitative aggression and reactive aggression. Where behaviours are suppressed by punishment and no appropriate alternative behaviours are explicitly strengthened, response substitution may occur — i.e., other undesirable behaviours may emerge. The suppressive effect of punishment may generalize to other, wanted, behaviours. Furthermore, the 'punishment contrast' effect may occur — when a behaviour is punished in one situation, it may increase above its baseline level in a situation where the punishment is not administered. The authors do report that there are sometimes positive side effects of punishment, but these are usually confined to very young and/or severely handicapped children. In addition, there are of course major ethical issues associated with the use of punishment.

Traditional Sanctions

The most widely used traditional sanction is undoubtedly the verbal reprimand, partially reflecting the predilection of teachers for verbal methods and partially the ease and convenience of delivery of the supposed 'punishment'. As with other punishments, the verbal reprimand sometimes works and sometimes doesn't, and may work for some children but not others. One study noted that verbal reprimand could work when it was very brief, directive and stern and included the pupil's name, and was coupled with praise for the whole group when everyone was behaving well. There was some evidence that non-verbal expressions of approval from the teacher were just as effective on their own as *verbal* reprimands. In a third study, it was found that quieter reprimands were usually more effective in reducing disruptive behaviour than loud reprimands. However, Rutter *et al.* (1979) noted that frequent disciplinary interventions in the classroom were associated with worse behaviour, although cause and effect were not easy to disentangle.

A useful review of the effectiveness of social reprimands is provided by Van Houten and Doleys (1983). In general, the evidence seems to support the view that repeated or very frequent verbal reprimands are not effective, that verbal reprimands delivered with appropriate supporting non-verbal behaviour are more effective, that reprimands are more effective at the beginning of undesirable behaviour than later, and that reprimand is more effective when a pupil is praised for behaving appropriately subsequent to the reprimand. It is likely that the effectiveness of verbal reprimand will be increased if it includes the pupil's name and specifies what the pupil should be doing which is incompatible with the undesirable behaviour. Furthermore, the nearer the teacher is to the target child when the reprimand is delivered, the more effective is the reprimand. Although sudden loud reprimands can produce a 'startle response', on the whole quiet reprimands are at least as effective and less likely to disrupt classroom procedure. There is some evidence that verbal reprimands delivered to one child in the classroom may also reduce the frequency of the undesirable behaviour reprimanded in other pupils. (This finding will not come as a great surprise to teachers, of course.)

Other sanctions commonly in use, especially in high schools, are 'lines', 'detention', and being 'on report'. A few schools use 'deprivation of privileges' as a punishment, but the deployment of this technique obviously requires that the children currently enjoy some privileges of which they can be deprived. If few privileges exist, or the supposed 'privileges' which do exist are not valued by the target child, then this sanction will not work. Very rarely have researchers scrutinized the effectiveness of these traditional sanctions *as they are used* in ordinary schools, i.e., with the usual attendant inconsistency, disorganization and confusion. Where research evidence exists on procedures akin to these traditional sanctions, they have usually been conducted in atypical situations where natural processes have often been interfered with and there is the additional complication of a great deal of direct observation possibly producing an 'experimenter effect'. This more 'academic' research will mostly be considered in greater detail in a later section on 'Precision Punishment'. It can be argued that as by no means all of these studies have demonstrated that punishment can be effective even in a controlled situation, there is much less chance of punishment proving effective in the day-to-day hurly-burly of school life. However, some teachers might take the view that the experimental settings in some of the academic research are so absurdly artificial that it is likely that punishment deployed in school is actually *more* effective than has been demonstrated by some experiments.

The *Fifteen Thousand Hours* study (Rutter *et al.*, 1979) did however provide considerable information on the impact of traditional sanctions deployed naturalistically. This study found that there was no association between the average number of detentions received by children and any of the various measures of outcome (attendance, behaviour, achievement, or delinquency rates). Likewise the number of times lines or extra work were dispensed by teachers as a form of punishment showed no association with behavioural, academic, or attendance outcomes. The pattern of association between punishment and outcome was generally weak and inconsistent. It has also been noted that there are serious practical problems inherent in the use of detention, in terms of pupil safety during late homeward journeys. A further factor is that if children are given extra academic work as a punishment, this is unlikely to improve their attitude to such work at other times, while penalties unrelated to the offence in question are likely to be resented. Hall *et al.* (1971) report on a study with sixteen-year-olds where low marks in lessons resulted in extra *tuition* after school to remedy the difficulty — this led to much higher marks being achieved in normal lessons. Scherer *et al.* (1984) describe a procedure wherein the teacher writes the pupil's name on the blackboard at the first incidence of disruption and puts a mark by it at every subsequent incident of disruption, the mark to represent one minute of detention. Detention commenced at the end of the lesson and was deemed to begin only when pupils were sitting quietly. After each minute one of the marks was wiped off the blackboard. This immediate and observable usage of 'detention' proved considerably more effective than the traditional way of deploying the punishment. Hall *et al.* (1971) report on a similar arrangement where disruptive children received five minutes detention for every out-of-seat behaviour, and this dramatically reduced the incidence of the behaviour in the short-term. It thus seems likely that it is possible to use 'detention' in an effective way, provided its use is immediate and carefully structured; whether it is possible to meet these requirements in the context of an ordinary teaching day is quite another matter. These issues will be considered in greater depth later. The use of 'lines' can be construed as an over-correction procedure, and although there is very little naturalistic work on the effectiveness of 'lines', the effectiveness of 'over-correction' will also be considered below.

The third punishment in the traditional repertoire is, of course, corporal punishment. Rutter *et al.* (1979) found high levels of corporal punishment (official *or* unofficial) associated with *worse* behaviour. For years, many schools claimed that corporal punishment was hardly ever used. Dr Johnson observed in 1775 that 'there is now less flogging in our great schools than formerly'. The Clarendon Commission on public schools noted in 1861 that 'corporal punishment has greatly diminished'. In 1937 the NUT stated that 'corporal punishment is rapidly disappearing from our schools', and in 1976 stated 'the use of corporal punishment in schools continues to diminish'. However, in that same year (1976) the National Children's Bureau showed that corporal punishment was still used in eighty per cent of Britain's secondary schools. Although it is likely that recent European legislation will eventually result in the abolition of corporal punishment throughout the United Kingdom, history warns us that this may not occur as quickly as might be assumed, and in any event unofficial corporal punishment may well continue. The United Kingdom has some way to go before it catches up with Poland, where corporal punishment was abolished in 1783. Some schools have been inconsistent in their use of corporal punishment even within themselves, and the DES report on one school where one 'house' used the cane three times more frequently than another of the same size. The DES further comment 'some schools reported that many children were so accustomed to severe beatings at home that they were impervious to corporal punishment at school, and indeed, that some children claimed to prefer it to other more inconvenient punishments'. There is other research evidence that the parents of deviant children are more likely to use physical than verbal punishment — with less effect. The British Psychological Society (1980) reviewed all the available evidence on the effectiveness of corporal punishment, and concluded 'We can find no evidence which shows that corporal punishment is of value in classroom management. We have found evidence of its disadvantages, although such evidence is not of the highest scientific rigour.' Furthermore, there is no evidence that where corporal punishment is abandoned by a school, pupil behaviour deteriorates, indeed in some circumstances an improvement in behaviour is reported.

Teachers sometimes advance the view that, even if corporal punishment is ineffective with frequent offenders, it serves to deter others, and the tenets of behavioural psychology lend a rationale to this view. Walters *et al.* (1965) certainly found that where children observed a peer punished for a behaviour, the probability of the observers' emitting this behaviour was reduced. However, there was no evidence as to the duration of this effect. Many people might find the prospect of beating children purely 'pour encourager les autres' unacceptable, particularly if they were the parents of the child on whom this demonstration was perpetrated. Rust and Kinnard (1983) report a study showing that heavy users of corporal punishment tended to be relatively inexperienced, closed-minded, neurotic and impulsive as compared to their peers who did not use corporal punishment. Teachers who had experienced corporal punishment when they themselves were school pupils were more inclined to use this form of punishment when they became teachers.

In fairness, some high schools have made efforts to systematize their use of punishments in the attempt to secure greater consistency of application. Kibble (1983) describes a system of punishing by numbers, wherein a hierarchy of punishments of increasing severity is given a numerical code which is easily and immediately recorded on a pupil's report or record. A similar system is advocated by Presland (1980), but while such numbered hierarchies have the advantage of making clear to teachers that there are a number of possible punishments at the lightweight end of the continuum of which they may not be aware, no data on whether the application of such a system improves pupil behaviour has been reported to date.

Suspension

There has been grave disquiet about the desirability and effectiveness of the practice of 'suspending' pupils. Research shows that more black students than white students are suspended and that the rates of suspension vary from school to school in a way which has no relationship with the objective difficulty of a school's catchment area. Suspension for truancy and missing classes, which accounts for a substantial proportion of suspensions, in fact rewards students with the very release from school that they are seeking. Students who are suspended are often those who can least afford to miss academic instruction. Suspension may not only harm pupils, but it can cause problems in communities where the pupils may loiter when not in school.

Occasional media headlines give the impression that suspension rates are rocketing. Wood (1983) noted that suspension rates in ILEA continue to increase despite the vast amount of spending in that authority on 'support centres'. However, evidence from national surveys, albeit of doubtful reliability, suggests that suspension rates are only showing a significant upward trend in the south of England. Further evidence on the various and erratic usage of suspension will be found in Topping (1983) and Gale and Topping (1986). It seems that suspension rates are much higher in the winter than in the summer, and tend to peak in the middle of a term. Schools undergoing or recently experiencing reorganization, particularly related to comprehensivization, are more likely to have high suspension rates. Schools vary enormously in the extent to which they suspend pupils for attendance violations and fighting each other. Bayliss (1982) reports an increase in one city of suspension for violence between pupils but no increase relating to confrontation between teachers and pupils. Some authorities have gone so far as to set up 'suspension units', both in and out of ordinary school (Topping 1983). Out-of-school suspension units tend to greatly increase the time suspended pupils spend out of mainstream education, and reintegration rates are very low. In-school suspension centres with limited duration of stay show better results than merely debarring children from school, but even here the results tend to be no better, or somewhat worse, than spontaneous remission.

Given the extremely inconsistent usage of suspension by schools, one might not expect the practice to be particularly successful in changing pupil behaviour for the better, and indeed research suggests that this is the case. In one study, only sixteen per cent of pupils suspended had been successfully maintained in ordinary school at follow-up one to three years later. Gale and Topping (1986) noted that more suspension incidents took place out of lesson time than in lesson time, and that contact with parents before and after the suspension incident was often unsatisfactory, while usage of support agencies was patchy and ill-coordinated. Although the vast majority of children were suspended only once, and usually for a short period, in only 42 per cent of cases did the schools perceive there to be evidence of improved child behaviour after suspension, in terms of a lack of subsequent problems of a *serious* nature. Of course, it may well be that schools do not suspend pupils with the objective of improving behaviour subsequently, but if this is not their objective, it would be interesting to have a clearer specification of what was. Gale and Topping (1986) found no significant correlations between suspension rates, size of school, and socio-economic status of a school's catchment area. Thus the usage of suspension was not significantly related to the objective difficulty of a school's catchment area, and other workers have published similar findings. Furthermore, schools' usage of suspension as a sanction is positively correlated with their use of corporal punishment. Thus schools tend to use either both or neither, and neither has a significant effect on pupil behaviour. If suspension rates do rise in any school after the abolition of corporal punishment, this effect can only be attributed to changes in teacher behaviour, as there is no evidence that children are affected one way or the other by either supposed sanction.

Nor is there much evidence that the removal of a specific problem pupil for a short period by suspension improves the lot of those left behind, although this is another popular myth in the teaching profession. Mortimore *et al.* (1983), in a survey of head teachers in the ILEA, reported that a number of head teachers of ordinary schools declined to use off-site units. Of those who did, a small majority reported vague 'beneficial effects', but a third reported no positive effects or a deterioration. Likewise, schools reporting that the absence of a 'unit' child improved the pupils left behind were only slightly more numerous than those reporting no significant difference. By contrast, Coulby and Harper (1985) report that the deployment of a peripatetic support service to intervene with the behaviour of difficult pupils in the ordinary school setting resulted in an improvement in the behaviour of the rest of the class in 44 per cent of cases, *and* 57 per cent of the class teachers involved reported feeling more confident about handling other similar situations in the future.

It seems clear that the practice of suspending pupils is deployed in an erratic and inconsistent way, wherein objectives are often ill-defined and future plans not well thought out. This is not to say that this traditional sanction might not be of some use, particularly where combined with better organized contact with parents and support agencies, and combined with some form of contracting with the child so that expectations are clear on return to school. On the other hand, it may well be that many disciplinary problems could be solved by activating the other components of this formula without including suspension.

Precision Punishment

If punishment is to work at all, it must be applied in a well-planned, structured and orderly way, and its effectiveness routinely evaluated with respect to each individual case. Serious ethical problems can arise here: it is debatable whether some teachers are sufficiently responsible to be given a technology of punishment which is actually effective. Again it is necessary to reiterate the constant finding that rewards are more effective than punishments, and are much less likely to have negative side effects. Teachers sometimes complain that it is organizationally difficult or inconvenient to establish reward systems, but this may only be true in the light of their long learning history of punishing first and asking questions afterwards. In fact, many punishments are more unwieldy to administer than many simple rewards. All that is needed is changed teacher behaviour and school procedures. If punishments are to be used at all, then just as rewards have to be individualized to be effective, particularly with children presenting difficult behaviour, then so must punishments. Individualization of punishments implies finding a punishment which is effective in reducing the problem behaviour of the pupil in question, not finding a punishment which 'fits the crime' with respect to some grand philosophical framework subscribed to by the teacher. Individualization of both rewards and punishments should increasingly lead teachers towards establishing individual contracts with specific children, specifying both rewards and (if necessary) punishments with relation to particular approved and disapproved behaviours. Such 'contingency contracting' is likely to be far more effective than the uniform application of homogenized sanctions which have already by definition failed, and may in the long run be no more time consuming.

The four sub-sections below will review the effectiveness of various well-structured and precisely applied methods of punishment, all of which represent more sophisticated versions of traditional sanction practice.

Response Cost

With more structure and immediacy, the traditional sanction of 'detention' can prove effective. Thus Broden *et al.* (1970), working with a special class of 13 to 15 year olds in an ordinary school, used a system of minus points leading to after-school detention, which could however be bought off by plus points gained for appropriate behaviour. The use of 'token' systems has been widespread to get over the problem of organizational inconvenience in delivering tangible rewards to children immediately, using the token as a sign or mediator of deferred gratification. There seems no reason why this principle should not be more widely applied to punishment, to help both teacher and pupil monitor the consequences of their behaviours. The prime requirements for effective application of punishment, i.e., immediacy, consistency and individualization, are perhaps most likely to be achieved where a token system is combined with some form of individual contracting. The behaviours to change, the rewards and possibly the punishments are negotiated with the pupil, and the teacher will also need to agree to change some behaviours of his/her own. The agreements reached can be written down and even signed in the presence of witnesses. There should preferably be penalty clauses, with consequences for infringements by both parties when these occur. White-Blackburn *et al.* (1977) found such a system successful with 12 and 13 year olds in an ordinary school, and Lane (1978) has reported applications in classrooms in the United Kingdom.

Pazulinec *et al.* (1983) provide a useful review of punishment via response cost. The term response cost was originally used to describe the loss of a reward which is either already in the individual's possession or was to be delivered at a later time, contingent upon the occurrence of a pre-specified problem behaviour. Some workers have chosen to give individual points non-contingently at the beginning of a day or class, but points are then lost based on the occurrence of problem behaviours — this can be referred to as loss-only response cost. A more commonly used procedure is to combine both reinforcement and response cost in a token programme where children can gain points for good behaviour but lose them for bad behaviour. The response cost has also been used as a group contingency, for example, Axelrod (1973) allocated a total number of points to a class at the start of a lesson, reducing this number by one for each occurrence of a problem behaviour by any of the pupils. At the end of each class session, all the pupils received reward proportionate to the remaining number on the board.

In general, the research carried out in classrooms shows that where response cost is used in a structured and methodical way, child behaviour certainly improves. Precise techniques are varied. One worker removed points from a child within the context of a points system if the child was out of seat when a timer rang, which it did at varying and unpredictable intervals. The child was then encouraged to share her points at the end of class with her classmates. Other workers have divided classes into teams and allocated 'bad' marks to a child at the occurrence of each undesired behaviour, with rewards being provided at the end of the lesson to the team with fewest bad marks. Although this procedure proved effective, it is not truly a response cost procedure, and other workers have preferred to award points before class and remove them one at a time for each undesirable behaviour, with equal effect. Response cost techniques have also been used to enhance academic performance as well as decrease problematic behaviour, and studies have shown that the procedure can result in a doubling of work output. In another interesting study, it was shown that both token earning and token response cost were equally effective in improving the intelligence test scores of delinquent adolescent boys, in comparison to a control condition. Witt and Elliott (1982) report on the use of a 'response cost lottery', in which students were given a fixed number of lottery tickets at the beginning of the week and had one removed for each occurrence of a problem behaviour. At the end of the week, all pupils entered a lottery draw for a prize, and the pupils who had retained most tickets obviously stood the greatest chance of winning. Compared to baseline observations, both appropriate behaviour and academic performance increased by a factor of between two and three times. Other workers have found response cost token systems to be effective in ameliorating minor behaviour problems even when the tokens have no extrinsic value or back-up rewards. The traditional sanction of 'deprivation of privileges' is of course a type of response cost procedure, but will work only where schoolchildren actually enjoy privileges of value to them of which they can be contingently deprived. Clarizio (1976) has reviewed research in the area of privilege deprivation. It seems clear that the effectiveness of this form of punishment depends not only on how much the pupil values what he or she is threatened with losing, but also on how clearly the way to regain the privileges is shown. Thus consultation with the pupils on the delineation of a menu of valued privileges is a desirable precursor to the establishment of a response cost programme. Privileges tend to occur naturalistically much more frequently in the home environment than the school environment, and a linkage of school behaviours to home contingencies on a response cost basis will be considered in a later section on 'Home-School Reporting'.

Pazulinec *et al.* (1983) report that response cost, in common with other punishments, has undesirable side effects. Escape and avoidance reactions have been noted, but not usually in programmes in classroom settings. Over-usage by certain members of staff can be a problem (just as with corporal punishment), and the effectiveness of the technique may reinforce teachers into using it more and more widely with increasingly trivial problem behaviours. Contrast effects can occur where one class-teacher of a group is using a stringent response cost programme with high criteria, where with another teacher the children are presented with much lower criteria.

Consistency between teachers, that unattainable goal, rears its head yet again. With some very problematic subjects, a response cost system can result in increased inappropriate behaviour, when costs have gone beyond a certain point. Some subjects refuse to 'pay a fine' and may try to accumulate 'debts'. Some individuals may become argumentative when tokens are removed or when back-up rewards become inaccessible, but clear specification of the rules and negotiation in advance with the subjects of the programme should usually obviate this problem. The authors conclude that response cost is socially acceptable, practical, efficient, specifiable and manipulable, amenable to research, not physically abusive and effective in reducing the occurrence of problem behaviour. Its application in a token micro-economy should not be beyond the compass of a reasonably well-organized teacher. It may be, of course, that well-organized teachers are not likely to need to use this kind of procedure. Pace and Forman (1982) report work in classrooms which suggests that the assumed degree of aversiveness of the cost procedure used does not necessarily correlate with the degree of behaviour change. Thus teachers experimenting with this procedure are to be encouraged to begin with relatively mild rewards and punishments, which of course are likely to be least organizationally stressful to deliver. As with other teaching activities, it may be that the imposition of an organizational structure on the problematic behaviour is quite as significant a factor in changing that behaviour as the size of any rewards or punishments involved in the programme. As with other teaching activities, what is significant may not be so much *what* you do, but *how* you do it.

Over-Correction

Over-correction is a blanket term for certain kinds of punishment, many of which are akin to the lay concepts of restitution and reparation, and associated techniques include 'Positive Practice' and 'Satiation'. An extremely thorough review of recent research on over-correction is provided by Foxx and Bechtel (1983). The general rationale of over-correction is to require the misbehaving individual to correct the environmental effects of the inappropriate act so that the environment is restored to a state as good as or better than previously existed, and/or to practise with some repetition the correct forms of relevant behaviour which are required in those situations where the misbehaviour commonly occurs instead. It is important to identify the specific and general disturbances created by the misbehaviour, to identify the behaviours needed to vastly improve the consequences of the disturbance, and to require the individual to perform these corrective actions *whenever* the misbehaviour occurs. For example, an individual who overturned a table might be required to set the table upright, dust and wax it, and straighten and dust all other tables in the room. A specification of a positive practice programme involves two steps: identifying appropriate behaviours that should be practised; and requiring the individual to perform these appropriate behaviours whenever the misbehaviour occurs. Thus, the positive practice for a table overturning problem might be to require the disruptor to perform an appropriate behaviour while seated at the table. Thus over-correction consequences are always directly related to the misbehaviour, and the misbehaving individual directly experiences the effort normally required of others to correct the products of the misbehaviour. Over-correction must be applied immediately to be effective, and this implies that the individual should have little or no time to enjoy the positive possible results of the misbehaviour. In other words, the over-correction and positive practice responses are incompatible with the pupil receiving alternative reinforcement for the misbehaviour. Over-correction usually implies that the subject performs the over-correction acts rapidly so that they constitute an inhibitory effort requirement. This relates to the application of contingent exercise (see Luce *et al.*, 1980) which is favoured as a punishment by some teachers. If necessary, the individual is instructed and manually guided through the required acts, with the amount of guidance adjusted on a moment-to-moment basis according to the degree to which the individual is voluntarily performing the act. In a high school classroom situation, the extent to which a teacher could afford to use physical prompting of this kind is more debatable. It is important that over-correction instructions are given in an unemotional way, and previous warning of the impending use of the technique may be desirable for all pupils, although the establishment of individual contracts would be even better.

To date, the bulk of research work on over-correction and positive practice has been done on children with special needs, sometimes in institutional or domestic settings. Relatively little work is reported on its use in educational establishments. However, there seems no reason why these procedures should not be applied to educational environments by imaginative, well-organized and socially responsible teachers. Types of over-correction in widespread use have included 'Required Relaxation' (also known as 'quiet training' or 'relaxation training'), all of which require an agitated child to remain quiet and relaxed in a supine or prone position until all signs of agitation have been absent for a pre-determined period. 'Cleanliness Training' is often used for children with toileting problems, involving comprehensive cleaning of soiled clothing and of the place where the accident occurred. 'Medical Assistance Training' has been used when the misbehaviour results in injury to another person, and involves the aggressor in assisting in all phases of the (elaborate) medical treatment that is provided to the victim. 'Social Apology Training' has been widely used when the individual's misbehaviour has frightened or annoyed others. The over-correction strategy suggests that the individual should reassure everyone in the immediate environment that the misbehaviour will not be repeated. Where the misbehaviour involves the disturbance of property, as in many incidents of vandalism, over-correction might be termed 'neatness training', for example, requiring a litter-dropper to pick up all paper scraps and other items from the floor. Positive practice procedures can usually be identified to relate specifically to the misbehaviour being modified.

Over-correction and positive practice procedures have been used successfully to treat a wide range of aggressive and disruptive behaviours, self-injurious and self-stimulatory behaviour, establish appropriate toilet behaviour and extinguish inappropriate oral behaviours. Educational applications include the use of positive practice by Barton and Osborne (1978) to increase the sharing behaviour of children with hearing impairment in a nursery class. Sharing of toys increased from 16 per cent during baseline to 67 per cent during the first positive practice condition. Foxx and Jones (1978) used a positive practice procedure in a remediation programme for spelling errors with 29 schoolchildren. Although the positive practice may seem tedious by modern standards, the children reported feeling that the programme helped them and at follow-up there was good evidence of generalization and maintenance of improved spelling. Other workers have since extended positive practice in this area. Matson *et al.* (1979) used a positive practice procedure to reinstate speech in an electively mute boy. The procedure required the boy to write the target word (which he had refused to speak) ten times.

Like other punishments, over-correction and positive practice have side effects, although these are as likely to be positive as negative. Negative side effects have included aggression towards the adult, temper tantrums or emotional behaviours, increases in non-targeted inappropriate behaviours, escape behaviour, passive resistance, active resistance, self-injurious behaviour, and resistance on the part of adults to carrying out the procedures consistently.

The concept of satiation is in many ways antithetical to that of positive practice, since it requires the pupil to repeat many times over (under controlled conditions) the misbehaviour which it is required to eliminate. Parents carry out satiation when they catch their children smoking for the first time and make them smoke the rest of the packet all at once until they turn green. However, there will be relatively few problems in a school setting to which satiation can be conveniently applied, as monitoring the controlled situation can be somewhat time-consuming. In any event, research on the effectiveness of satiation is much less well developed than that on other punishment procedures discussed above.

Time-Out

Some high schools have established 'isolation rooms' or other areas in the school where pupils are sent to 'cool off' after a confrontation. This may be for a pre-specified period or until acceptable behaviour is demonstrated by the pupil. Some systems expect the child to continue with classwork while in isolation (the work supplied by the ordinary classteacher), while others require that the child sit in silence and ponder. The isolation area may be supervised directly or indirectly by teachers, usually by senior and/or experienced members of staff. Some schools establish a rota so that the room or area is always manned by a teacher with a free period.

Very few of the arrangements currently existing in secondary schools bear much relationship to the original behavioural concept of 'time-out', providing yet another example of how schools can misapply psychological research — and then often complain that it doesn't work. The essential concept of time-out, from whence it draws its name, derives from learning theory. The assumption is that the disruptive student must be getting something out of being disruptive (for example, attention, peer group status, avoidance of work), therefore the best way to reduce the disruptive behaviour should be by removing the student to 'time-out from reinforcement' — away from those things which are currently reinforcing the disruptive behaviour in the situation in which it is occurring. It may be expected that on the pupil's return to the original situation, the same reinforcers will again operate, and disruptive behaviour will recur. However, this may not happen if the pupil is aware that any recurrence will again automatically and consistently result in time-out. It is obviously essential that 'time-out from reinforcement' is just that — it is no use whatsoever removing the pupil to a situation where alternative reinforcers are available. Having a pupil sit outside the head teacher's office where he or she can act the fool, chat to passers-by and overhear confidential information is unlikely to help the situation.

Time-out is not intended as a punishment. Learning theory proposes that the removal of the child from the contingencies which are currently reinforcing his or her disruptive behaviour will result in that disruptive behaviour 'extinguishing'. Nevertheless, many pupils (and some teachers) certainly see time-out as used in their situation as distinctly punishing to them. However, it is worth stressing that time-out is not intended to be experienced as highly unpleasant and aversive by the pupil, but it does involve removal from all the factors tending to reinforce disruptive behaviour. These latter are of course likely to be different for different pupils. As with other interventions, there is a need for individualization, as it has been shown that for some children time-out can actually be rewarding, especially if they find social interaction stressful and have difficulty bearing future possible contingencies in mind.

A useful review of recent research on time-out is provided by Brantner and Doherty (1983). The authors identify three different types of time-out. In 'isolation TO', the child is physically isolated from the source of reinforcement and typically another room is used. Less restrictive, and with fewer punitive overtones, is 'exclusion TO', in which the subject is removed from the immediate area of reinforcement. For example, disruptive behaviour in the classroom might result in the child having to face into a corner or sit behind a screen or piece of furniture, excluding the child from classroom activities but maintaining their physical presence in the classroom. Another form of time-out has been called 'contingent observation'. Children who are disruptive in a classroom can be made to sit and watch on the periphery and observe the appropriate social behaviour of the other children for a brief period of time before rejoining the activity. This procedure clearly combines TO with modelling. Another form of 'non-exclusion' TO is the 'time-out ribbon', and children in the classroom are taught that wearing a ribbon (or other marker) is a cue for appropriate behaviour. When a child is disruptive the marker is removed and during this period the child can view classroom activities but is not allowed to participate. The teacher ignores the child and removes any objects and materials near the child. This procedure thus involves ostentatious ignoring signalled by the removal of a 'permit to participate' which is visible to the other children.

In practice, teachers may devise highly effective organizational variants on these techniques, but they must take great care to incorporate the fundamental tenets of TO and evaluate the effectiveness of their idiosyncratic procedure. Thus, teachers of small children will often reserve a special chair in a quiet corner of the classroom, and children becoming over-excitable are directed to sit on this chair. The chair itself often quickly acquires a magical aura, the mere sight of which is sufficient to calm some children. The question of ending time-out is highly relevant in this context. In true TO, the child is removed from all stimulation, and thus is not provided with work materials. Clearly, children cannot be left in this situation for any length of time, or their work output would be severely reduced thereby. Release from time-out can operate on either a timed or a contingent basis. With time release the child stays in TO for a pre-specified period of time, which may be as short as one minute and is most unlikely to be longer than ten minutes. In 'contingent release' the child earns release from TO by demonstrating appropriate or improved behaviour. Teachers need to be clear about which system of release from TO they are operating, and also make this clear to the children.

A problem with the TO procedure is that it does not necessarily involve the prior establishment of positive reinforcement. Therefore its effects may be due to the aversive qualities of isolation alone and bear little relationship to any supposed reinforcing qualities of a classroom. By definition, for disruptive pupils the naturalistic rewards for conforming behaviour in the classroom must be less than the reinforcement available from other sources for disruptive behaviour. To tackle disruptive behaviour, increasing the supply of the former is likely to be a more potent intervention than removal from the latter.

There is very substantial evidence on the effectiveness of TO in modifying disruptive and aggressive behaviour, but by no means all of this research concerns pupils in ordinary schools. Unlike more obvious 'punishments', TO does not usually show an immediate suppression of the problem behaviour, and this can generate a problem if teachers are not immediately reinforced into applying the procedure consistently. The child's previous learning history and constitutional sensitivity to certain reinforcers will influence the effectiveness of the technique. The environmental context both in and out of the TO situation may have a profound impact on its effectiveness. In practice, teachers have often failed to monitor TO procedures carefully, implement them consistently over a period, and evaluate the results. Like the punishments to which it is related, TO is not necessarily as simple to apply effectively as it may initially seem from the simplicity of the basic idea. Particularly in high schools, the sheer organizational complexity of the environment often militates against the effective application of the procedure, and relatively few high schools have as yet managed to organize themselves to apply the technique really effectively. Some workers have used signals to indicate the onset of TO within the applied setting (including an electronic tone, a bell, counting aloud, a ribbon, a clock, coloured cards and an alarm), but there is little evidence that these signals defiinitely improve the effectiveness of the procedure.

Various studies have investigated the effects of manipulating different parameters of the TO situation. Three studies have demonstrated that TO is considerably more effective where the 'time-in' environment was enriched in stimulation, although these studies were not with normal children. For some children, TO may have a novelty effect which is reinforcing, at least initially. Longer durations of TO tend to have more impact than shorter durations, but short durations of TO should always be tried first. Short durations of TO can be very effective on their own, but if there is inconsistency in managing the procedure, and short durations of TO are presented after longer durations have been utilized, the effectiveness of the shorter durations will be comprehensively sabotaged. There is some evidence that the use of time-out as an intermittent or random intervention can be as effective as using it for every occurrence of the problem behaviour, but its application does need to be unpredictable and random to produce this effect. There is some evidence that contingent release time-out is more effective in some circumstances than fixed duration time-out. Child self-regulation of the duration of the TO has proved just as effective as teacher stipulation of TO duration.

One of the dangers of the use of TO is that it may not work quickly and may thus be abandoned. The research evidence suggests that this is likely to be associated with a return to disruptive behaviour by the pupil which is actually worse than at baseline. Periods of continuous application as short as one month have been reported as maintaining successful long-term suppression with TO. A number of long-term follow-up studies have reported that the procedure has effectively changed behaviour over periods as long as twelve months and three years. Many of these studies have been with children with severe special needs, so it would be reasonable to expect TO to be effective with normal children within an initial trial period of about two months if it were going to be effective at all. Generalization to different settings has been demonstrated as a result of TO intervention, but this seems to be confined to variants within similar environments. The generalization of TO effects from home to school and vice versa has not been consistently demonstrated. It seems clear that time-out must be used carefully, ethically and responsibly, and in a planned, organized and consistent way. In particular, any tendency for the duration of TO to extend incrementally should be closely monitored and guarded against.

Physical Restraint

Needless to say, some disruptive pupils do not go willingly to time-out when instructed. It may be necessary for the teacher to prompt the child physically to proceed to time-out — i.e., drag the child there if necessary. The ease with which this may be accomplished is naturally to some extent a function of the size, strength and determination of the subject. Van Houten and Doleys (1983) discuss 'physical response termination'. In general, physical restraint tends to be applied to gross motor responses that are dangerous to the child, to the adult, or to others. Although researchers have not demonstrated experimentally that physically preventing or terminating a child's response adds to the effectiveness of a simple reprimand in the long run, there are several studies in which researchers have coupled physical restraint with a verbal reprimand. These studies demonstrated a high level effectiveness for the dual procedure, but the contribution to this effectiveness of the physical interruption remains unclear. For many teachers, scientific objectivity in this matter will be irrelevant, since dictates of safety will usually be paramount in necessitating interruption of the problem behaviour. There is some evidence that where a more severe punishment is paired occasionally with a less severe punishment, the effect of the less severe punishment on its own is enhanced, so it may well be that a teacher need only demonstrate the capacity and determination to interrupt a problem behaviour physically on a few occasions in order to be able to inhibit that kind of child behaviour on a more widespread basis.

Unfortunately, particularly with very excited or very large children, teachers are often very poor at applying physical restraint successfully. The adult needs a clear idea of when intervention by physical restraint is indicated, because such restraint must be used decisively and quickly at the staff member's initiative, not when the child forces it. Physical restraint should be implemented before the child has attempted to strike the adult and certainly before the child has succeeded in striking the adult — in general, the rule is to restrain the child before restraint is fully expected. Adults should only attempt to restrain children physically when they are confident of their ability to do so. A half-hearted attempt is doomed to failure and will result in even greater disruption subsequently. With practice of course, an adult's confidence will quickly grow — it is desirable to practise on the smaller disruptive children first. Thus physical restraint must be on the adult's initiative — decisive, determined and quick. The physical shock to a child of being speedily restrained and removed at some velocity is frequently in itself highly salutory. Once the adult has demonstrated the ability to overpower disruptive children at speed, the need to actually do it is often found to virtually disappear overnight. The children can be relied upon to pass the word around. A useful pamphlet has been produced by Topping and Brindle (1979) which details a variety of means of physically holding children and reviews the more common methods of child counter-attack. However, this is not the place for detail of that kind.

The Ecology of the Sanction System

Disruptive behaviour in schools does not take place in isolation, but is set in a complex social and organizational context. This is particularly true in high schools. Any attempt to 'cure' the problem behaviour of a disruptive pupil solely by direct 'therapy' with the child is most unlikely to be successful. However, manipulating the many variables impinging on that disruptive behaviour in a complex organization can be extremely difficult and time-consuming. Nevertheless, the effort must be made, and better systems thought out. It is all too easy to attribute a child's problem behaviour solely to 'within-child' variables, when in fact some very simple modification in the physical environment may greatly ameliorate the difficulty.

Environmental Antecedents

Deprivation of privileges can be used as a punishment, but its use is dependent on the existence of privileges of which the child can be deprived, and this has resource implications. It may imply the availability of space, money and staff supervisory time to provide a coffee bar, access to the art room during lunch-breaks, a favourable staff-pupil ratio to permit flexibility in the timetable to enable children to earn additional periods of favoured subjects, and so on. Rutter *et al.* (1979) note that in schools where more pupil work is displayed in public places, there tends to be less pupil graffiti — this implies that a simple environmental modification can elicit more desirable behaviour. Within the classroom, the layout of furniture may have a profound effect on child behaviour. Wheldall *et al.* (1981) noted that child on-task behaviour was significantly higher when children sat in formal rows of desks than when they sat round cooperative tables, and this was particularly true for children with low initial on-task behaviour. Timmins (1981) studied the effect of noise on child behaviour. There is considerable evidence that high noise levels impair successful learning. A noise meter was used which gave pupils a signal when class noise level rose above a pre-set criterion. Feedback from this signal markedly reduced noise levels in the class and reward for quietness reduced it further — the overall reduction was from 91 breaches of criterion in a half hour period to five per half hour period. Similar work is reported by Greene *et al.* (1981).

Demonstrations of environmental control over problematic behaviour can be found in the literature on vandalism and littering. O'Neill *et al.* (1980) doubled the rate of deposition of litter in bins by providing novel shapes of litter bins. Bacon-Prue *et al.* (1980) comparatively evaluated increasing the numbers of litter bins, employing two litter-pickers, and running a 'litter lottery' in which marked pieces of litter were exchangeable for money if brought in to headquarters by members of the public. The litter lottery was the most effective intervention. Schools with flat roofs with easy access and a multitude of hidden alcoves have been found to result in high levels of vandalism, and many teachers may feel that the configuration of play spaces around a school is a large factor in disruptive behaviour at breaktime. Some schools in America have a 'vandalism fund' from which the costs of remediating any vandalism are drawn, and the surplus in which at year end is made available to the pupils. This latter arrangement was found to reduce vandalism by 82 per cent.

Although the literature on the effect of the physical environment on other forms of disruptive behaviour within the school building is much more sparse, many teachers would feel that narrow corridors, obstructive fire doors, narrow staircases, buildings which are difficult to supervise, rooms with poor acoustic qualities, long corridors which encourage pupil racing, a lack or excess of ventilation or daylight, and a host of other environmental features can certainly affect a pupil behaviour.

Effective Monitoring

Many punishments depend on immediacy of application for effectiveness, and of course this implies that the children must be very rapidly 'found out'. Only half of incidents of disruptive behaviour occur in direct confrontation with teachers (Gale and Topping, 1986), and for the other 50 per cent of incidents the first management problem is that of determining when the behaviour occurs — i.e., of monitoring. Many high schools have systems of placing disruptive pupils 'on report', and for many pupils this is a reasonably cost-effective measure, so far as their behaviour in class is concerned. The extension of this kind of report system to less structured and supervised situations is organizationally very problematic. Teachers clearly have little time for close supervision of children outside of class, and this kind of monitoring must perforce be taken over by non-professional adults or by peer volunteers, in those specific cases where disruptive behaviour is causing great concern.

However, adult volunteers are rarely consistently available, and the payment of para-professionals incurs the expenditure of scarce resources. A more cost-effective alternative may be the deployment of members of the peer group to monitor the behaviour of particular problematic pupils. Teachers often tend to underestimate the capabilities of members of the peer group in this respect. There are many examples in the literature of programmes which have sought to arrange for highly sociometrically ranked members of the peer group to model appropriate behaviours for disruptive pupils, monitor the disruptive behaviours of these pupils and provide both positive and negative reinforcement to such pupils. This has been effectively done in both primary and secondary schools. Strain *et al.* (1976) review much of the work in this field. There is some evidence that maintenance and generalization of improvements is more reliable in peer reinforcement programmes than in those where the programme is managed and contingencies dispensed by an adult. There is no evidence that using peers in this way results in any detriment to them, and indeed there is some evidence that an improvement in rates of desirable behaviour in the peer volunteers can occur. For those wishing to pursue this area of work, further references are given in Topping (1983) and in a helpful review by McGee *et al.* (1977).

Maintenance and Generalization

Changing the disruptive behaviour of a problem pupil in one situation at one time is all very well, but teachers commonly look for improvements which endure over time and transfer to other situations in which the child may find himself. This is not necessarily easy to achieve, since the rewards and punishments relevant and specific to one situation may not be widely generally available in others or at other times. Some interventions do produce spontaneous maintenance and generalization, but where this occurs the teacher must consider himself lucky, for as a general rule these effects must be planned for and deliberately elicited.

Stokes and Baer (1977) reviewed 270 behaviour change studies and noted how few had programmed for generalization. These authors went on to describe 'an implicit technology of generalization'. Strategies discussed included sequential modification of behaviours approximating to the ideal, introduction of the child to naturally occurring maintaining contingencies, ensuring training of sufficient various exemplars of required behaviour, ensuring desirable behaviour was elicitable in various stimulus conditions, testing the child by usage of indiscriminate contingencies, the programming of common stimuli or signals into other situations, ensuring that other change agents were trained and available to mediate generalization, and other forms of training for generalization. This classic paper is highly recommended reading. An evaluative review of transfer of training in behaviour modification programmes is also provided by Wehman *et al.* (1977). Peer programming has already been referred to as a means of ensuring transfer of training, and the training of parents coupled with the establishment of home-school reporting, and the alternative procedures of self management training, are considered in more detail below.

Home-School Reporting

It can be argued that for the most disruptive pupils in a school, by definition the naturally occurring contingencies have not proved reinforcing. Thus even to establish initial behaviour change, let alone ensure generalization and maintenance, it may be necessary to look beyond the school for reinforcers which are potent enough to change disruptive behaviour within the school. Powerful reinforcers may exist in the home environment, and a system of recording the child's behaviour at school and reporting this to the parents, who apply reinforcers at home as appropriate, may serve to get round such difficulties with minimal time investment by the school. Many schools have some form of 'reporting' system, but few have gone so far as to seek detailed and specific parental cooperation in backing up such a scheme. The majority of parents, even the parents of disruptive pupils, can be relied upon to be cooperative when told of a simple straightforward way in which they can be of great help. If nothing else, it should be good for their self-image to know that they can do something where the school has failed.

Workers such as Hall *et al.* (1970) and Schumaker *et al.* (1977) report effective use of home-school reporting to improve the behaviour of disruptive adolescents aged up to nineteen years. A study by Lahey *et al.* (1977) showed that the procedure was effective in modifying the in-school behaviour of children at nursery school. A useful review of this subject is provided by Taylor *et al.* (1984). These authors urge that positive contingencies should be delivered at home so long as they are effective in reducing problematic behaviour, and note that interventions of this kind tend to be highly cost-effective.

Parents have access to a much wider range of reinforcers than the schools, and have much greater opportunities to individualize reinforcement. As is the case with in-school reporting systems, impact can often be improved by precise specification of desired and undesired behaviours. All too many school reporting schemes degenerate into collections of vague subjective description of problem behaviour, often revealing more about the emotional reaction of the teacher than about what the pupil actually did. To maintain parental cooperation and consistency, and to ensure that the pupil involved sees a home-school reporting scheme as reasonably fair, it is essential that precise specifications of, and criteria for, problematic and desired behaviour are negotiated and agreed with all parties beforehand.

Self-Management

With all behaviour change programmes, the hope is that the pupil's improved behaviour will be sustained less and less by artificial reinforcers and more and more by naturally occurring reinforcers, to the point where no special effort has to be made to keep the pupil's behaviour within bounds, and it could be said that the pupil had achieved 'self-control'.

There has been a good deal of work into 'cognitive self-instruction' to help children develop self control. Meichenbaum and Goodman (1971) trained impulsive children to talk to themselves, initially overtly and then covertly, in an attempt to increase their self control. The children were effectively required to rehearse verbally the consequences of their intended actions before carrying them out. The procedure proved effective, including at one month follow up, and appeared more effective than merely describing the required behaviour to the children. By 1979, Snyder and White had elaborated this procedure and were employing it with severely disturbed institutionalized adolescents.

Although many secondary schools utilize some form of report system in which teachers record their observations of pupil behaviour, relatively few have explored 'self-recording', in which pupils make their own recordings based on their own observations of their own behaviour. While it may seem implausible that the behaviour of severely disruptive pupils could be changed by such a simple device, many research studies have been encouraging. Some disruptive pupils are not actually aware of how obnoxious their own behaviour is, and a period of self-recording can bring this home to them with embarrassing clarity. Of course, this method will not work with all disruptive pupils, and where it is tried it may well be desirable to have some element of less frequent teacher recording continuing in parallel with the pupil's self-recording as a cross check on the reliability of the observations of *both*. Scherer *et al.* (1984) describe a successful programme where pupil self-recording was alternated with teacher recording. A helpful review of the use of self-recording in behaviour modification in the secondary school has been provided by McNamara (1979).

It is a relatively small step from self-instruction and self-recording to self-reinforcement. It may seem improbable to expect pupils who have clearly enjoyed being disruptive to show the ability to consistently and reliably reward themselves for behaving appropriately, yet there is a considerable body of research which demonstrates that reward administered to themselves by school pupils is as effective as reward administered to them for improved behaviour by external agents such as teachers. Even less probable, Salend and Allen (1985) found pupils were also able to self-punish, in the context of a response cost system for decreasing inappropriate behaviour. The self-managed response cost system was quite as effective in improving pupil behaviour as was a similar system managed externally by adults. A recommended review of the field of behavioural self-control was provided by Thoresen and Coates (1976), who noted a marked increase in books and manuals on the subject.

Finally, it should be noted that pupils can be successfully trained to manipulate teacher behaviour as a survival strategy. Children have been trained to 'recruit reinforcement' from the potential generalization setting (Stokes and Baer, 1977). This approach involves teaching children to emit behaviours which have a high probability of being reinforced by teachers, and to suppress behaviours which tend to result in aversive consequences. Graubard *et al.* (1971) taught adolescent pupils in ordinary classrooms to make eye contact with teachers, ask for help, react positively to teacher instructions, ask for extra work, sit up straight at their desks, and to break eye contact and not react when being scolded by the teacher. These procedures dramatically increased positive teacher contacts with these pupils.

While some practitioners may be concerned about the prospect of teaching children to alter the behaviour of their adult managers, in fact this procedure often proves less costly and time consuming than attempting to influence the adults (often unsuccessfully). Furthermore, in terms of the ecology of the sanction system, it recognizes the reciprocity of human social behaviour, and by teaching children to attend to the effects of their own behaviour, emphasizes self-control.

Conclusion

Disruptive pupil behaviour is a product not only of within-child factors, but also of teacher behaviour, school ethos and organization, and the nature of the physical environment. Many traditional 'punishments', as usually applied, are of doubtful effectiveness or known ineffectiveness. More precise forms of punishment include response cost, over-correction, positive practice, time-out and physical restraint, and these are of known effectiveness, while containing elements familiar to many teachers. However, no punishment will be effective unless individualized and applied in an organized manner with immediacy and consistency. This implies delivering the punishment in a planful and structured way (resisting any urge to 'shoot from the hip'), and building in monitoring procedures and strategies to promote generalization and maintenance (home-school reporting and self-management training may be helpful here). However, punishment has undesirable side effects and is generally less effective than reward, and teachers would be better employed utilizing their time developing reward systems in schools rather than elaborating complex punishment procedures.

References

AXELROD, S. (1973) 'Comparison of individual and group contingencies in two special classes', *Behaviour Therapy*, 4, pp. 83–90.

BACON-PRUE, A., BLOUN, R., PICKERING, D. and DRABMAN, R. (1980) 'An evaluation of three litter control procedures', *Journal of Applied Behaviour Analysis*, 13, 1, pp. 165–70.

BARTON, E.S. and OSBORNE, J.G. (1978) 'The development of classroom sharing by a teacher using positive practice', *Behaviour Modification*, 2, pp. 231–50.

BAYLISS, S. (1982) 'Rise in suspensions for playground fights', *Times Educational Supplement*, 15th October, p. 10.

BRANTNER, J.P. and DOHERTY, M.A. (1983) 'A review of time out: A conceptual and methodological analysis', in AXELROD S. and APSCHE J. (Eds) *The Effects of Punishment on Human Behaviour*, New York, Academic Press.

BRODEN, M., HALL, R.V., DUNLOP, A. and CLARK, R. (1970) 'Effects of teacher attention and a token reinforcement system in a junior high school special education class', *Exceptional Children*, 36, pp. 341–9.

BRITISH PSYCHOLOGICAL SOCIETY (1980) *Report of a Working Party on Corporal Punishment in Schools*, Leicester, B.P.S.

COULBY, D. and HARPER, T. (1985) *Preventing Classroom Disruption: Policy, Practice and Evaluation in Urban Schools*, London, Croom Helm.

FOXX, R.M. and BECHTEL, D.R. (1983) 'Overcorrection: A review and analysis', in AXELROD S. and APSCHE J. (Eds) *The Effects of Punishment on Human Behaviour*, New York, Academic Press.

FOXX, R.M. and JONES, J.R. (1978) 'A remediation programme for increasing the spelling achievement of elementary and junior high school students', *Behaviour Modification*, 2, pp. 211–30.

GALE, I. and TOPPING, K. (1986) 'Suspension from high school: The practice and its effects', *Pastoral Care in Education*.

GRAUBARD, P.S., ROSENBERG, H. and MILLER, M. (1971) 'Student applications of behaviour modification to teachers and environments, or ecological approaches to social deviancy', in RAMP E.A. and HOPKINS B.L. (Eds) *A New Direction for Education: Behaviour Analysis*, Lawrence, Kansas, Centre for Follow Through.

GREENE, B.F. *et al.* (1981) 'An analysis and reduction of disruptive behaviour on school buses', *Journal of Applied Behaviour Analysis*, 14, 2, pp. 177–92.

HALL, R.V., CRISTLER, C., CRANSTON, S.S. and TUCKER, B. (1970) 'Teachers and parents as researchers using multiple baseline designs', *Journal of Applied Behaviour Analysis*, 3, 4, pp. 247–55.

HALL, R.V., AXELROD, S., FOUNDOPOULOS, M., SHELLMAN, J., CAMPBELL, R.A. and CRONSTON, S. (1971) 'The effective use of punishment to modify behaviour in the classroom', *Educational Technology*, 2, 4, pp. 2–6.

HOGHUGHI, M. (1983) *The Delinquent*, Burnett Books Limited.

KIBBLE, B. (1983) 'Punish by numbers', *Times Educational Supplement*, 26th August.

LANE, D.A. (1978) *The Impossible Child*, volume 2, London, I.L.E.A.

LUCE, S.C., DELQUADRI, J. and HALL, R.V. (1980) 'Contingent exercise: A mild but powerful procedure for suppressing inappropriate verbal and aggressive behaviour', *Journal of Applied Behaviour Analysis*, 13, 4, pp. 583–94.

MCGEE, C.S., KAUFFMAN, J.M. and NUSSEN, J.L. (1977) 'Children as therapeutic change agents: Reinforcement intervention paradigms', *Review of Educational Research*, 47, 3, pp. 451–77.

MCNAMARA, E. (1979) 'The use of self-recording in behaviour modification in a secondary school', *Behavioural Psychotherapy*, 7, 3, pp. 57–66.

MATSON, J.L., ESRELDT-DOWSON, K., and O'DONNELL, D. (1979) 'Over-correction, modelling and reinforcement procedures for reinstating speech in a mute boy', *Child Behaviour Therapy*, 1, pp. 363–71.

MEICHENBAUM, D.H. and GOODMAN, J. (1971) 'Training impulsive children to talk to themselves: A means of developing self-control', *Journal of Abnormal Psychology*, 77, 2, pp. 115–26.

MILBURN, C.W. (1980) 'A positive rewards system', in UPTON G. and GOBELL A. *Behaviour Problems in the Comprehensive School*, Cardiff, Faculty of Education, University College Cardiff.

MORTIMORE, P., DAVIES, J., VARLAAM, A. and WEST, A. (1983) *Behaviour Problems in Schools: An Evaluation of Support Centres*, London, Croom Helm.

NEWSOME, C. *et al.* (1983) 'The side effects of punishment', in AXELROD S. and APSCHE J. (Eds) *The Effects of Punishment on Human Behaviour*, New York, Academic Press.

O'NEILL, G.W., BLANCK, L.S. and JOHNER, M.A. (1980) 'The use of stimulus control over littering in a natural setting', *Journal of Applied Behaviour Analysis*, 13, 2, pp. 379–81.

PAGE, D.P. and EDWARDS, R.P. (1978) 'Behaviour change strategies for reducing disruptive classroom behaviour', *Psychology in the Schools*, 15, pp. 413–18.

PAZULINEC, R., MEYERROSE, M. and SAJWAJ, T. (1983) 'Punishment via response cost', in AXELROD S. and APSCHE J. (Eds) *The Effects of Punishment on Human Behaviour*, New York, Academic Press.

POWER, M.J., ALDERSON, M.R. and PHILIPSON, C.M. (1967) 'Delinquent schools', *New Society*, 10, 264, pp. 542–3.

PRESLAND, J.L. (1980) 'Behaviour modification and secondary schools', in UPTON G. and GOBELL A. *Behaviour Problems in the Comprehensive School*, Cardiff, Faculty of Education, University College Cardiff.

REYNOLDS, D. (1975) 'When teachers and pupils refuse a truce: The secondary school and the creation of delinquency', in MUNGHAM G. and PEARSON G. (Eds) *Working Class Youth Culture*, London, Routledge and Kegan Paul.

REYNOLDS, D. (1976) 'The delinquent school', in HAMMERSLEY M. and WOODS P. (Eds) *The Process of Schooling: A Sociological Reader*, London, Routledge and Kegan Paul.

REYNOLDS, D., JONES, D., ST. LEGER, S. and MURGATROYD, S. (1980) 'School factors and truancy', in HERSOV L. and BERG I. (Eds) *Out of School*, London, Wiley and Sons.

REYNOLDS, D. and SULLIVAN, M. (1981) 'The effects of school: A radical faith restated', in GILLHAM B. (Ed.) *Problem Behaviour in the Secondary School: A Systems Approach*, London, Croom Helm.

ROTTER, J.B. (1966) 'Generalized expectancies for internal versus external control of reinforcement', *Psychological Monographs*, 80, 1.

RUST, J.O. and KINNARD, K.Q. (1983) 'Personality characteristics of the users of corporal punishment in the schools', *Journal of School Psychology*, 21, pp. 91–105.

RUTTER, M. *et al.* (1979) *Fifteen Thousand Hours: Secondary Schools and Their Effects on Children*, London, Open Books.

SALEND, S.J. and ALLEN, E.M. (1985) 'Comparative effects of externally managed and self-managed response-cost systems on inappropriate classroom behaviour', *Journal of School Psychology*, 23, pp. 59–67.

SCHERER, M., SHIRODKAR, H. and HUGHES, R. (1984) 'Reducing disruptive behaviours: A brief report of three successful procedures', *Behavioural Approaches with Children*, 8, 2, pp. 52–7.

SCHUMAKER, J.B., HOVELL, M.F. and SHERMAN, J.A. (1977) 'An analysis of daily report cards and parent-managed privileges in the improvement of adolescents' classroom performance', *Journal of Applied Behaviour Analysis*, 10, 3, pp. 449–64.

SHARPLEY, C.F. and SHARPLEY, A.M. (1981) 'Contingent versus non-contingent rewards in the classroom: A review of the literature', *Journal of School Psychology*, 19, 3, pp. 250–8.

STOKES, T.F. and BAER, D.M. (1977) 'An implicit technology of generalization', *Journal of Applied Behaviour Analysis*, 10, pp. 349–67.

TAYLOR, V.L., CORNWELL, D.D. and RILEY, M.T. (1984) 'Home-based contingency management programmes that teachers can use', *Psychology in the Schools*, 21, pp. 368–74.

THORESEN, C.E. and COATES, T.J. (1976) 'Behavioural self-control: Some clinical concerns', in HERSEN, M. *et al.* (Eds) *Progress in Behaviour Modification: Volume 2*, New York, Academic Press.

TIMMINS, P. (1981) *Classroom Noise: Its Control and Effects.* Unpublished M.Sc. thesis, University of Southampton.

TOPPING, K.J. (1983) *Educational Systems for Disruptive Adolescents*, London, Croom Helm.

TOPPING, K.J. and BRINDLE, P. (1979) *Physical Restraint of School Children*, Halifax, Calderdale Psychological Service.

VAN HOUTEN, R. and DOLEYS, D.M. (1983) 'Are social reprimands effective?', in AXELROD S. and APSCHE J. (Eds) *The Effects of Punishment on Human Behaviour*, New York, Academic Press.

WALTERS, R.H., ROOKE, R.D. and CANE, V.A. (1965) 'Timing of punishment and observation of consequences to others as determinants of response inhibition', *Journal of Experimental Child Psychology*, 2, pp. 10–30.

WEHMAN, P. *et al.* (1977) 'Transfer of training in behaviour modification programme: An evaluative review', *The Journal of Special Education*, 11, 2, pp. 217–31.

WHELDALL, K., MORRIS, M., VAUGHAN, P. and NG, Y.Y. (1981) 'Rows versus tables: An example of the use of behavioural ecolgoy in two classes of eleven-year-old children', *Educational Psychology*, 1, 2, pp. 171–82.

WHITE-BLACKBURN, G., SEMB, S. and SEMB, G. (1977) 'The effects of a good-behaviour contract on the classroom behaviours of sixth-grade students', *Journal of Applied Behaviour Analysis*, 10, 2, pp. 312–20.

WITT, J.C. and ELLIOTT, S.N. (1982) 'The response cost lottery: A time efficient and effective classroom intervention', *Journal of School Psychology*, 20, 2, pp. 155–61.

WOOD, N. (1983) 'ILEA secondary school suspension figures spiral', *Times Educational Supplement*, 18th March.

WOOLRIDGE, P. and RICHMAN, C.L. (1985) 'Teachers' choice of punishment as a function of a student's gender, age, race and I.Q. level', *Journal of School Psychology*, 23, pp. 19–29.

Further Reading

AXELROD, S. and APSCHE, J. (eds) (1983) *The Effects of Punishment on Human Behaviour*, New York, Academic Press.

AZRIN, N.H. and HOLZ, W.C. (1966) 'Punishment', in HONIG W.K. (Ed.) *Operant Behaviour*, New York, Appleton Century Crofts.

HARROP, A. (1983) *Behaviour Modification in the Classroom*, London, Hodder and Stoughton.

JOHNSTON, J.M. (1972) 'Punishment of human behaviour', *American Psychologist*, 27, pp. 1033–54.

LASLETT, R. and SMITH, C. (1984) *Effective Classroom Management: A Teacher's Guide*. London, Croom Helm.

LEACH, D.J. and RAYBOULD, E.C. (1977) *Learning and Behaviour Difficulties in School*, London, Open Books.

PRESLAND, J.L. (1980) 'Behaviour modification and secondary schools', in UPTON G. and GOBELL A. *Behaviour Problems in the Comprehensive School*, Cardiff, Faculty of Education, University College Cardiff.

ROBSON, J. (1981) *Effective Classroom Control*, London, Hodder and Stoughton.

RUTTER, M. *et al.* (1979) *Fifteen Thousand Hours: Secondary Schools and their Effects on Children*, Shepton Mallet, Open Books.

TOPPING, K.J. (1983) *Educational Systems for Disruptive Adolescents*, London, Croom Helm.

What is the Behavioural Approach to Teaching?

Kevin Wheldall and Frank Merrett
University of Birmingham

Problems of classroom behaviour and motivation are, as the editors of this book make clear, endemic in education. Teachers consistently cite difficulties in these two areas as their main classroom concerns and traditionally they have been dealt with in the same way, that is, by punitive methods. Both unacceptable or troublesome behaviour and idleness or lack of interest represent threats to the teacher's role which he or she commonly seeks to excise or avoid by aversive means. One consequence of this may be the daily litany of desist commands heard in many classrooms: 'Sit down, Sarah. Talking again, Barry. Leave Brendon alone, Nigel — get on with your own work. Something of interest outside, Mary? Eyes on your work please,' and so on, endlessly. As the research reviewed by Schwieso and Hastings in this volume shows, teachers the world over spend a considerable proportion of their teaching time reprimanding children for troublesome and/or non-work-related behaviours and hardly ever comment approvingly on appropriate behaviour (Merrett and Wheldall, 1986a). Moreover as our surveys in both primary and secondary schools (reviewed in our previous chapter in this volume) clearly show, teachers are mostly concerned with high frequency but relatively trivial troublesome behaviours such as 'talking out of turn' and 'hindering other children'. These are the behaviours which help to cause teacher stress as they occur with monotonous regularity and call for immediate action which usually takes the form of reprimands and sanctions. In this chapter we will consider an alternative approach to such problems based on behavioural psychology: the behavioural approach to teaching. We will describe the basic operating principles and then illustrate the effectiveness of this approach with demonstration studies of its application with both younger and older children in schools.

Kevin Wheldall and Frank Merrett

The Behavioural Approach to Teaching

The behavioural approach to teaching refers to the application(s) of behavioural psychology to promote good classroom practice by, almost exclusively, positive methods. In this chapter we shall concentrate primarily on its use with the social behaviour of children since it is generally accepted that good social behaviour in the classroom is necessary for academic learning to take place. The application of behavioural psychology is sometimes referred to as *behaviour modification*.

Behaviour modification is a generic term referring to the applied use of behavioural psychology to bring about changes in human behaviour by workers in the helping professions (clinical and educational psychologists, social workers, teachers and so on). Based on the operant conditioning model of B.F. Skinner, its central tenet holds that all behaviour is primarily learned and maintained as a result of an individual's interactions with his environment, which includes other individuals, and is hence susceptible to change by exerting control over features of that environment. Behaviour change may be achieved by manipulating the consequences following behaviour, in line with the 'law of effect'. Simply stated, this means that, within any particular context, whether a behaviour is repeated or not depends upon the consequences following it.

Behaviour modification has proved an effective technique for teaching more appropriate behaviour and reducing the frequency of inappropriate behaviour, with a variety of populations in many different settings. Such techniques have been found to be efficient and effective procedures for instituting and maintaining more appropriate behaviours but have not been without their critics who have questioned the ethics of such procedures. In reply to criticisms that behaviour modification is repressive and constitutes 'mind control', its advocates have claimed that it is ethically neutral, can be used for good or evil, by devil or saint, and merely formalizes and enhances the natural learning processes of the everyday world. Unhappily the term 'behaviour modification' has acquired an unfortunate public image. Hence, in the rest of this paper we employ the currently preferred term, 'behavioural approaches'.

In our book *Positive Teaching* (Wheldall and Merrett, 1984), we defined the behavioural approach to teaching in terms of five key principles. These are as follows:

1 Teaching is concerned with the observable. Teachers using the behavioural approach concern themselves with what a child actually does rather than speculating about unconscious motives or processes which may be thought to underlie behaviour. The only evidence we have about what people can do or will do and about what they believe comes to us by observing their behaviour. Consequently, careful definition and observation of behaviour are central to the behavioural approach.

Frequently, people propose explanations for behaviour which are not reasons at all. These are 'explanatory fictions' and some examples are innate aggression, language acquisition device and, dare we say it, dyslexia. To say that a child is often out of his seat *because* he is hyperactive is, quite simply, circular and gets us nowhere fast; hyperactive is just another way of describing the same behaviour. It does nothing to explain it.

2 Almost all classroom behaviour is learned. This is not to decry genetic inheritance nor to assume that anybody can be taught to do anything given time. Genetic inheritance sets the limits for what an inidvidual can learn, but behaviour is still the result of learning. Certainly this applies to the sort of behaviour that parents and teachers are chiefly concerned with, for example, knowing how to respond politely to others and being able carry out academic tasks like reading. Of course, children learn bad behaviour as well as good behaviour, a fact which parents and teachers are less ready to accept. The good news is that bad behaviour can be unlearned and new, more appropriate, behaviour learned in its place.

3 Learning involves change in behaviour. The only way that we know (that we can know) that learning has taken place is by observing a change in the child's behaviour. Teachers should not be satisfied with vague statements such as, 'Gemma has a better attitude towards school now'. Evidence is needed that she now attends on time, answers more questions, completes her homework or whatever. These are all clear examples of behaviours which can, if necessary, be counted and compared.

4 Behaviour change depends mainly upon consequence. This means that children (and adults and other animals, for that matter) learn on the basis of tending to repeat behaviours which are followed by consequences which they find desirable or rewarding whereas they tend not to repeat behaviours, the consequences of which they find aversive or punishing. The emphasis should be upon desirable consequences following appropriate behaviour. It has been shown repeatedly that rewarding good behaviour is more effective than punishing undesirable behaviour.

5 Behaviours are also influenced by the contexts within which they occur. In any situation some behaviours are more appropriate than others. If a child's behaviour is appropriate for a particular circumstance then it is likely to be rewarded by the people (adults or peers) who are around. If it is inappropriate to the situation it is less likely to be rewarded and may even be punished. As a result children rapidly learn not only how to perform certain behaviours but also when and where they are appropriate. Similarly, certain behaviours are more likely in some situations rather than others simply because there is more opportunity to engage in them. There is far more chance to chatter and to interfere with others when seated in classroom table groups than when in rows, for example, whilst young children are more likely to push and jostle when crowded together around the teacher than when spread out. It is important to emphasize that it is necessary to consider classroom ecological variables and setting events for behaviour as well as consequences.

This is what is meant by the behavioural approach to teaching. The main assumption is that children's behaviour is primarily learned and maintained as a result of their interactions with their environment, which includes other children and teachers. Consequently, children's behaviour can be changed by altering certain features of that environment. As we have said, the key environmental features are events which immediately precede or follow behaviour. This means that classroom behaviours followed by consequences which the pupils find rewarding will tend to increase in frequency. Similarly, certain changes in behaviour may be brought about merely by changing the classroom setting (for example, seating arrangements or classroom rules). The five points set out above may be seen as the essential features of the behavioural approach to teaching.

If we believe that teaching is concerned with helping children to learn new skills and gain new information, and if we believe also that learning implies a change or changes in behaviour, then it follows logically that teaching is about changing children's behaviour, whether we are talking about the acquisition of appropriate social skills or the learning of new academic information. Moreover, if teaching is about changing behaviour then the role of the teacher is, quite simply, to bring about changes in the behaviour of the children in his or her class.

The basic model embodying the crucial elements of the behavioural approach is known as the three term analysis of behaviour or the ABC model. It provides a basis for the analysis of, and intervention in, any particular teaching situation. 'A' refers to the antecedent conditions, i.e., the context in which a behaviour occurs or what is happening in that environment prior to a behaviour occurring. 'B' refers to the behaviour itself, i.e. what a child is actually doing in real physical terms (not what you think he is doing as a result of inferences from his behaviour). 'C' refers to the consequences of the behaviour, i.e., what happens to the child after the behaviour. Let us look at these three elements again in a little more detail, beginning with behaviour.

Behaviour. We have already said that a child's behaviour refers to what she is actually doing and we attempt to say what a child is doing in as precise a way as possible. If we observe a child building a tower with bricks, we would not write down 'creative play' since another observer or someone else reading our notes might interpret 'creative play' differently. It is too vague and imprecise. We would record that the child constructed a tower of four bricks. To say that it is 'creative' and/or that it is 'play' is to interpret, is prone to inaccuracy and vagueness and is unlikely to be useful.

Similarly, if a teacher tells us that Jason is always 'messing about' in class, we have to ask the teacher to define the behaviour more clearly. What you regard as 'messing about' may not be what he regards as 'messing about'. Moreover, if we use a vague definition there is no guarantee that it is the same sort of behaviour we are categorizing in this way two days running. So we would ask the teacher to list any of Jason's behaviours which he finds objectionable and then to define them as precisely as possible. A behaviour which is frequently found at the top of many teachers' lists is 'talking out of turn'. If we define this as 'any talking by a child when the teacher has requested the class to get on with set work in silence', then we are moving closer towards an objective definition. The more objective our definition, the easier it is for two observers to agree that a certain behaviour has occurred and the easier it is to count instances of such behaviour. Counting instances of behaviour can be an extremely useful, if not essential, component of the behavioural approach to teaching.

Precise definition of behaviour also helps us to avoid the danger of over-interpretation and giving explanatory fictions as causes of behaviour. These are generally unhelpful and give a veneer or gloss of 'scientific' explanation. For example, if Darren keeps hitting other children his teacher may describe him as being 'aggressive', but if we ask her how she knows this, she may reply 'He keeps hitting other children'. The word 'aggressive' is simply a label for a child who frequently hits other children but is sometimes used as if it were an explanation of this behaviour.

Consequences. As we said earlier, this refers to the fact that we tend to repeat behaviours which bring us what we want and to refrain from repeating behaviours leading to occurrences which we want to avoid. This appears to be a characteristic of all animals but we differ from animals, and also from each other, in terms of what we seek out and what we seek to avoid. In common with other animals, we tend to seek out food and will repeat behaviours which have led to the provision of food when we are deprived of it. Moreover, many, if not most of us, will work for money. Similarly, the majority of people find praise and approval rewarding and tend to behave in a way which is likely to be followed by praise or approval. On the other hand, perhaps few of us go out of our way to collect train numbers and, thankfully and more seriously, even fewer seek out and behave in a way likely to secure the 'reward' of drugs such as heroin. A major concern within the behavioural approach to teaching is with the identification of things and events which children find rewarding and to structure the teaching environment so as to make access to these rewards dependent upon behaviour which the teacher wants to encourage in his class.

In simple, everyday language consequences may be described as 'rewarding' or 'punishing'. Rewarding consequences, which we call positive reinforcers, are events which we seek out or 'go for', whilst we try to avoid punishing consequences; neutral consequences are events which affect us neither way. Behaviours followed by positive reinforcers are likely to increase in frequency. Behaviours followed by punishers tend to decrease in frequency whilst neutral consequences have no effect. In the behavioural approach to teaching, infrequent but desired behaviours (for example, getting on with the set work quietly) are made more frequent by arranging for positive reinforcers, such as teacher attention and approval, to follow their occurrence. Undesired behaviours may be decreased in frequency by ensuring that positive reinforcers do *not* follow their occurrence, i.e., a neutral consequence is arranged. Occasionally it may be necessary to follow undesired behaviours with punishers (for example, a stern 'telling off') in an attempt to reduce the frequency of behaviour rapidly, but there are many problems associated with this procedure. Contrary to popular belief, punishment plays only a minor and infrequent role in the behavioural approach, not least because what we believe to be punishing could, in fact, be reinforcing to the child. For example, the child who receives little attention from adults may behave in ways which result in adult disapproval. This child may prefer disapproval to being ignored and will continue to behave like this because adult attention is positively reinforcing. This is known as attention-seeking behaviour.

We should note that terminating a punishing consequence is also reinforcing and can be, and often is, used to increase desired behaviours. This is known as negative reinforcement. Again this has problems associated with its use since the child may rapidly learn other, more effective, ways of avoiding the negative consequence than you had in mind. For example, a teacher may continually use sarcasm and ridicule with his pupils. He ceases only when they behave as he wishes. Another way of avoiding this unpleasant consequence, however, other than by doing as the teacher wishes, is to stay away from school.

Finally one can punish by removing or terminating positive consequences (for example, by taking away a child's sweets). This is known as *response cost* but again there are similar problems associated with this approach. The following diagram shows the relationships between these various consequences and their effects.

Antecedents. Antecedent events or conditions, i.e., events which precede behaviour, may also influence its occurrence. They can serve to prompt a certain behaviour. Consider the situation when a teacher leaves the room and his class is left alone. For some classes this occurrence will have become a cue for noisy, disruptive behaviour since there is no-one around to reprimand the children. When the teacher does return the noisy disruptive behaviour will cease. We can see that a specific antecedent condition has control over this particular behaviour which is derived from association with certain consequences. Let us take another example which highlights how this might occur.

The teacher asks a child a question in class (antecedent stimulus), the child gives a silly answer (the behaviour), and his classmates laugh (the

Table 1

	To Increase Behaviour(s)	*To Decrease Behaviour(s)*
Delivery of	'Good things' i.e., rewarding with smiles, sweets, toys, praise, etc. Technical term: *Positive reinforcement*	'Bad things' i.e., punishing with smacks, frowns, reprimands, etc. Technical term: *Punishment*
Removal of	'Bad things' i.e., allowing escape from pain, noise, nagging, threats, etc. Technical term: *Negative reinforcement*	'Good things' i.e., losing privileges, house points, money, opportunities to earn 'good things'; etc. Technical term: *Response Cost*

consequence). If this consequence is positively reinforcing, we may expect the child to produce silly answers upon subsequent similar occasions. He will probably be less likely to do so, however, when his classmates are not there. The presence of his peers has become a stimulus for his misbehaviour. This example gives some of the idea behind the need to consider the context in which behaviours occur. The relationships between A, B, and C, the antecedent conditions, the behaviours and the consequences are known as the contingencies of reinforcement. Another important consideration which we must bear in mind, however, is the frequency of reinforcement.

When we want to teach a child to do something new, or to encourage him to behave in a certain way more frequently than he normally does, it is important that we ensure that he is positively reinforced every time he behaves as we want him to. This normally leads to rapid learning and is known as continuous reinforcement. When he has learned the new behaviour and/or is behaving as we want him to do regularly, then we may maintain this behaviour more economically by reducing the frequency of reinforcement. Another important reason for wanting to reduce the frequency is that the child may become less responsive if the positive reinforcer becomes too easily available. Consequently, once a child is regularly behaving in a desired way we can best maintain that behaviour by ensuring that he is now reinforced only intermittently. Intermittent reinforcement can be arranged so that a child is reinforced every so often (i.e., in terms of time) or, alternatively, after so many occurrences of the behaviour. These different ways of organizing the frequency of reinforcement are known as reinforcement schedules.

Following this summary of basic behavioural theory, we can now turn to a consideration of what the behavioural approach to teaching is all about. With some children the behaviour that concerns us has not yet been learned, with others the behaviour is learned but does not occur frequently enough whilst other children frequently behave in inappropriate ways. The behavioural approach to teaching is about changing the frequencies of behaviour. It can be used to teach new skills or to increase or decrease existing rates of behaviour. It is important to emphasize that the behavioural approach to teaching is primarily concerned with increasing the frequency of desirable behaviour in the classroom.

The effectiveness of the behavioural approach to teaching in the normal classroom has been demonstrated in a wide variety of experimental studies. Our own studies have demonstrated how to bring about changes in the problem behaviour of single children, small groups and even whole classes of children from a wide range of educational populations (Merrett, 1986; Wheldall and Merrett, 1984). More importantly, we have shown teachers how to encourage and increase the kinds of behaviour they want to see children in their classes engaged in and which are of educational benefit to them.

The methods advocated are all firmly based on behavioural principles and have all been carefully and rigorously tried and tested in work with teachers. Simple and straightforward interventions by teachers using positive methods can bring about dramatic results in terms of improved classroom atmosphere and the quantity and quality of work produced. Both antecedents and consequences can be engineered to good effect. Moreover, these methods, illustrated in the case studies below, have been shown to yield more satisfying and rewarding classroom experiences for both teachers and children.

Case Studies in the Behavioural Approach to Teaching

The behavioural approach can be applied in the management of classroom social behaviour in an endless variety of ways, calling for imagination, inventiveness and initiative on the part of teachers. There is no single prescriptive nostrum. The behavioural approach to teaching requires the consistent application of basic principles to unique and personal classroom problems. Behavioural methods work with all ages and in all subject areas; their operationalization, however, necessarily changes from situation to situation. Moreover, demonstrations of the effectiveness of behavioural interventions differ in terms of the formality with which they are carried out and evaluated. The rigorous designs beloved of researchers cut less ice with practical teachers for whom simple 'suck it and see' methods are enough. Both forms of demonstration study are necessary. First, let us consider a study which is little more than an anecdote, but which nevertheless proved a very rewarding lesson for the teacher, nursery assistant and parents involved.

Helping an Individual Child in a Nursery Class

In the nursery class in our Centre for Child Study, the two staff were concerned about a four year old boy, whom we will refer to as Gavin. Gavin came from a caring, professional family, but in comparison with the other children in the nursery, he seemed to our staff to be 'rather immature'. Pressed to be more specific, the nursery teacher and nursery assistant described how he very rarely played with the other children, never initiated interactions and, in fact, did not seem to do very much for himself at all. He behaved, they said, in some ways more like a two year-old than a four year-old and was 'babied' by his parents.

Casual observation certainly confirmed the worries of the nursery staff. Gavin spent most of his time standing on the fringe of the nursery action, watching or daydreaming, with this thumb in his mouth. Both nursery class staff employ positive methods and are au fait with our behavioural approach but they reported that praise seemed to have little effect on Gavin. It certainly did not seem to encourage him to participate more. Consequently, we suggested that a more powerful form of reward might be necessary in the form of tokens. The usual sort of star chart is not appropriate for young children and so the 'snake' programme was suggested. A long snake was drawn for him on a stiff card, divided up into a number of sections. It was explained to Gavin, in simple terms, that whenever he completed an activity, he would be allowed to colour in one of the segments of his snake. When his snake was complete he would receive a prize, a small model vehicle which, in common with most small boys, he was very keen to have.

It is only fair to add that our staff were not, at this stage, totally convinced that this scheme would work for Gavin. Nevertheless, they enthusiastically put the scheme into operation and began by suggesting activities to him, for example, painting a picture or building a Lego model. Gavin, to his credit, responded to these suggestions and consequently earned his points and the right to colour succeeding segments of the snake. Later on, the staff asked him what he wanted to do next, as a prompt, and he continued to be rewarded every time he completed an activity. Finally, he began gradually to initiate activities himself, pausing only to tell the staff that he had finished and to colour another segment.

Gavin's progress was remarkable and by the end of the first week he had completed his snake and was delighted to receive his prize, a model tractor. Another snake programme was immediately initiated, at his request. No formal data were collected apart from the implicit recording of completed activities in the colouring-in of the snake. This visual record of progress confirmed casual observations of Gavin's increased activity level. Instead of almost literally 'doing nothing' Gavin was now clearly seen to be engaging in several different activities every morning, to the satisfaction of the nursery staff. An unplanned bonus for the staff came from Gavin's parents, who had been told about the programme and who had been encouraged to praise Gavin for his progress on the snake. Shortly after the programme began they reported improvements in his social behaviour at home. He rapidly began to change from being a passive child with little interest in his world to a far more active individual with a lively curiosity. In spite of being more active he began to sleep *less* and was not nearly so sluggish as he had previously been. As Gavin was approaching the age to begin formal schooling these were important developments.

A 'Game' Approach to Improve the Behaviour of a Top Junior Class

The informal report above illustrates how in some situations hard data collection is not essential. The changes were sufficiently large and obvious to impress both nursery staff and parents. In the next example, however, more objective data collection was carried out in the context of a study carefully designed to demonstrate the effectiveness of a behavioural intervention with primary aged pupils.

Ways of maintaining control in an unruly classroom are many and various, but the key principle using the behavioural approach is basically to praise the good and try to ignore the bad. Becker, Madsen, Arnold and Thomas (1967) and Madsen, Becker and Thomas (1968) in classic studies on this, compared 'rules, praise and ignoring': i.e., set a series of simple, positively phrased rules which are made known to the class, for example, 'we sit quietly while working'; ignore all behaviour contravening these rules where possible; catch the children being good and reinforce them. They compared various combinations of these three basic procedures. The first condition, rules only, had little effect in reducing undesirable behaviour. The results were still inconsistent when 'ignoring' was added. But the third combination in which praise was added to 'rules' and 'ignoring' was shown to be a highly effective procedure for maintaining classroom control. Hence they concluded that 'praise for appropriate behaviour was probably the key teacher behaviour in achieving effective classroom management'.

Similarly, an experiment by Thomas, Becker and Armstrong (1969) showed how 'good' teachers who normally maintain a well ordered classroom by ignoring inappropriate behaviours and by consistently reinforcing appropriate behaviours, can, by altering these contingencies, produce dramatic deterioration in classroom behaviour. In one study disruptive behaviour was raised from the normal low level of around eight to nine per cent to over forty per cent accompanied by an appreciable rise in noise level. This was 'achieved' by the teacher frequently expressing disapproval for inappropriate behaviours. Thus it has been shown experimentally that whilst reinforcing (by expressing approval of) desirable behaviours leads to increased good behaviour, attending to inappropriate behaviour, even by expressing disapproval, may increase the very behaviours it is attempting to reduce. It has similarly been shown that increasing the number of 'sit down' commands increases the amount of out-of-seat behaviour, whilst praising for in-seat behaviour reduces out-of-seat behaviour.

In our own study demonstrating one approach to behavioural classroom management, we wanted to devise a positive approach which the children would actually find enjoyable. Consequently, rather than concentrating on trying to eliminate undesirable behaviours, which is known to be ineffective, we decided to concentrate on the behaviour we wanted, i.e., getting on with school work or 'studying behaviour' and to try to raise the frequency of what was, in the class we studied, relatively infrequent behaviour. As we make clear in our original paper reporting this study (Merrett and Wheldall, 1978), the approach was not totally original, being based on several other studies employing 'game' strategies, but it was highly successful.

The subject was a young, relatively inexperienced, female teacher, who was having a lot of trouble in controlling her class of thirty intellectually below average 10–11 year olds attending a state primary school. Classroom seating was arranged around four tables and we decided to make use of this in our intervention strategy.

However, initially we needed more specific and accurate information about the children's behaviour in the classroom. A cassette-tape was prepared to give a clear 'ping' on a 'variable interval' schedule of sixty seconds, i.e., at irregular intervals but on average once per minute. On hearing the sound the teacher would look at one of the four tables of children, indicated in random order on a pre-prepared sheet, and note the behaviour of the target child for that table by ticking the appropriate column. The target child was chosen afresh for each observation session on a random basis and thus all children in the class were observed during the study. Every time she heard the 'ping' the teacher had to glance at the schedule to see which table was next and record the behaviour of the target child by ticking appropriately. She could do this whilst working at her desk and, with experience, whilst walking around the room advising individuals and commenting on their work. The reliability of the teacher's results was checked from time to time by the experimenter using an identical record sheet and the same target children, and there was found to be very high agreement.

After several weeks of practice, 'baseline' data was collected, i.e., data collected prior to the teacher being given any instruction in behavioural methods (she also had no prior knowledge of the behavioural approach). By averaging over sessions we calculated that the children were 'on-task', i.e., quietly getting on with their work, only forty-four per cent of the time. The teacher was then given some basic instruction in the behavioural approach and an intervention strategy was suggested to her. She readily

Figure 1: Average On-task Behaviour Over the Three Phases of the Study.

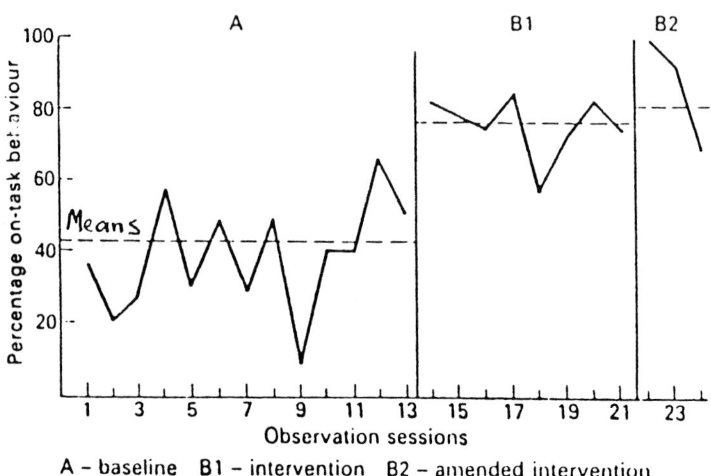

agreed since she was well aware of the rather 'chaotic' state of her classroom.

Briefly, the children were told the rules of a 'game' which were: we stay in our seats whilst working; we get on quietly with our work; we try not to interrupt. Whilst the game was in progress, the cassette would be switched on and every time the 'ping' sounded the teacher would look at one of the tables. If everyone on the table was keeping the rules, then each child on the table would score a house point. (They were assured that all tables would get equal turns but that the order would be random.) Each time a team point was given it was accompanied by verbal praise. This procedure lasted for five weeks when an amendment was announced. In future points would be awarded on only fifty per cent of the signals (pings), again on a random basis. The pings continued to serve the teacher as a signal for observing and recording the behaviour of the target children as well as a signal for reinforcement.

The results were remarkable and immediate, as Figure 1 shows. From the baseline on-task behaviour of only 44 per cent, it rose to 77 per cent following the intervention. Moreover, when the amendment to the schedule of reinforcement was made, after five weeks, the on-task behaviour rose even higher to between 80 and 100 per cent. Interestingly the quality of 'off-task' behaviour also changed. Whereas before the intervention disruptiveness was mainly shown in loud talking and quite a lot of movement around the room, after intervention off-task behaviour consisted mainly of passive inattention, daydreaming, watching other children and so on.

A purely subjective estimate of the classroom after the intervention was of great improvement in terms of orderliness and quiet during classroom work periods. An attempt was also made to measure academic output both before and after intervention. For example, samples of written work taken from the class during the collection of baseline data showed a mean output of approximately five written words per minute. During one of the first intervention sessions this had improved to a mean of approximately thirteen written words. However the number of spelling errors, despite the big increase in output, had hardly changed.

Comment was invited from the teacher once the project was completed. She used the term 'harrowing' to describe her problems with class control in her first (probationary) year. The recording of baseline data had proved 'tedious and time-consuming' at first but she thought that it became easier and less distracting after practice. She said she 'felt silly' about putting up the wall chart of rules, but she agreed that the effect of the intervention was immediate and very effective and said that she would continue using behavioural techniques especially in providing positive reinforcement for good behaviour. Some of the children were also asked their opinion of the game. Of the thirteen who responded, twelve were approving. All of those approving commented upon the fact that the quietness that prevailed enabled them to concentrate and get on with their work without interruption.

One issue which was surprising was the effectiveness of house points. It had been supposed that some stronger back-up reinforcement would be needed to make the game effective. Perhaps the house points worked so well because the intervention took place shortly after the system had been introduced and because it, in turn, was backed up by the award of badges to be worn in school.

However, as was stated earlier, it is not enough to attempt to analyze children's behaviour merely in terms of responses and reinforcers. As well as considering what happens following a behaviour (the consequence) we must also consider what happens before the behaviour occurs (the antecedent conditions). We can bring about changes in classroom behaviour by altering the antecedents, as the following study shows.

Changing Children's Classroom Behaviour by Changing the Seating

Most teachers will have noticed how the behaviour of a certain class varies depending on who is teaching them or even depending on where they are being taught. In other words, the behaviour of classes of children comes under what behavioural psychologists call stimulus control, whereby different stimulus conditions are followed by different forms of behaviour. Being in Softy Simpson's room may become the stimulus for unruly behaviour, for example, whilst few would dare even to breathe loudly in Biffer Barnes' class. Similarly, academic lessons, held by necessity in the art and craft room by the same teacher, may lead to more off-task or disruptive behaviour than when held in a regular classroom. Being in the art and craft room has become associated with a different form of behaviour, involving more movement around the room, perhaps.

It has been shown, for example, that location, where children sit in class, dramatically affects the number of questions they are asked (Moore, 1980). Other studies have shown that during story sessions and demonstrations, kindergarten children's on-task behaviour (paying attention to the teacher) was higher when the children were placed so as to allow space between each child and his neighbours, than when they clustered around their teacher. On-task behaviour was also higher if the session was preceded by a rest period rather than by a session of vigorous activity, giving the lie to the commonsense view of children being quieter after 'having got it out of their systems', (Krantz and Risley, 1977).

In Britain, classroom seating whereby desks or tables are arranged in rows is the norm in secondary schools and this was also the case in primary schools until the sixties. The influential Plowden report advocated a generally less formal approach to primary education favouring learning by discovery via topic and project work. This appears to have been accompanied by a move towards less formal seating arrangements, away from rows to a preference for table formations. In this latter arrangement, desks or tables are arranged so that four to eight children sit around a common work area. This new seating arrangement was widely adopted and is still the most commonly found being employed for overtly academic, individual, task orientated work (for example, workcards), as well as group work. To our knowledge, however, no empirical evidence was ever adduced to support this change of seating arrangement. Our own research comparing the effects of different seating styles in classrooms was inspired by, and replicates and extends, work by Axelrod, Hall and Tams (1979).

We carried out two parallel studies comparing 'tables' and 'rows' type seating arrangements in two state junior schools, (reported fully in Wheldall, Morris, Vaughan and Ng, 1981). In both schools a fourth year class of 10–11 year old children was chosen. One class consisted of 28 mixed sex and ability children attending a school in an urban residential area whereas the other class consisted of 25 similar children from a school on a council housing estate. In both classes the children normally sat around tables in groups of four, five or six. The design, procedure and, indeed, results of the two studies were very similar.

The children were initially observed for two weeks (ten days) in their normal seating arrangements around tables. An observation schedule using a time sampling procedure (described below) was employed to obtain estimates of on-task behaviour. This was defined, by the teachers, as doing what the teacher instructed, i.e., looking at and listening to her when she was talking to them, looking at their books or workcards when they were required to complete set work, only being out of seats with the teacher's permission, and so on. The observation schedule required each child to be observed twice per lesson in random order for 30 seconds. This was broken down into six five-second periods. If the child was on task for the whole five seconds he scored one point; if off task for any of the five seconds he did not score. Hence, this yielded a score out of six for each 30 second period and a score out of twelve for the two observation periods per child per lesson combined, which was subsequently converted to a percentage. This gave us an estimate of percentage on-task behaviour for each child for each lesson which, when averaged, gave an estimate of on-task behaviour for the whole class.

After observing the class for two weeks sitting around tables (baseline data), the desks/tables were moved into rows without comment from the teacher and the children were observed for a further two weeks (eight days in the first study, ten days in the second study) using the same procedure. Finally, the desks were moved back to their original positions, again without comment, for a further two weeks of observation (seven days in the first study, ten days in the second study). This time there were a few complaints from the children since they preferred sitting in rows.

In short, on-task behaviour rose by around 15 per cent overall when the children were placed in rows and fell by nearly as much when they returned to tables. Note how similar the general picture is for the two classes (see Figure 2). Looking at individual children, the most marked improvements in on-task behaviour occurred within those children whose on-task behaviour was previously very low. As we might expect, the effect was lessened in the case of children with high initial on-task behaviour. One or two children in each study showed higher on-task behaviour in groups; especially one child in the second study, the noisy ringleader of an anti-school group, who spent most of his time in rows trying to regain contact with his group!

We subsequently carried out a similar study on seating arrangements in a special school for ESN (M) children with behaviour problems (described in more detail in Wheldall, 1981). In this study we also included observations of disruptive behaviour and teacher behaviours. Three classes were observed for four phases of ten observations spread over approximately two week intervals. Again, seating was normally arranged around tables. In the first phase, observation was carried out in the usual (tables) conditions to provide baseline data, followed by phase 2 in which the class was moved into rows. Phase 3 constituted a return to the tables seating arrangement, followed by phase 4, in which seating was again arranged in rows. All lessons took place in the same room and were maths lessons given by the same teacher to all three classes: a junior class of 11 children, a middle class of 11 children and a senior class of 12 children.

The results dramatically confirmed and extended our previous findings. For every class on-task behaviour doubled during rows and fell during tables conditions. Similarly, rate of disruptions trebled during tables and fell during rows (results for the junior class are shown in Figure

Figure 2: Average On-task Behaviour for Two Classes Over the Three Phases of the Study.

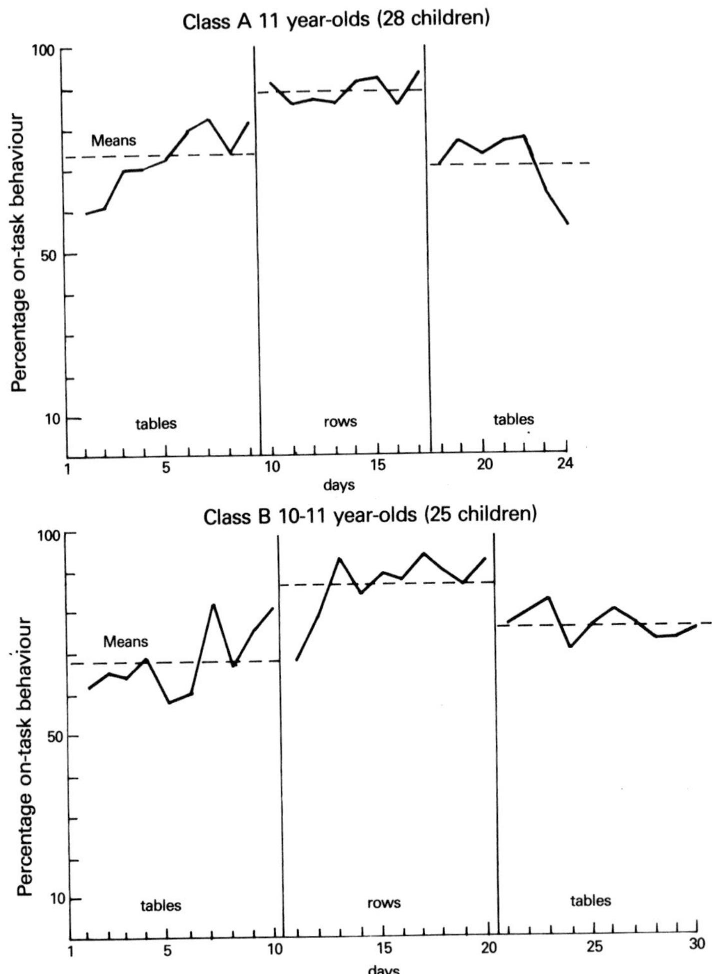

3). We also observed changes in teacher behaviour. Positive comments consistently went up during rows conditions whilst negative comments decreased. Thus the teacher apparently found it easier to praise and to refrain from disapproval when the children were seated in rows.

Before commenting on the conclusions to be drawn from these studies we must attempt to answer the question 'Why does seating around tables lead to more disruption, less on-task behaviour and less desirable teacher behaviour?'. We believe that the answer is quite simple. A table arrangement is geared towards enhancing social interaction. It facilitates eye contact, a prime means of initiating a social encounter, and provides a setting for increased participation in such encounters by involving the whole group. After all, we engineer such seating arrangements in precisely this way when we wish to encourage social interaction, in committees or when playing bridge, for example. Moreover, tables provide ideal cover for

Figure 3: Average On-task Behaviour and Number of Disruptive Behaviours for Class 2U Over the Four Phases.

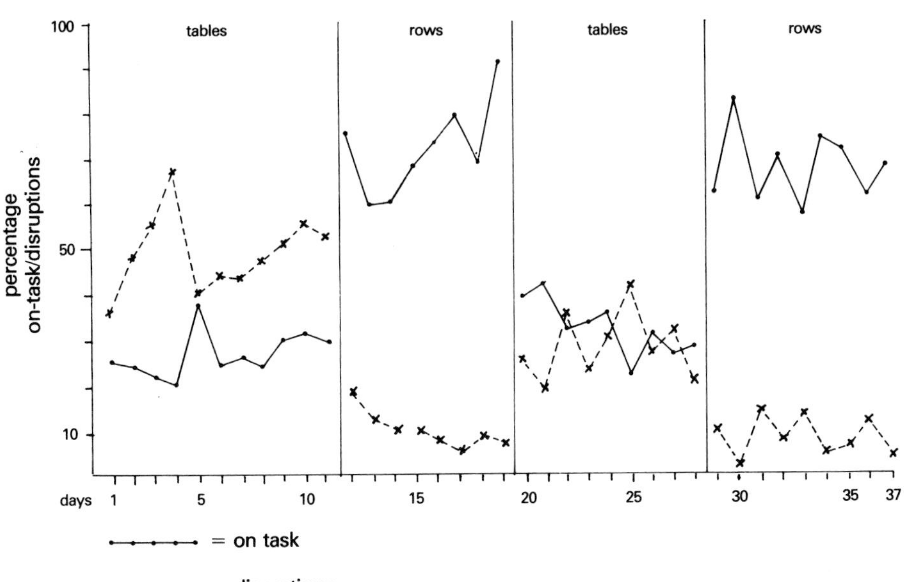

covert aggression or teasing, by means of kicking or pinching under the table, thereby increasing disruption. Rows formations, on the other hand, minimize either form of social contact, allowing fewer occasions for the teacher to comment adversely and more instances of desirable behaviour for him or her to comment upon favourably. In short, it could be argued that it amounts to little short of cruelty to place children in manifestly social contexts and then to expect them to work independently. It must immediately be emphasized, however, that we are not advocating a return to rows for all work. It is offered only as a possible strategy to encourage academic work which requires the child to concentrate on the specific task in hand without distractions. Rows would be totally inappropriate, for example, for small group discussions or group topic work, where table arrangements might prove more effective.

These results on seating arrangements constitute just one lesson to be learned from the behavioural approach to teaching. Certainly they should cause us to doubt our current preoccupation with fixed classroom seating arrangements and to encourage us to experiment with seating so as to optimize the appropriate behaviour for the task in hand and to discourage inappropriate behaviours.

Improving Behaviour in Secondary Home Economics Lessons

Far fewer experimental studies have been conducted in secondary schools, but simple behavioural methods work just as effectively here as they do in schools for younger children. In this study the widely-used behavioural procedure known as RPI ('rules, praise and ignoring') described earlier, was employed in four secondary home economics lessons. The rules used, which could be a little more complicated with these older pupils, were as follows: we try to work quietly and put up our hands when we need help; we listen carefully to instructions and read the board and our recipe sheets carefully; we try to work tidily in our units and share the jobs when clearing away; we get on with our cooking without disturbing others.

Thinking in terms of the ABC model we outlined earlier it will be appreciated that rules are being employed here as they are important antecedents for behaviour. They act, in fact, as a form of 'prompt' and teachers operating RPI are encouraged to draw attention to the rules regularly. This is best done when the pupils are clearly keeping the rules or at 'neutral' times such as the beginning of each session, but *not* when they are being infringed. This leads us logically to the second and third components, praise and ignoring.

Praise and ignoring refer to the consequences aspect of this procedure. Quite simply, teachers are required to praise pupils for keeping the rules and to ignore infractions of the rules. Praise may refer to the whole class or to individuals but should refer specifically to their behaviour in keeping the rules. Ignoring is often more difficult for teachers and is frequently misunderstood. It refers only to the behaviours governed by the rules (this is made easier by the fact that the rules are positively phrased) and does not mean that teachers should not intervene if a fight breaks out or if pupils are about to do something dangerous. The idea is to avoid responding to rule related misbehaviours since it may draw unnecessary attention to the miscreants (which they may find rewarding) and since it detracts from the overall positive approach, reducing the teacher's positive power.

It must be emphasized that ignoring on its own (that is, without rules and praise) has been shown to be ineffectual and as a technique it has certainly been 'over-sold' to teachers. 'Ignore it and it will go away' is the sloppy advice sometimes given to teachers by those with a superficial knowledge of the behavioural approach. Such a procedure is obviously nonsense to a teacher who knows he or she cannot permit certain behaviour excesses to continue without intervention and who recognizes that his or her attention to certain behaviours, such as those involved in showing off to peers, has little effect in comparison to peer approval or attention. An unsuccessful or unpopular child who gets a little begrudging acceptance or a laugh from his peers for fooling about is often not going to be much affected by teacher reprimand or by ignoring. The technique of ignoring is at least partly predicated upon the assumption that teacher attention (even if negative) may be rewarding. The hard truth is that teacher response may be irrelevant.

In view of the points made above and especially since the RPI procedures were employed in home economics practical (cookery) lessons in this study, reprimands for potentially dangerous behaviour were not excluded. Teachers were, however, instructed to ignore rule infringements wherever possible and to concentrate on praising rule-keeping and on-task behaviours. To back up RPI in this study, the teachers were also asked to make a general evaluative summary statement at the end of each lesson concerning the behaviour of their classes during that lesson, if it was warranted; for example, 'You have all worked much harder today than last week. Let's see if you can do even better next time.'

These then were the RPI procedures used in this study with four mixed second-year classes of twelve and thirteen year olds and their three experienced teachers (one teacher taught two classes). All four classes had gained a reputation for noisiness, untidiness and not listening. The aims of the study were to demonstrate that simple behavioural methods could be used effectively in home economics practical lessons, to encourage more attention to the task in hand, and especially, to reduce the excessive noise levels commonly experienced in such practical classes. To this end all four classes were systematically observed for thirty minutes during the practical component of their weekly lesson over an eight week period. These observations were completed by our student who had been carefully trained to use our classroom behaviour observation schedule, OPTIC (Merrett and Wheldall, 1986c). OPTIC (Observing Pupils and Teachers In Classrooms) allows objective data to be collected on both teachers' use of approval and disapproval and, in addition, on children's level of on-task behaviour. As those interested can read about the schedule in Merrett and Wheldall (*op. cit.*) we will not dwell on detail here. The use of a second observer in a sample of lessons showed that the reliability of these observations was very high (around 90 per cent). In addition, the observer was also able to obtain objective measures of 'noise level' by using a decibel meter.

In order to demonstrate the effectiveness of the procedures clearly and rigorously, RPI was introduced successively at two-week intervals with the four classes. All classes were observed operating normally for the first two weekly lessons and the intervention was then introduced in the first class. Two weeks later it was introduced into the second class and after a further two weeks into the third class. The fourth class remained under normal conditions throughout. This procedure is known technically as multiple baseline design and is employed to show how the intervention consistently and unequivocally exerts its effect upon behaviour. The graphs (Figures 4 and 5) show clearly the effectiveness of the RPI intervention on both on-task behaviour and noise levels.

In each of the three experimental classes on-task behaviour is seen to rise following the introduction of the intervention; in the first class from (on average) around 78 per cent to 83 per cent, more markedly in the second class from around 75 per cent to 89 per cent and in the third class from about 75 per cent to 85 per cent. In the fourth class, on-task behaviour averaged about 83 per cent throughout, since no intervention was attempted with this (control) class.

The effects of the intervention are shown even more clearly on noise level (Figure 5). Again, in each of the three experimental classes noise level was shown to fall markedly following the introduction of the intervention; in the first class from an average of around 66*db*. to 62*db*., in the second class from 68*db*. to 63*db*. and in third class from 69*db*. to 61*db*. In the fourth (control) class noise level remained roughly constant at around 63*db*.

This study, then, provides convincing evidence of the effectiveness of behavioural methods with secondary aged children in a potentially difficult practical work setting, most previous studies in secondary schools having been carried out in academic lessons. Our results add to the body of experimental data confirming that the behavioural approach is applicable to older, secondary aged pupils just as much as it is with younger children.

One of the legitimate reservations about using behavioural methods with older children, however, is the need for more powerful back-up reinforcers with more difficult or poorly motivated pupils. The disenchanted, potentially troublesome, teenage pupil is less likely to find the traditional privilege of 'feeding the guinea pig' rewarding and we are unlikely to be able to offer the traditional teenage delights of 'sex 'n' drugs 'n' rock 'n' roll'! So it is reasonable to ask, 'What do secondary aged pupils find reinforcing?'.

We recently carried out a study with an Australian colleague, Dr Peter Sharpe, referred to earlier, (Sharpe, Wheldall and Merrett, 1986) following up his earlier work carried out with Australian adolescents (Sharpe, 1986). Briefly, we surveyed the attitudes and opinions of nearly 400 secondary pupils aged 12 to 16 years attending two comprehensive schools in the West Midlands. Our 'Praise and Rewards Attitude Questionnaire' (PRAQ) inquired into pupils' preferences for various types of reward for both academic and social behaviour. In brief, we found that most British secondary pupils *do* perceive rewards and praise as appropriate outcomes for

Figure 4: The Effects of RPI on On-task Behaviour

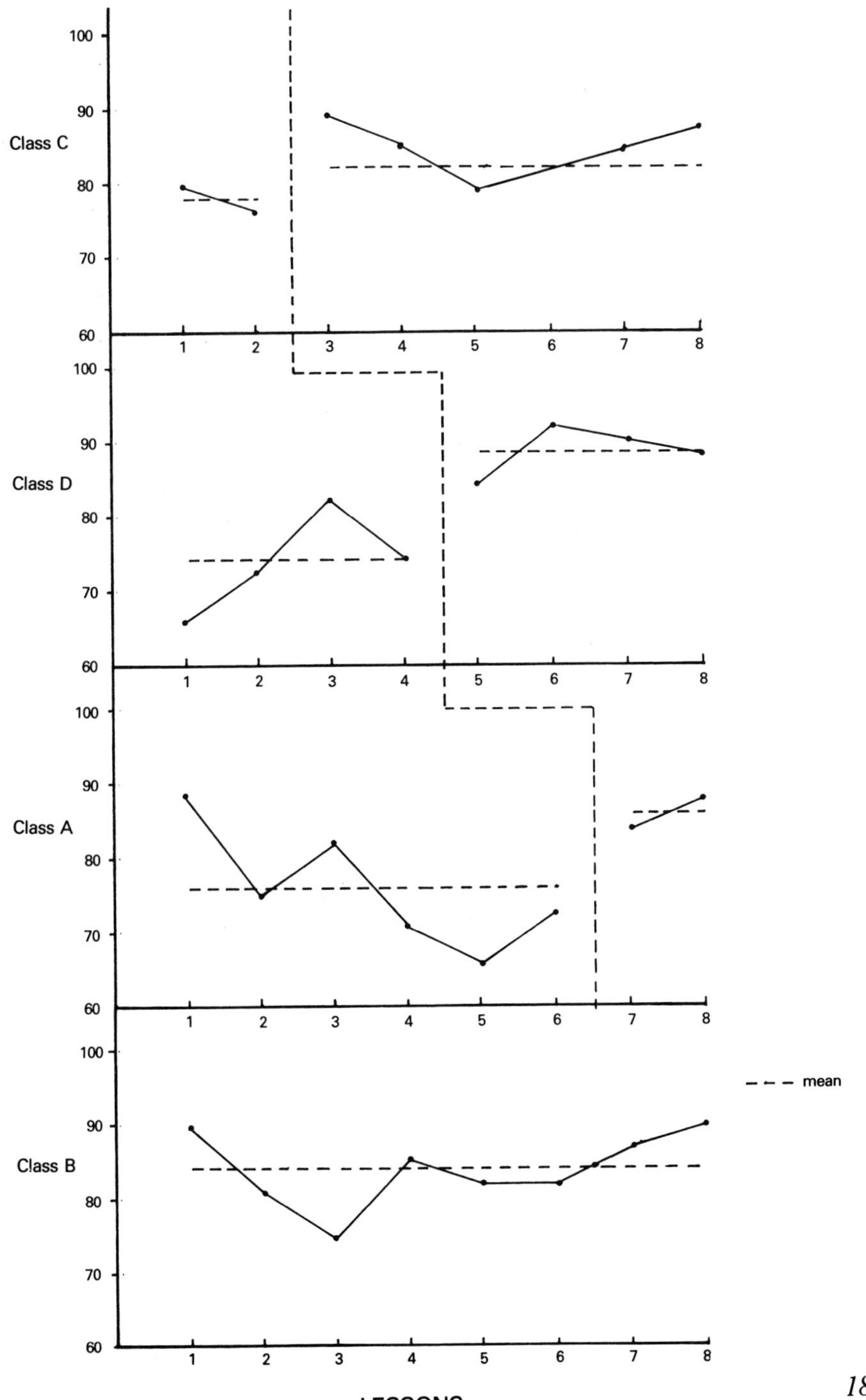

Figure 5: The Effects of RPI on Noise Level

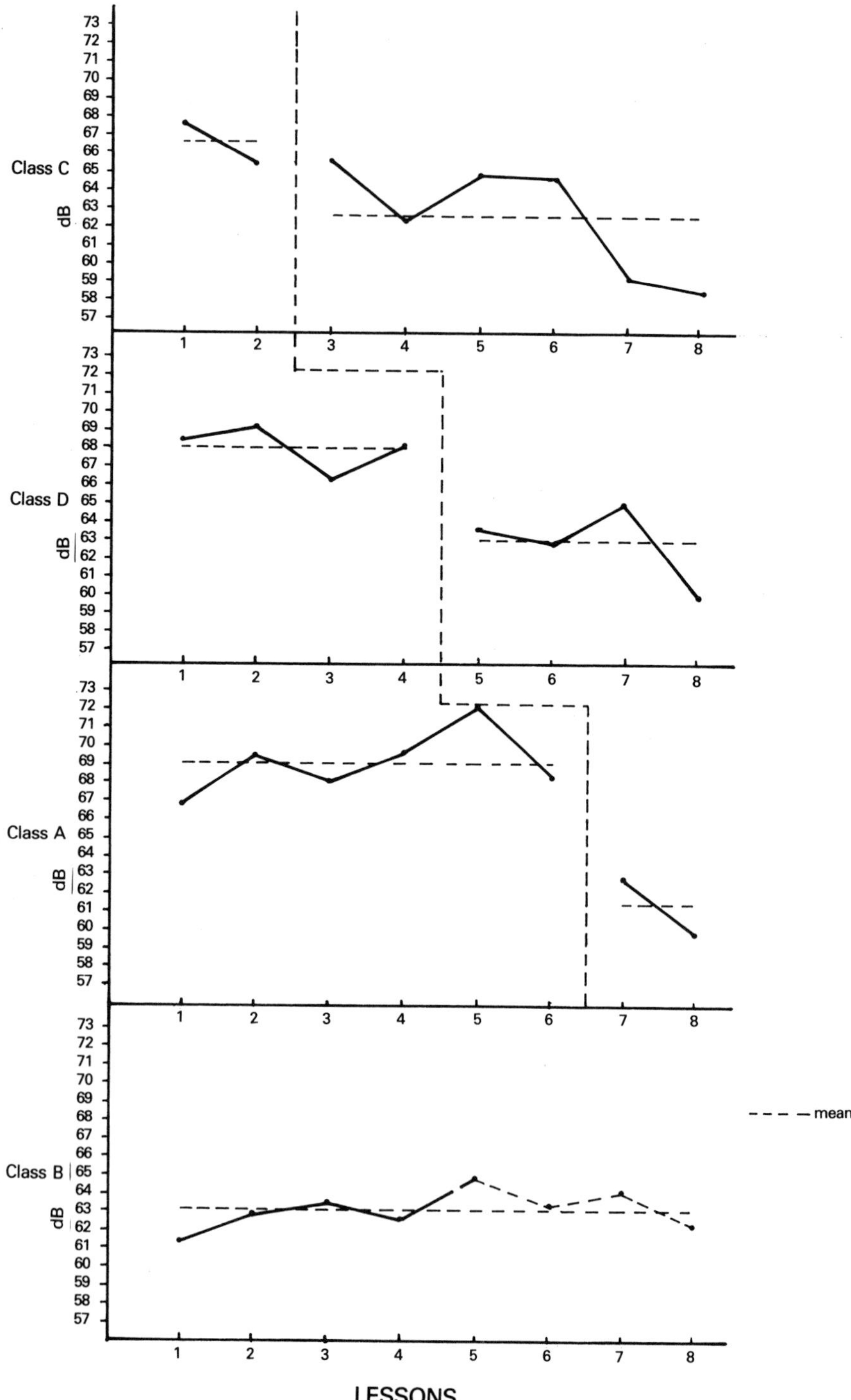

both academic and social behaviour, although older pupils tend to regard them as more appropriate for academic behaviour alone. Our results also showed that when offered a choice of six alternative rewards (sweets, free time, no reward, praise, points or a positive letter home), free time and a positive letter home were most highly regarded. Free time is perhaps predictable. It is relatively easily arranged and has certainly been shown to be effective (see, for example, Wheldall and Austin, 1980). A positive letter home was much less predictable and is certainly hardly ever employed in British secondary schools. A letter home is normally only ever used to convey disapproval of social or academic behaviour. Its use in a positive form as a reward needs to be explored experimentally but it is certainly a 'cheap' option which can readily be arranged. It should be noted that free time and a positive letter were the favoured choices of pupils for both social and academic behaviour. People of all ages respond to a range of internal and external reinforcers. Secondary school pupils are no exception and respond favourably to various forms of praise and reward which are available for use by the teacher.

In this chapter we have attempted to outline a positive, behavioural approach to improving classroom discipline. The central focus has been on encouraging the types of behaviour which teachers consider to be most appropriate for effective learning to take place. What should be taught and in what order and how it should be taught are decisions for teachers to make as expert and professional educationists. The behavioural approach to teaching provides the means for achieving whatever teachers decide is in the best interests of their pupils.

References

AXELROD, S., HALL, R.V. and TAMS, A. (1979). 'Comparison of two common classroom seating arrangements', *Academic Therapy*, 15, pp. 29–36.

BECKER, W.C., MADSEN, C., ARNOLD, C.R. and THOMAS, D. (1967) 'The contingent use of teacher attention and praise in reducing classroom behaviour problems', *Journal of Special Education*, 1, pp. 287–307.

KRANTZ, P.J. and RISLEY, T.R. (1977) 'Behaviour ecology in the classroom', in O'LEARY, K.D. and O'LEARY, S.F. (Eds) *Classroom Management: The Successful Use of Behaviour Modification* (second edition), New York, Pergamon.

MCNAMARA, E. (1986) 'Behavioural approaches in the secondary school', in WHELDALL, K. (Ed.) *The Behaviourist in the Classroom*, London, Allen and Unwin in association with Positive Products.

MADSEN, C.H., BECKER, W.C. and THOMAS, D.R. (1968) 'Rules, praise and ignoring: Elements of elementary classroom control', *Journal of Applied Behaviour Analysis*, 1, pp. 139–50.

MERRETT, F. (1986) *Encouragement Works Better Than Punishment*, (second edition) Birmingham, Positive Products.

MERRETT, F. and WHELDALL, K. (1978) 'Playing the game: A behavioural approach to classroom management', *Educational Review*, 30, pp. 391–400.

MERRETT, F. and WHELDALL, K. (1986a) 'National rates of teacher approval and disapproval in British primary and middle school classrooms', *British Journal of Educational Psychology*.

MERRETT, F. and WHELDALL, K. (1986b) 'British teachers and the behavioural approach to teaching', in WHELDALL, K. (Ed.) *The Behaviourist in the Classroom*, London, Allen and Unwin in association with Positive Products.

MERRETT, F. and WHELDALL, K. (1986c) 'Observing Pupils and Teachers in Classrooms (OPTIC): A behavioural observation schedule for use in schools', *Educational Psychology*, 6, pp. 57–70.

MOORE, D. (1980) 'Location as a causal factor in the unequal distribution of teacher questions: An experimental analysis', *Proceedings of the Third Australian Conference on Behaviour Modification*, Melbourne, Australian Behaviour Modification Association.

SHARPE P. (1986) 'Behaviour modification in the secondary school: A survey of students' attitudes to rewards and praise', *Behavioural Approaches with Children*, 9, pp. 109–12.

SHARPE, P., WHELDALL, K. and MERRETT, F. (1986) 'The attitudes of British secondary pupils to praise and reward'. (Submitted for publication.)

THOMAS, D.R., BECKER, W.C. and ARMSTRONG, M. (1969) 'Production and elimination of disruptive classroom behaviour by systematically varying teacher's behaviour', *Journal of Applied Behaviour Analysis*, 1, pp. 35–45.

WHELDALL, K. (1981) 'A before C or the use of behavioural ecology in classroom management', in GURNEY, P. (Ed.) *Behaviour Modification in Education, Perspectives No. 5.*, Exeter, School of Education, University of Exeter.

WHELDALL, K. and AUSTIN R. (1980) 'Successful behaviour modification in the secondary school: A reply to McNamara and Harrop', *Occasional Papers of the Division of Educational and Child Psychology of the British Psychological Society*, 4, pp. 3–9.

WHELDALL, K. and MERRETT, F. (1984) *Positive Teaching: The Behavioural Approach*, London, Allen and Unwin.

WHELDALL, K., MORRIS, M., VAUGHAN, P. and NG, Y.Y. (1981) 'Rows versus tables: An example of the use of behavioural ecology in two classes of eleven year-old children', *Educational Psychology*, 1, pp. 171–84.

3

Understanding and Fostering Motivation in the Classroom

Introduction

The last four chapters provide a variety of perspectives upon current understandings of the role of motivation in the classroom. Two of the contributors approach the issue from the perspective of attribution theory, two from that of behavioural psychology. Nevertheless, all four papers can be seen to agree in the following of current trends in educational psychology, in as much as the dichotomy between motivation and behaviour, and between intrinsic and extrinsic motivation, which differing theoretical traditions so emphasized in the past, is now accepted as having been overstated. Moreover, if previous sections have emphasized ways in which the teacher can establish more precise control over her pupils, the theme of this section is about ways of promoting the independence and autonomy of the individual learner.

Colin Rogers provides a good example of the way in which social psychology is providing new insights into educational practices as well as deepening understanding of the traditional concerns of psychology. He uses attribution theory to provide a pupil's view of motivation in the classroom. Attribution theory is concerned with how commonsense explanations of life events actually influence people's behaviour. For instance, a child who believes that his failure at school is the result of lack of effort will be likely to try harder next time, whereas one who believes that failure stems from lack of ability will be more likely to give up trying, regardless of the actual effort or talent involved. Rogers demonstrates that the teacher will need to be as attentive to pupils' interpretations of the causes of academic achievement as they are to facilitating attainment. If Rogers shows how attribution can be used to understand children's motivation, Grolnick and Ryan's chapter uses this perspective to suggest new approaches to achieving traditional educational goals. Within education, and indeed philosophy as a whole, there has been a longstanding debate about the differing merits of intrinsic and extrinsic motivation. Nevertheless, most educators have concurred in placing a high value upon developing self-directed, mature learners. Grolnick and Ryan demonstrate how different phrasing of instructions can promote either independence or conformity learners who are, otherwise, being set very similar tasks. They sound a necessary note of caution concerning the effect of powerful extrinsic controls, of the sort discussed in many of the chapters in our book, upon the learner's growth into autonomy.

The last two chapters approach the issue of the learner's own motivation from a more behavioural perspective. Dale Schunk's concern is with the changing of perceived self efficacy, the belief held by an individual concerning his ability to achieve certain goals. For Schunk, the dichotomy between extrinsic and intrinsic motivation may be better seen as a dialectic. Objective aspects of a learning situation affect subjective ones, and these in turn affect performance. Schunk reviews evidence, much of it from his own research, as to how a person's sense of self efficacy — an internal factor — can be enhanced in education by the structuring of the external learning environment. Thus his chapter provides a bridge between the practices described elsewhere in this volume by Schwieso and Hastings, Topping and Wheldall and Merrett, and the pupil and teacher cognitions which interest Rogers, Grolnick and Ryan. Ted Glynn clearly shares Grolnick and Ryan's concern that the school environment may not foster independence in learning. He demonstrates, however, how the behavioural approach, which has often been accused of reducing the learner to a stimulus-response mechanism, is perfectly capable of sustaining a more sophisticated educational perspective. His particular interest is in responsive environments which provide the classroom situations that foster such self-directed learning, provide settings which support the learning in progress and supply appropriate consequences to support performance. The implied contrast is with much current practice which might be regarded as presupposing a reactive learner whose role is simply that of responding to teachers.

Attribution Theory and Motivation in School

Colin G. Rogers
University of Lancaster

All teachers and most pupils will have a working conception of motivation. Motivation is the thing that explains why one person does better at a task than another even though both appear to have equal ability. Motivation is the thing that leads to one person working long and hard at a task while another stops at the first excuse. Motivation is the thing that enables one pupil to work with the minimum of direction and guidance from the teacher, while another child has to be constantly monitored and directed.

Most readers with some teaching experience will be able to recognize the above and add to the list. Motivation is a powerful explanatory concept that would appear to be deeply embedded in the thinking and folk wisdom of members of the teaching profession. However, push at the concept of motivation a little, ask a few awkward questions concerning its more precise nature and, often, its explanatory power seems to melt away. Notice that the paragraph above offered not so much definitions of motivation itself, but definitions of the things that motivation supposedly does. They tell us much more about the differences between those who apparently have a lot of it, and those who do not, than they do about the entity itself.

If the concept of motivation is to fulfil its apparent promise regarding its power to explain differences in educational success and failure, then it is necessary to begin to build up a working model of motivation itself. It is necessary to have an understanding of the concept that not only informs us as to the consequences of having different levels or types of motivation, but also explains why such differences might occur and how they operate. Furthermore, if this understanding is to have educational consequences, in the sense of providing teachers with practically useful conceptual tools, then it must provide an analysis of motivation that is relevant to classroom processes.

These points have not escaped the attention of psychologists to date and there have been several attempts to conceptualize motivation, to develop theoretical accounts of its development and operation and to devise programmatic interventions from these theories (useful and comprehensive accounts of the development of the major strands in psychological thinking can be found in Weiner, 1980; Ames and Ames 1984).

Perceptions of Causes and Motivation

This chapter looks at one of these conceptualizations, that developed by Weiner (1972, 1974, 1979, 1984) and his various associates. This model draws on one of social psychology's currently dominant theoretical systems, attribution theory (Hewstone, 1983; Jaspars, Fincham and Hewstone 1983). Attribution theory attempts to develop a model of the ways in which people will ordinarily make judgments concerning the causes of events. Attribution theorists regard these judgments as significant as, in common with other 'cognitive' approaches to the study of human behaviour (Eiser, 1980) it is an individual's understanding of a situation, rather than the situation itself, that is held to determine the ways it which they react. From the early work of Heider (1958) onwards, attribution theorists have held that people's beliefs concerning the causes of events are critical in determining the understanding that they have of those events.

A simple example will serve to illustrate the point. Two pupils have both attempted a maths test at school. Each does badly on the test in comparison to other members of the class. Let us assume that each child is concerned about his performance and asks himself why it came about. One child decides that his performance is the result of his idleness over the last couple of weeks. He had not attended to the lessons that the test was related to, he had not done his homework. The second child decides that his performance was the result of a basic lack of mathematical ability. He is simply the kind of person who does not do well at maths tests. Attribution theorists will go on to claim that these two differing explanations of what was, objectively, the same level of performance, make the performance levels quite different in terms of their subjective import for the pupils concerned. The first pupil is likely to conclude that future improvements are possible. If he attends to future lessons, if he does his homework, there is no need for him to perform as poorly again. The second pupil is likely to conclude that extra work and effort will be a waste of time. If you can't do it you can't do it and that is that. To put it another way — the first child's failure provides a motivationally useful 'kick-in-the-pants' while the second's proves to be debilitating.

The Contribution of Weiner

'Attribution theory' is in many respects a poor descriptive term. As generally understood by present day social psychologists, the term refers not so much to a single articulated theory, but rather to a somewhat loose collection of research studies and attempts to explain the data thus produced. Some social psychologists have more or less abandoned the term and refer instead to the psychology of ordinary explanations (Antaki, 1981). These approaches all share one basic concern, however, which is an examination of the ways in which people explain or attempt to explain events that have happened to them or to others about whom they are concerned to some notable degree.

The approach taken by the attribution theorists has been classified into two broad categories (Weiner, 1974), each of which is capable of further subdivision. The first group is referred to as 'theories of attribution'. Here the concern is with the ways in which individuals make decisions concerning the causes of events that they wish to explain. Given that an event has taken place, just how does a person decide what caused it to happen, and why might one individual arrive at a different conclusion from another? The second category, of 'attributional theories', concerns attempts to explain the consequences of a decision to attribute an event to a particular cause. As will be clear from a reexamination of the example given above, concerning two pupils' reactions to the results of a maths test, any attempt to use attribution theory to explain reactions to success and failure within the school context will need to incorporate elements of both categories.

Initially we will need to know whether attributing instances of success and failure to different causes seems to have any bearing on performance, then we will need to know why, and to what extent, apparently similar circumstances might be explained differently.

Classifying the Causes of Success and Failure

Weiner's approach to beginning to untangle this was to assume that whereas the list of causes to which an instance of success or failure *might* be attributed is potentially longer than the number of people making the attributions, there may well be certain features of causes that are critical in their consequences and that would reappear in a number of apparently differently described causes. If this were to be the case, then it ought to be possible to classify causes for success and failure along dimensions that are related to these key features, and then to assume that all causes that share a location on the resulting classification system will be essentially similar in their effects.

Full details of the reasoning that has guided the development of the classificatory systems can be seen elsewhere (Weiner, 1972, 1974, 1979, 1984). A brief summary will suffice here.

The 1979 statement of theory by Weiner is the one that currently guides most work in the area (but the interested reader is strongly encouraged to examine Weiner's contribution to the excellent 1984 volume edited by Ames and Ames). In the 1979 publication Weiner identified four dimensions that seemed to account for the majority of attributions made by individuals in a variety of situations. It ought, however, to be pointed out that it is still the case that much of the evidence for this claim is drawn from laboratory studies rather than from those carried out in the field, in our case the school classroom. There is now evidence (Little, 1985) to show that attributions made under classroom conditions are very varied and may possibly require a different category system.

The first is the internality dimension. Causes of success and failure can vary according to the degree to which they can be seen to reside within the actor (the person whose success or failure we are concerned with) or within the situation. A success seen to be determined by the ability or effort of the actor would be an internally caused success, whereas one seen to be caused by the ease of the task or the actions of others would be externally caused. In the majority of cases (Weiner claims) there will be agreement among individuals as to where any cause ought to be located. Ability would be seen by most members of our culture as being internal, something to do with the actor and not the situation. Weiner does concede that such consensus is not always apparent. Luck, for example, may be seen by some as residing in the situation (the will of the gods) whereas others might see themselves as being typically lucky people (we create our own luck in life). The crucial point, however, is the location of a cause in each case. As we shall see later, internal causes and external causes are held to have different consequences.

The second dimension that Weiner refers to is stability. A stable cause of success and failure will be one that remains the same and has a constant effect over a period of time. Unstable causes, on the other hand, are subject to change. Ability and the difficulty of the task are typically seen as examples of stable causes of success and failure, while effort and luck are typical examples of unstable causes. Again it is important to realize that an apparently similar cause, that is, one given the same descriptive label by two or more people, might be seen by them to have different properties that will lead it to have different places on a dimension. Effort, for instance, would seem to be seen by most people as an unstable cause. No doubt we can all recall instances where the effort we put into a particular task has varied considerably over time. For some people, however, effort will be seen to be a stable cause of success and failure. They would regard themselves as being typically lazy or typically industrious. Ability, as we shall see later, can be seen in quite different ways by children at different stages of development.

The third dimension is that of controllability. Some causes of success and failure can be varied at will, others cannot. Ability is generally regarded as being uncontrollable. Either you have it or you don't. (Again, however, we shall be noting some developmental exceptions to this later.)

Effort, on the other hand, is often regarded as being a controllable cause.

Finally, Weiner's fourth dimension is globality. A global cause is one that has far-reaching effects, whereas a specific one is limited in respect to the range of events that it will influence. Ability is a cause that can be seen to vary along the globality dimension. In some cases, or to some people, a lack of ability might be seen to have global consequences. One believes oneself to be hopeless at everything. On other occasions, or when a different person is making the judgment, the ability judged to be lacking is seen to be specific to one particular task. To return briefly to the example given above, the pupil who attributed the failure to a lack of ability might assume that this deficiency was peculiar to maths. In this case the cause of the failure would have been judged to be specific. Alternatively, the pupil might have decided that the lack of ability was global in which case it would be seen to apply to most areas of endeavour.

In his most recent statement of the complete theory, Weiner (1984) expresses these dimensions somewhat differently, describing them in terms of three main dimensions: locus (whether the cause is internal or external); constancy (divided into temporal stability — constancy over time, and cross-situational generality — globality as defined above); and responsibility (divided into controllability and intentionality). While not having any great impact on the implications of the theory this classification is clearer and more internally consistent than the earlier and better known one, and will doubtless come to supercede it. The 1979 formulation, however, is, for the moment at least, the account of the theory that the majority of published work will make reference to.

The Antecedents and Consequences of Attributions

As will be recalled from above, attribution theorists have concerned themselves with theories of attribution and attributional theories. In respect to the present discussion, these two major lines of enquiry reduce to a concern with the factors that lead an individual to attribute an instance of success or failure to any one particular cause, or combination of causes, rather than to any other, and to a concern with the consequences of having done just that. To the practising teacher, both are of equal concern. In order to emphasize the importance of the claims that are being made here, we will begin by looking in greater detail at the claimed consequences of attributing an instance of success or failure to any particular cause.

The Consequences of Attributions for Success and Failure

Weiner has identified two major types of consequences both of which he sees as having important implications for the motivational reactions of the individual concerned. The first of these concerns the expectations for the future that an individual might have, while the second relates to that individual's affective (or emotional) reaction to the success or failure.

The effects on expectations are the more clearly understood, indeed Weiner (1984) goes as far as to claim that the relationship described by attributional theory has the status of a fundamental law of psychology. Weiner's concern is with the effect that attributions will have on *expectancy shifts*, rather than on the expectancy itself. The major determinant of the expectancy would seem to be the outcome of the event itself. In other words, following success we are likely to expect more success and following failure, more failure. However, the *degree* to which this is true will depend upon the attribution made to explain the success or failure.

The relevant dimension is constancy. The more constant the cause of a success or failure is assumed to be, over time or place, the greater will be the degree to which we will expect more of the same. For example, an instance of failure, attributed to a lack of effort (a cause at the low end of the constancy dimension), will produce a relatively low expectation for future failure. After all, all we have to do to avoid a repeated failure is to work harder. An apparently similar failure, attributed to a more constant cause, such as ability, would give rise to a more confirmed expectation of future failure. The research supporting this claim need not be explored in any detail here (the interested reader will be able to access most of it via Weiner, 1984).

A moment's reflection will lead to the conclusion that there is a clear advantage, from the motivational point of view, to adopting a certain pattern, or style of attributions for success and failure. The pupil who consistently attributes his or her successes to stable causes, but their failures to unstable causes, will progressively come to hold higher and higher expectations for future success. Every success will confirm the view that more success is on the way, while failures will not carry a similar implication. At the other extreme, there is a clear motivational disadvantage to adopting a style that leads to stable attributions for failure, but unstable ones for success. For such an individual each failure will bring with it doom laden predictions for continuing lack of success, while successes, when they do come, will be seen as only temporary respites.

The claimed existence of these different, *typical* responses to success and failure lies at the heart of the attributional approach to the study and understanding of motivation in the school context. Pupils are seen as responding not just to instances of success and failure themselves, but to their own interpretation of them. These interpretations will help to determine the way in which that individual then goes on to respond to future situations in which success or failure appear as possible outcomes. Further reflection leads to the conclusion that the factors that determine the attributions are themselves likely to be the most critical part of the process from the school teacher's point of view. This will be particularly so if these factors turn out to be, to some degree, controllable by the teacher. However, before turning attention to the antecedents of attributions, let us examine some further consequences.

The second major type of consequence, identified by Weiner, is concerned with the affective responses to success and failure. Most people would react to failure with a negative affect, say shame, and to success with positive affect, say pride. Weiner's initial (1972) conception was a straightforward one. To the degree that an outcome was attributed to an internal cause the affect associated with it would be heightened. To the degree that it was associated with an external cause the associated affect would be reduced. So, everyone will be likely to feel proud following success, but those who believe that the success was caused by something about themselves (such as their effort) will experience the greatest pride. Similarly, failure makes us all feel bad, but never more so than when we are convinced that the failure was the result of something to do with us (a lack of ability or effort, for example). On the other hand, of course, if we can equally confidently attribute a failure to something to do with the situation our feelings of shame will be considerably reduced.

This argument has a convincing ring to it, but it has been shown to be only part of the story. A study by Weiner, Russell and Lerman (1978) demonstrated what, with the benefit of hindsight, ought to have been obvious beforehand. That is, that while pride and shame may be the major affective reactions to success and failure they are not the only ones. The 1978 study is important for two reasons. Firstly, it reveals a more complex pattern of relationships between attributions and affect than the one initially suggested. Secondly, and in the long term more significantly, it has important implications for research methods. In this study, Weiner and colleagues allowed the participants to respond freely with descriptions of their affective states over a number of different situations. Previously the concern had been to demonstrate that the logically derived relationships held up in practice, an approach that frequently excluded the discovery of other relationships.

The present position seems to be that a variety of affects will follow success and failure, and that the particular attribution made will influence the one that is experienced. For instance, guilt is likely to follow if a failure is attributed to a personally controllable cause whereas gratitude will follow if a success is seen to be due to factors personally controllable by others.

The link between attributions and affect has been taken up in a somewhat different manner by Covington and his colleagues (Covington and Beery, 1976; Covington and Omelich, 1979a; Covington and Omelich, 1979b; Covington and Omelich, 1979c; Covington, 1984). Covington's researches have led him to the conclusion that affect ought to be seen not so much as a consequence of attributions but rather as one of their major determinants. Covington and Beery (1976) and Covington (1984) provide good and more detailed accounts of self-worth theory for those who wish to pursue the matter further, but at this point it is important for the reader to be clear that not all cognitive approaches to motivation assume an essentially rational information-processing approach as does Weiner.

The link with affect for Weiner is, nevertheless, still very important. If different individuals do develop consistent ways of attributing success and failure then they are likely to come to hold, increasingly, expectations for either success or failure, and to have certain affects more clearly associated with those outcomes. The individual who regularly attributes success to a stable and internal cause, can be assumed to be much more likely to anticipate success confidently and to relish that success than does the individual who consistently attributes success to unstable causes. Attributing failure to a stable, internal cause is likely to generate very negative attitudes towards achievement situations.

The Antecedents of Attributions for Success and Failure

What has been outlined above shows how attributions influence reactions to success and failure. In order to understand why different individuals experience varying reactions to success and failure it is necessary to outline in a similar manner the factors held to influence the process of making these attributions.

Bar-Tal (1982) has presented an outline of the processes which influence the attribution process. He argues that antecedents of attributions for success and failure can be divided into two major categories, each of which can be further subdivided. The first major category is the pupil's own dispositions and history, while the second concerns the information currently available to him or her.

This major subdivision carries with it some possibly important implications for the teacher. To the extent that personal dispositions play a part in determining the pattern of attributions produced by any one individual, we may be obliged to conclude that any resulting motivational patterns will be difficult, if not impossible, for the teacher to influence. To the degree that the information available to the pupil from the current context is the major influence, however, teacher influence becomes more feasible.

For some significant degree of teacher control to be a realistic proposition some important conditions need to be met. First, that pupils' attributions are indeed influenced by the current context. Secondly, that the relevant aspects of this context are potentially controllable by the teacher. Thirdly, that the potentially controllable is put under *actual* control. This final assumption is an important one that is often overlooked in discussions of the educational implications of attribution theory. Rogers (1982) has argued that attribution theorists need to concern themselves much more with educational issues defined in the way that educationists themselves would define them, if their work is to have any impact on educational practice. In respect to present concerns, this would seem to reduce to first attempting to communicate the concerns of attribution theory to the teaching profession and second, ensuring that research attends to the practicalities of manipulating the context of real classrooms.

Personal dispositions clearly do play an important part in determining the nature of attributions for success and failure. One of the first concerns of attribution theorists, wishing to establish an account of motivational behaviour in attributional terms, was to demonstrate links between patterns of attributions and established measures of achievement motivation or the need for achievement (Atkinson, 1964; Atkinson, 1980; Atkinson and Raynor, 1974; Atkinson and Raynor, 1978). Relatively early reports (for example, Kukla, 1972) have shown that those high in the need for achievement will tend to attribute success to effort or ability and failure to lack of effort. Those low in the need for achievement will have no clear attributional pattern for success but will tend to attribute failure to a lack of ability. Results such as these are essential as far as development of the theory is concerned for they allow the attributionists to demonstrate links with the mass of research that has been generated by the need for achievement literature (see Ball, 1977; Fyans, 1980; Spence, 1983; Ames and Ames, 1984, for examples).

Following closely from this in conceptual terms, was the concern to demonstrate links between the pattern of attributions that an individual now demonstrates, and that individual's history of success and failure. A fuller introductory account of this work can be seen elsewhere (Rogers 1982). The major conclusion is that individuals are likely to attribute expected outcomes to stable causes and unexpected outcomes to unstable causes (Chaikin, 1971; Frieze and Weiner, 1971; Ames, Ames and Felker, 1977). From this general principle it clearly follows that those with a history of success are more likely to attribute further successes to a stable factor (for example, ability). It will also be recalled that Weiner argues that attributions to stable factors generate more confident expectations that the outcome will be repeated. In this way a beneficent cycle is set up — success breeds success.On the other hand a history of failure makes success unexpected, leading to an attribution to an unstable cause in turn making further successes seem relatively unlikely. This can also be seen to be part of a cyclic process only this time the effects are vicious rather than beneficent. Expected and unexpected failure, determined by the degree to which past failure can be considered to be characteristic, gives rise to similar and complementary effects. One of the challenges that attribution theory provides for the teacher concerns attempts to break these cycles when to do so would be to the pupil's advantage.

Various demographic factors, such as race and socio-economic class have also been shown to be related to attributional patterns (for example, Friend and Neale, 1972; Raviv *et al.*, 1980). Those in ethnic minority groups (from the British point of view) and from lower social-class groups tend to demonstrate attributional patterns that would be disadvantageous educationally.

A further demographic factor that is currently generating considerable research interest is the sex (or gender) of a pupil. Rogers (1985) has reviewed some of the literature on this (see also Deem, 1984; Delamont, 1980; Sutherland, 1981). A number of studies have demonstrated the existence of sex differences in the attribution of success and failure (Lochel, 1983; Dweck *et al.*, 1978; Deaux, 1976; Frieze, 1980; Bar-Tal and Frieze, 1976; Nicholls, 1978). Broadly these studies indicate that girls and women across a number of different tasks and situations are more likely to attribute failures to lack of ability and less likely to recognize the presence of ability as a cause of their own successes. As with race and class effects, those who tend to do less well in the educational system also seem to have the less adaptive attributional patterns.

The brief discussion of sex-differences in attributional style above serves to lead us into a discussion of the ways in which the present situation might influence the attributional patterns of pupils. The sex of the pupil is, of course, something that the teacher does not influence. It is fixed prior to the commencement of school and the study by Lochel (1983), referred to above, shows that attributional patterns also become associated with gender before compulsory schooling starts. However, while teachers cannot influence the sex of their pupils they can, and apparently do, react to it. These reactions will form part of the information that is available to a pupil at any one time and might therefore influence the ways in which attributions are formed.

Studies by Dweck and her colleagues (1978), which are now widely cited in the literature examining the different performance patterns of boys and girls at school, are indicative of a link between patterns of teacher-pupil interaction, and the patterns of attributions that those pupils come to demonstrate.

Dweck's research demonstrated two things. Firstly that patterns of interaction between teachers and young pupils varied according to the sex of the pupil. Secondly, that such patterns of interaction could influence attributions for success and failure. In essence the research showed that in the early stages of schooling teachers would appear to be creating a more favourable environment for girls in that the female pupils received fewer instances of criticism relating to non-academic aspects of their school behaviour. However, this lack of general criticism helps to establish a situation where the criticism that a young girl pupil does receive is highly likely to be criticism directed at the actual quality of her work. Such concentrated criticism is thought to have an influence different from the criticism that the typical boy pupil would receive. When criticized for aspects of his work, the boy will perceive this against a background of a relatively high level of criticism for a whole range of activity. The girl is therefore more likely to take the teacher's criticism of her work as an indicator of a lack of ability. The boy is more likely to see it as something else, perhaps just another sign of the bias that teachers seem to have against boys.

A second piece of research in the same paper demonstrates that both boys and girls would be influenced, in terms of the attributions that they made, by the pattern of feedback directed at them. Those that received feedback similar to that shown to be typical for girls in classrooms (that is, feedback that concentrated criticism on to strictly work-related matters) were more likely to attribute failure to a lack of ability. Those that received more generalized criticism were more likely to attribute failure to a lack of effort or to the hostility of the judge. This latter finding strongly suggests that it is the patterns of interaction established between pupils of each sex and their teachers that are important for the determination of attributional styles and not the sex of the pupils *per se.*

Research of this kind is important, as it shows the ways in which an attributional approach to the analysis of classroom practices can be beneficial. The paradox uncovered by the Dweck research is this. While girls in the early years of their schooling would appear to be developing within an environment that is more favourable than that experienced by the boys (girls are less frequently criticized and are typically chosen by teachers as their 'favourite' pupils in the early years of schooling at least), this same environment is actually encouraging girls to assume that failure implies a lack of ability. Remember from our earlier discussion of the consequences of attributions that one likely outcome of this would be girls coming to believe that they are less likely to be successful in subject areas that are believed to be difficult and therefore to demand high levels of ability. (See Rogers, 1982, 1985, for introductory discussions of the way in which this analysis might be extended to account for the gradual withdrawal of girls from subjects such as physics and maths in the later years of schooling.)

Interactions with teachers then are likely to be an important source of information for the pupil that will be used by the pupil in the process of making decisions about the causes of instances of success and failure. Bar-Tal (1982) catalogues a variety of ways in which teachers will influence the attributions of their pupils.

The first of these is verbal appeals and covers the kind of pattern that Dweck unearthed. Different types of verbal feedback will have different effects. There is also evidence to suggest that the instructions given to pupils regarding a task will have an influence on attributions. Kukla (1972) has demonstrated that subjects will respond differently on a task dependent upon their level of achievement motivation and the degree to which they have been led to believe that the task is one that requires ability and/or effort to successfully complete. Research currently being undertaken by Rogers (1986) that will be briefly discussed later indicates other ways in which the means of instruction used by the teacher might influence attributions.

Bar-Tal's third category of teacher behaviour is referred to as reinforcements. Of greatest concern here is the degree to which a teacher uses cooperative or competitive reward systems. Extensive research is now available concerning the effects of cooperative and competitive forms of instruction (Johnson *et al.*, 1984; Slavin, 1983). Ames (1984) and Nicholls (1984b) have produced evidence showing that attributions will be influenced by these different reward systems. In particular it is claimed that cooperative reward systems are more likely to produce attributional patterns that are associated with a relatively high level of intrinsic motivation. That is, pupils that are less fearful of failure, and more willing to engage in tasks without the teacher having to continually dangle carrots or wield sticks.

The fourth category of teacher behaviour is verbal feedback. Evidence from the classroom seems to be very limited here, but Bar-Tal cites laboratory based studies (Meyer *et al.*, 1979) to show how comments following success or failure can influence attributions. For example, there would seem to be a tendency for people to assume that someone who receives some degree of criticism after success must have a high level of ability. Rogers (1980) in a similar vein, demonstrates the somewhat patronizing attributions that are made by boys with respect to the successes and failures of girls.

Finally Bar-Tal points out that teachers can quite deliberately influence attributions. Work by Dweck (1975), Andrews and Debus (1978) and DeCharms (1976, 1984) shows that it is possible to systematically influence patterns of attribution by setting up an attribution retraining programme (such programmes have also had some success in the clinical world — see Antaki and Brewin, 1982).

To summarize so far, the work by attribution theorists has demonstrated that attributional patterns and motivational patterns seem to be related to each other. Attributions are held partially, at least, to determine motivational patterns by influencing a pupil's expectations for success and failure and the affective reactions that he or she has towards those events. In turn, it is possible to determine the factors that influence the makings of attributions (and therefore the origins of motivational style). What is most encouraging from the teacher's point of view is that many of these factors seem to be located within the classroom and are potentially under the control of the educational system, if not the individual teacher.

Developmental Factors

One element that is not given sufficient attention in many accounts of the attribution process in schools, including some of Weiner's own accounts, is the effects of development. Rogers (1982) outlines some of the research that indicates general age-related changes in the ways in which children understand causal relationships and the values that they put upon different causes of success and failure (in addition see Weiner and Kun, 1976; Rogers, 1980; and Frieze, 1980). More recently, however, research more sharply focused on developmental changes within the school context has been producing results that have some very important implications for an analysis of the development of motivational style over the schooling period. One of the leading workers in this area has been Nicholls (1984a, 1984b; Nicholls and Miller, 1983) and it is his research that will be focused on here.

As has been made clear above, attribution theorists believe that instances of success or failure influence the motivation of individuals through the ways in which those individuals interpret success and failure events. It is clearly the case, therefore, that a success attributed to ability will be likely to have different motivational implications from one attributed to luck, or to effort. If this is actually to be the case then it must follow that each individual has concepts of ability, effort, task difficulty and all the other possible causes of success and failure, that are clearly differentiated from each other. One of the more significant claims made by Nicholls is that young children frequently will not have fully differentiated from each other concepts such as ability and effort. Further, he goes on to claim that the process of obtaining fully differentiated concepts has, in its own right, important implications for the operation of motivation in educational settings. His case will be illustrated here by outlining parts of the developmental process that he has identified.

There are two key aspects of development according to Nicholls (1984a). The first of these concerns the development of the concept of difficulty. Nicholls identifies three levels here. During the first, the egocentric stage, the child assumes that those things which he or she expects to be able to succeed on are easy and those where they do not are difficult. No reference is made to the successes of others or to any other aspects of the task.

In the second stage, the objective level, difficult tasks are seen to be ones that have the appearance of complexity. A jigsaw puzzle, for example, that had many small pieces would be judged to be more difficult than one that has a few large pieces. Adults, of course, will also use such a mode of judgment (not least when it comes to choosing jigsaws for their offspring). The point that Nicholls is making is that younger children will not be able to operate at any more sophisticated levels.

The final stage, the normative conception of difficulty, comes when the child begins to define task difficulty in terms of the proportion of people attempting it that would gain success. An easy task is now seen to be one on which most people would be successful, and a difficult one would be a task at which most would fail. These judgments are clearly independent of your own assessment of your own chances of success. Whereas at the first level it was, by definition, impossible to expect to fail an easy task, by the third level this is no longer so. The key point that emerges from this analysis is that by the final stage the degree of difficulty attributed to tasks undertaken has implications for the self-concept.

Central to this self-concept will be assessments of levels of effort and ability. These are also subject to developmental change. Four stages are identified by Nicholls representing a development from a position where effort, outcome and ability are hardly distinguished at all (people who do well are clever, people who try hard are clever) through finally to the adult view of ability as a capacity. At this final level ability is seen to be a relatively fixed aspect of a person's nature that will set an ultimate limit upon what they can achieve, irrespective of the amount of effort they may exert. While it is still possible to achieve below this maximum level, it is deemed to be impossible to exceed it on a regular basis. A run of good luck may produce some exceptional results in some circumstances, but this does not last.

Taken together, these two developmental patterns have some important implications for the ways in which a pupil will perceive failure at various tasks. As the child moves towards the normative view of difficulty, he will become increasingly concerned with how others have performed (for it is the performance of others that defines the difficulty of the task). This growing concern with the performance of others also leads the child to be increasingly concerned with the reasons for his own performance, *relative* to that of others. This relative perspective heightens the importance of internal causes (what is it about me that leads to my performance differing from that of other people when we all apparently share the same classroom environment?).

At the same time the child becomes increasingly concerned to avoid concluding that failure is caused by lack of ability (this follows from the increased tendency to regard ability as a capacity that will set an absolute ceiling upon levels of attainment), while also becoming more likely to conclude that his prospects are poor if he does attribute failure to a lack of ability. In an argument that develops increasingly close links with the work of Covington (Covington and Beery 1976; Covington 1984), Nicholls states that the older child will be increasingly concerned to avoid failures that might imply a lack of ability. One clear way of doing this is to not try very hard, thereby providing a built-in explanation for failure. Alternatively the pupil could select only very difficult tasks (failure being attributed then to difficulty and not to lack of ability) or very easy tasks where failure is highly unlikely to occur. These various strategies are not well suited to the maximization of the child's school progress.

This analysis by Nicholls, even in the very abbreviated form provided here, presents some intriguing possibilities. One of these is that the oft noted decline in intrinsic motivation as the child progresses from primary to secondary school has more to do with the development of the concepts of ability than it does with the differing modes of teaching and organization employed at the two levels of the school system.

Prospects for the Future of an Attributional Approach to Motivation

Work on attribution theory as related to schooling continues apace. From what we know already it is clear that there is a link between the motivational patterns that a child will display and the way in which that child attributes success and failure. Furthermore there are links between these attributional patterns and various school-related experiences including actions of the teacher and the degree to which school work is set up on cooperative or competitive lines. Overriding this, it is now clear that aspects of the child's cognitive development during the years of schooling will have an important impact on the implications of the explanations of success and failure that the child devises.

Work in the future is likely to concentrate on three main areas. The first of these will be the development of motivational style. Nicholls' (1984a) collection reveals a large number of research avenues that seem ripe for further exploration. The second will be the further development of attribution retraining programmes. The third will be the increased examination of the types of attributions made by children across a variety of different kinds of school work and across a variety of different organizational frameworks.

This latter work is very much in its infancy at present. However, it does seem to show promise. Little (1985) has shown that when allowed to express their attributions for success and failure in their own words, schoolchildren in the 5–14 age range will use a much wider variety of causes than those typically covered by attributional research. Rogers (1986) is beginning the task of examining the ways in which these wider and more complex categories of causes are employed across a variety of different kinds of school work. For example, early results seem to imply that children are more likely to attribute success or failure in maths to ability when the maths work is presented to them in the form of a test than when presented in the form of work completed individually at the child's own pace. If such effects can be reliably and systematically demonstrated, then it ought to become possible for attribution theory to provide the basis for a system of examining various schemes of work with a view to identifying their likely motivational impact.

Above all else, attribution theory provides teachers with a conceptual framework with which they can begin to analyze their own classroom practices and the reactions to those practices of their pupils. At the outset of this chapter it was stated that if we are to be able to realize the apparent explanatory power of the concept of motivation, then we have to be able to define motivation in terms other than those relating to differences in the consequences of two pupils having different motivational levels. In attributional terms, motivation *is* the pattern of causes that each pupil judges to be responsible for their own successes and failures. Understanding these judgments, the consequences of them and the factors that influence them is a task to be undertaken by each teacher concerned with the motivation of their pupils.

References

AMES, C. (1984) 'Competitive, cooperative and individualistic goal structures: A cognitive-motivational analysis', in AMES, R.E. and AMES, C. (Eds) *Research on Motivation in Education. Volume 1. Student Motivation*, London, Academic Press.

AMES, R.E. and AMES, C. (Eds) (1984) *Research on Motivation in Education. Volume 1. Student Motivation*, London, Academic Press.

AMES, C., AMES, R. and FELKER, D.W. (1977) 'Informational and dispositional determinants of children's achievement attributions', *Journal of Educational Psychology*, 69, pp. 1–8.

ANDREWS, G.R. and DEBUS, R.L. (1978) 'Persistence and the causal perception of failure: Modifying cognitive attributions', *Journal of Educational Psychology*, 70, pp. 154–66.

ANTAKI, C. (Ed.) (1981) *The Psychology of Ordinary Explanations of Social Behaviour*, London, Academic Press.

ANTAKI, C. and BREWIN, C. (1982) *Attributions and Psychological Change: Applications of Attributional Theories to Clinical and Educational Practice*, London, Academic Press.

ATKINSON, J. (1964) *An Introduction to Motivation*, Princeton, N.J., von Nostrand.

ATKINSON, J. (1980) 'Motivational effects in so-called tests of ability and educational achievement', in FYANS, L.J. (Ed.) *Achievement Motivation: Recent Trends in Theory and Research*, London, Plenum Press.

ATKINSON, J. and RAYNOR, J. (1974) *Motivation and Achievement*, Washington D.C., Winston.

ATKINSON, J. and RAYNOR, J. (1978) *Personality, Motivation and Achievement*, Washington D.C., Hemisphere.

BALL, S. (Ed.) (1977) *Motivation in Education*, London, Academic Press.

BAR-TAL, D. (1982) 'The effect of teachers' behaviour on pupils' attributions: A review', in ANTAKI, C. and BREWIN, C. *Attributions and Psychological Change: Applications of Attributional Theories to Clinical and Educational Practice*, London, Academic Press.

BAR-TAL, D. and FRIEZE, I.H. (1976) 'Attributions of success and failure for actors and observers', *Journal of Research in Personality*, 10, pp. 256–65.

CHAILIN, A.L. (1971) 'The effects of four outcome schedules on persistence, liking for the task and attributions of causality', *Journal of Personality*, 29, pp. 512–26.

COVINGTON, M.V. (1984) 'The motive for self-worth', in AMES, R.E. and AMES, C. (Eds) *Research on Motivation in Education. Volume 1. Student Motivation*, London, Academic Press.

COVINGTON, M.V. and BEERY, R. (1976) *Self-worth and School Learning*, New York, Holt, Rinehart and Winston.

COVINGTON, M.V. and OMELICH, C.L. (1979a) 'Are causal attributions causal? A path analysis of the cognitive model of achievement motivations', *Journal of Personality and Social Psychology*, 37, pp. 1487–504.

COVINGTON, M.L. and OMELICH, C.L. (1979b) 'It's best to be able and virtuous too: Student and teacher evaluative responses to successful effort', *Journal of Educational Psychology*, 71, pp. 688–700.

COVINGTON, M.L. and OMELICH, C.L. (1979c) 'Effort: Double-edged sword in school achievement', *Journal of Educational Psychology*, 71, pp. 169–82.

DEAUX, K. (1976) 'Sex: A perspective on the attribution process', in HARVEY, J.H., ICKES, W.J. and KIDD, R.F. (Eds) *New Directions in Attribution Research. Vol. 1*, Hillsdale, N.J., Erlbaum.

DECHARMS, R. (1976) *Enhancing Motivation: Change in the Classroom*, New York, Irvington.

DECHARMS, R. (1984) 'Motivation enhancement in educational settings', in AMES, R.E. and AMES, C. (Eds) *Research on Motivation in Education. Volume 1. Student Motivation*, London, Academic Press.

DEEM, R. (1984) *Co-education Reconsidered*, Milton Keynes, Open University Press.

DELAMONT, S. (1980) *Sex Roles and the School*, London, Methuen.

DWECK, C.S. (1975) 'The role of expectations and attributions in the alleviation of learned helplessness', *Journal of Personality and Social Psychology*, 31, pp. 674–85.

DWECK, C.S., DAVIDSON, W., NELSON, S. and ENNA, B. (1978) 'Sex differences in learned-helplessness: II. The contingencies of evaluative feedback in the classroom. III. An experimental analysis', *Developmental Psychology*, 14, pp. 268–76.

EISER, J.R. (1980) *Cognitive Social Psychology: A Guidebook to Theory and Research*, London, McGraw Hill.

FRIEND, R.M. and NEALE, J.M. (1972) 'Children's perceptions of success and failure. An attributional analysis of the effects of race and social class', *Developmental Psychology*, 7, pp. 124–8.

FRIEZE, I.H. (1980) 'Beliefs about success and failure in the classroom', in MCMILLAN, J. (Ed) *The Social Psychology of School Learning*, London, Academic Press.

FRIEZE, I.H. and WEINER, B. (1971) 'Cue utilization and attributional judgements for success and failure', *Journal of Personality*, 39, pp. 591–606.

FYANS, L.J. (Ed.) (1980) *Achievement Motivation: Recent Trends in Theory and Research*, London, Plenum Press.

HARVEY, J.H., ICKES, W.J. and KIDD, R.F. (Eds) (1976) *New Directions in Attribution Research. Vol. 1*, Hillsdale, N.J., Erlbaum.

HEIDER, F. (1958) *The Psychology of Interpersonal Relations*, New York, Wiley.

HEWSTONE, M. (Ed.) (1983) *Attribution Theory: Social and Functional Extensions*, Oxford, Basil Blackwell.

JASPARS, J., FINCHAM, F. and HEWSTONE, M. (1983) *Attribution Theory and Research: Conceptual, Developmental and Social Dimensions*, London, Academic Press.

JASPARS, J., HEWSTONE, M. and FINCHAM, F. (1983) 'Attribution theory and research: The state of the art', in JASPARS, J., FINCHAM, F. and HEWSTONE, M. (1983) *Attribution Theory and Research: Conceptual, Developmental and Social Dimensions*, London, Academic Press.

JOHNSON, D.W., JOHNSON, R.T., HOLUBEC, E.J. and ROY, P. (1984) *Circles of Learning: Cooperation in the Classroom*, Virginia, ASCD.

KUKLA, A. (1972) 'Attributional determinants of achievement-related behaviour', *Journal of Personality and Social Psychology*, 21, pp. 166–74.

LITTLE, A.W. (1985) 'The child's understanding of the causes of academic success and failure: A case study of British schoolchildren', *British Journal of Educational Psychology*, 55, pp. 11–23.

LOCHEL, E. (1983) 'Sex differences in achievement motivation', in JASPARS, J., FINCHAM, F. and HEWSTONE, M. (1983) *Attribution Theory and Research: Conceptual, Developmental and Social Dimensions*, London, Academic Press.

MEYER, W.U., BECHMANN, M., BIERMANN, U., HEMPLEMANN, M., PLOEGER, F.O.

and SPILLER, H. (1979) 'The informational value of evaluative behaviour: Influences of praise and blame on perceptions of ability', *Journal of Educational Psychology*, 71, pp. 259–68.

NICHOLLS, J. (1978) 'The development of the concepts of effort and ability, perception of academic attainment, and the understanding that difficult tasks require more ability', *Child Development*, 49, pp. 800–14.

NICHOLLS, J. (1980) 'A re-examination of boys' and girls' causal attributions for success and failure based on New Zealand data', in FYANS, L.J. (Ed.) *Achievement Motivation: Recent Trends in Theory and Research*, London, Plenum Press.

NICHOLLS, J. (Ed.) (1984a) *Advances in Motivation and Achievement: Volume Three. The Development of Achievement Motivation*, London, JAI Press.

NICHOLLS, J.G. (1984b) 'Conceptions of ability and achievement motivation', in AMES, R.E. and AMES, C. (Eds) *Research on Motivation in Education. Volume 1. Student Motivation*, London, Academic Press.

NICHOLLS, J.G. and MILLER, A.T. (1983) 'The differentation of the concepts of difficulty and ability', *Child Development*, 54, 951–9.

RAVIV, A., BAR-TAL, D., RAVIV, A. and BAR-TAL, Y. (1980) 'Causal perceptions of success and failure by advantaged, integrated and disadvantaged pupils', *British Journal of Educational Psychology*, 50, pp. 137–46.

ROGERS, C.G. (1980) 'The development of sex differences in evaluations of others' successes and failures', *British Journal of Educational Psychology*, 50, pp. 243–52.

ROGERS, C. (1982) *A Social Psychology of Schooling*, London, Routledge and Kegan Paul.

ROGERS, C. (1985) 'Sex roles in education', in HARGREAVES, D.J. and COLLEY, A. (Eds) *The Psychology of Sex Roles*, London, Harper and Row.

ROGERS, C.G. (1986) *Attributions for Success and Failure: The Effects of Classroom Activity*, British Educational Research Association Annual Conference, Bristol, September.

SLAVIN, R.E. (1983) *Cooperative Learning*, London, Longman.

SPENCE, J. (Ed.) (1983) *Achievement and Achievement Motives: Psychological and Sociological Perspectives*, San Francisco, W.H. Freeman.

SUTHERLAND, M. (1981) *Sex Bias in Education*, Oxford, Blackwell.

WEINER, B. (1972) *Theories of Motivation: From Mechanism to Cognition*, Morristown, N.J., General Learning Press.

WEINER, B. (1974) *Achievement Motivation and Attribution Theory*, Morristown, N.J., General Learning Press.

WEINER, B. (1979) 'A theory of motivation for some classroom experiences', *Journal of Educational Psychology*, 71, pp. 3–25.

WEINER, B. (1980) *Human Motivation*, New York, Holt, Rinehart and Winston.

WEINER, B. (1984) 'Principles for a theory of student motivation and their application within an attributional framework', in AMES, R.E. and AMES, C. (Eds) *Research on Motivation in Education. Volume 1. Student Motivation*, London, Academic Press.

WEINER, B. and KUN, A. (1976) 'The development of causal attributions and the growth of achievement and social motivation', in FELDMAN, S. and BUSH, B. (Eds) *Cognitive Development and Social Development*, Hillsdale N.J., Erlbaum.

WEINER, B., FRIEZE, I., KUKLA, A., REED, L., REST, S. and ROSENBAUM, R.M. (1972) 'Perceiving the causes of success and failure', in JONES, E.E., KANOUSE, D.E., KELLEY, H.H., NISBETT, R.E., VALINS, S. and WEINER, B. *Attribution: Perceiving the Causes of Success and Failure*, Morristown N.J., General Learning Press.

WEINER, B., RUSSELL, D. and LERMAN, D. (1978) 'Affective consequences of causal ascriptions', in HARVEY, J.H., ICKES, W.J. and KIDD, R.F. (Eds) *New Directions in Attribution Research. Volume 2*, Hillsdale, N.J., Erlbaum.

Autonomy Support in Education: Creating the Facilitating Environment

Wendy S. Grolnick and Richard M. Ryan
University of Rochester

One of the major directions along which development proceeds is towards greater autonomy. Movement away from the absolute dependence of early infancy and toward the relative independence of adulthood is the universal path along which all persons must travel. Most developmental psychologists and educators assume that there are natural or inherent tendencies that can be found in every child, which lead him or her in the direction of decreased heteronomy and greater self-direction (for example, Dewey, 1938; Bruner, 1962; Rogers, 1969; Piaget, 1971). However, once that is assumed, the *practical* question remains of identifying and creating those conditions which facilitate rather than forestall this process.

Schools represent the most important context in middle childhood and adolescence for this development of autonomy (Grolnick and Ryan, 1986b). Through education a child presumably acquires competencies and skills which make possible later economic and social adaptation. However, perhaps more significant than skills *per se* is the growth of the motivation and interest in exercising, elaborating, and applying them (Ryan, Connell and Deci, 1985). Stated differently, successful education breeds more than technical competence; it deepens an individual's confidence and sense of agency, which is so essential to self-direction and self-respect as an adult. This is the affective aspect or goal of education: to facilitate the personality development of children in a direction of greater motivation and independence in the process of learning, achievement and social relatedness. Yet on the topic of this affective component of education many educational theorists are notably mute.

The purpose of the present chapter is to focus on this more enigmatic aspect of educational practice. Our task is to examine the role of teachers and parents in facilitating (or blocking) the development of autonomy and self-regulation in children. To do so we will call upon a variety of research and field studies in the academic context. It will be argued that only through a classroom and school community context which supports the exercise of autonomy is the child likely to grow to identify with the values of that community and what it has to offer. Further, only insofar as autonomy and self-regulation are fostered will praise and esteem for actions be adequately internalized as 'self'-esteem, and therefore contribute to confidence and self-direction in adulthood.

Many people become wary when it is suggested that autonomy be promoted. They suspect something uncivilized or chaotic will emerge when autonomy is advanced. Thus, rather than support and guide the natural trend toward autonomy, they instead battle with nature. Autonomy in this view is something to be curtailed, shaped, or controlled lest it conflict with pre-ordained values. Yet such a view neglects the fact that autonomy does not mean the absence of values; it means instead learning to identify with and independently exercise them (Ryan, Connell, and Grolnick, in press). Similarly, autonomy does not mean escape from work or achievement. Rather it means the acquisition of an interest and sense of importance for the activity of one's work, and thus of self-motivation and choice within it. Autonomy does not mean the neglect of all discipline; it means growing away from dependence on external controls toward self-regulation and self-management.

Reciprocally, the promotion of autonomy involves not an avoidance of activity on the part of a teacher or parent but rather great subtlety and expertise (Grolnick and Ryan, 1986a,b). Autonomy develops and is strengthened only insofar as it is exercised, and eliciting that exercise requires skilled and creative practice. One cannot push someone to be self-directed without unwittingly undermining that goal. Similarly, one cannot teach another to be responsible without first giving over some responsibility. In this sense, autonomy promotion is a facilitative rather than a training process. It requires attending to the internal frame of reference of the child or student and supporting responsible action as it emerges from within (Ryan, Connell, and Deci, 1985). It means affording opportunities for action rather than assigning them. It means nurturing independent solving of problems rather than dictating the search for answers (Deci, Nezlek and Sheinman, 1981). Thus autonomy grows when there is, from parent and teacher, support for autonomy.

Finally, autonomy progresses only when the challenges to its exercise are themselves optimal (Deci and Ryan, 1985). Challenges that are too great and result in pervasive failure only lower confidence and willingness to try. The exercise of autonomous capacities can proceed only from what one can already do. Under conditions of optimal challenge, those current capacities can be strengthened and elaborated. Finally, challenges which are too easy simply will not be engaged without outside prompt or reward. They are, in fact, experienced as boring and thus will be engaged only for extrinsic reasons. In sum, to facilitate autonomy, conditions for its exercise must be tailored to the developmental level and skill from which the individual starts.

The reasoning employed here then suggests a set of propositions capable of empirical exploration. They include the following:

1 Autonomy is essential to self-motivation. When autonomy is experienced, motivation, interest and desire for challenge are associated characteristics.
2 Children develop autonomy, self-motivation, and self-regulation to a greater degree under conditions where adults support autonomy.
3 Emphasis on controlling behaviour and salient use of external pressures and rewards undermines the sense of autonomy, and leads to lower self-regulatory capacities.
4 Autonomy is essential to self-esteem. Self-esteem develops, that is, only when one's own actions and interactions are valued and supported.
5 The development of autonomy is a transactional process. The more it is supported the more it obtains. However, the less it is in evidence the less likely adults are to support autonomy and the more likely they are instead to control or enforce compliance.
6 Autonomy will tend to be exercised under conditions of optimal challenge. Challenges too great or too easy are inimical to its expression.

These and other related propositions are what are explored in the research detailed herein.

Autonomy in the Classroom — Does It Matter?

So far, we have suggested that the movement toward autonomy is a natural developmental process. We have stated that it is important to capitalize on children's innate tendencies in this direction by providing educational experiences congruent with them, i.e., circumstances in which learning is experienced as autonomously motivated and in which feelings of effectance can take root. In our first proposition, the empirical evidence for which we will explore in this section, we suggested that whether or not children experience support for their autonomy in the classroom can have important concomitants, not only for children's achievement and learning per se, but also for their emotional adjustment and motivation. Schools, because they are such a pervasive socializing influence, shape many aspects of development including children's self-esteem, perceptions of control, and values (Grolnick and Ryan, 1986a). Viewed in this way, experience of autonomy can have far-reaching consequences.

Deci, Nezlek and Sheinman (1981) explored children's experiences of support for autonomy versus of being controlled within the classroom. They used a measure developed by DeCharms (1976) to assess the extent to which children experience their teachers' behaviour and the classroom climate as supportive of autonomy or as controlling (which he termed 'origin' and 'pawn' experiences, respectively). The experience of an autonomy-supportive climate involved children's seeing themselves as initiating their learning behaviour and as active participants in the classroom. Experiencing the classroom as controlling, on the other hand, involved experiencing the teacher as directing their learning behaviour, and themselves as more passive. Deci *et al.*, administered this questionnaire to 610 children from 35 classrooms. They also had children complete a survey developed by Harter (1981) which assessed children's motivation in the classroom. This scale measures three motivational tendencies: preference for challenge, curiosity, and independent mastery attempts, which are combined to provide an index of children's mastery motivation. Children's descriptions of their classrooms on the autonomy-support to control dimension were then correlated with children's mastery motivation (Harter, 1981), perceived competence in school (Harter, 1982), and self-esteem (Harter, 1982). The results of this study indicated significant relations between children's experiences of the classroom and intrinsic motivation. Children experiencing the classroom as more autonomy supportive described themselves as more intrinsically motivated for school than those experiencing the classroom environment as more controlling. Further, there were relations between perceptions of the environment and both perceived competence and self-esteem. Children describing the classroom as more supportive of their autonomy viewed themselves as more competent in school and had higher self-esteem than those seeing the classroom as more controlling.

In a related study (Ryan and Grolnick, 1986), we attempted both to replicate these important findings as well as expand upon them by investigating possible sources of children's perceptions of the classroom environment as either supportive of or controlling autonomy. In this study, we administered DeCharms' origin-climate questionnaire. We found that children's experiences of themselves in the classroom on this autonomy-support dimension had important consequences not only for their intrinsic motivation but for other self-related cognitions and affects. These results suggested that the more autonomy supportive the children perceived their classroom environments to be, the more mastery motivation they reported for school. Furthermore, children describing their classrooms as higher on the autonomy-support dimension described themselves as more competent in school and had higher self-esteem more generally than those seeing the classroom as more controlling. Thus, this study replicated that of Deci, Nezlek and Sheinman (1981). In addition, the more autonomy supportive in nature the children perceived their classroom to be, the more they perceived school success and failure to be internally controlled and the less they saw control of outcomes in school in the hands of powerful others such as the teacher or reported that they did not know who or what controlled success and failure outcomes in school (Connell, 1985).

In a second phase of the study these children were asked to write a projective story about an ambiguous classroom scene. Those who had previously reported a more controlling atmosphere depicted more passive students and more authoritarian teachers in their stories than children who saw their classroom as more autonomy supportive. Thus, the perceived classroom environment has ramifications for how children organize and interpret their environment more generally.

The Ryan and Grolnick study thus demonstrated that there is great variability in the extent to which children experience themselves as autonomous in the classroom and that children's perceptions of themselves on this dimension have important consequences for motivation and affects with regard to both school and the self. If facilitating experiences of autonomy in the classroom is a goal for education, it would be important to understand the sources of these individual differences. How is it that some children feel more autonomous in school than others? In the same study, we explored two sources of variance in the way in which children experience their classrooms: differences *between* classrooms and individual differences between children *within* classrooms. Between-classroom differences were described by the average classroom climate score for all children in a given classroom while within-classroom differences referred to within-classroom variations from the particular classroom mean. We found, first, that there were average differences between classrooms in experienced autonomy. Such between-classroom differences suggest that teachers provide certain contexts for learning which facilitate differing experiences of autonomy for the children in their classrooms. These results, then, point to the importance of the climate provided by the teacher for children's experiences of autonomy or lack thereof.

However, the results also showed that even within classrooms there was great variability in the extent to which self-determination or autonomy was experienced. In fact, the individual difference component of experiences in the classroom largely accounted for relations between the classroom climate measure and self-related variables. This finding suggests that, irrespective of the teacher, there are aspects of the children which lead them to experience themselves as more or less autonomous. One possibility for understanding these individual differences in perceived autonomy is that children may behave in such a way that they are actually treated differentially by the teacher and so feel more or less self-determined in the classroom. A second possibility is that children come into the classroom with tendencies toward experiencing themselves as more or less autonomous and these tendencies affect how they experience the teacher and classroom. One possible explanation for the latter account is that experiences of home environments may shape tendencies to see other environments and caretakers in particular ways. Thus, some of the experience of autonomy in the classroom appears to be derived from classroom experiences while another part is derived from children's characteristics and possibly their histories with caretakers. In the next sections of the chapter, we will explore the importance of teachers and parents in facilitating autonomy in children.

Facilitating Autonomy — The Role of the Classroom Environment

The Ryan and Grolnick (1986) study revealed that there are differences between classrooms in the extent to which children experience themselves as self-determining or autonomous. These findings suggest that teachers may have an important role in facilitating such classroom experiences. There have been a number of studies focusing on one particular aspect of teachers: the extent to which they are supportive or controlling of children's autonomy. Deci, Nezlek and Sheinman (1981) suggested that teachers have characteristic tendencies toward dealing with children that can be viewed as ranging from supporting children's autonomy to controlling children's behaviour. These authors reasoned that some teachers believe that children should be controlled and that they know what is best for the children. These teachers tend to use controls such as rewards, evaluations or grades, and threats to get children to learn and to solve problems that come up in the classroom. These techniques lead children to experience their behaviour and learning in school as instrumental to achieve such rewards or grades rather than as self-determined. Other teachers believe that it is important for children to be able to solve their own problems and see their role as to facilitate such independent thought and decision making. They tend to try to involve children in the process of learning by giving them choices. These teachers tend to support children's problem-solving attempts by using discussion and other autonomy-promoting techniques rather than by imposing their own solutions onto the children.

Before examining the effects of teachers' orientations on the autonomy-support to control dimension, it is important to clarify that an autonomy-supportive context for learning is not a permissive one. The autonomy-supportive classroom is not one where there is complete freedom for children to do whatever they want. Rather, there is a good deal of consistent structure imposed by teachers. The determining factor in autonomy-supportive versus controlling classrooms is, then, not whether there are rules, disciplinary techniques and directives, but, rather, the way in which these structures are imposed and the extent to which choices and independence are encouraged when possible. The issue of imposing limits in an autonomy-supportive context will be discussed at greater length later in this section.

Deci, Schwartz, Sheinman and Ryan (1981) developed a measure of teachers' orientations on the autonomy-support to control dimension.

Teachers' orientations, as measured by this scale, were then correlated with the mastery motivation (Harter, 1981) and self-evaluations (Harter, 1982) of the children in their classrooms. The results of these analyses revealed significant relations between teacher orientations and these variables such that the more autonomy-supportive the teacher, the higher the mastery motivation children reported and the higher their perceived competence in school and in general. Although these findings suggest that teachers' orientations on the autonomy-support to control continuum can have important consequences for the motivation and self-related affects of children, the correlational nature of this study leaves the direction of influence undetermined. One explanation for these findings is that teachers affect children's thoughts and feelings but another is that the motivational orientations of the children in the classrooms leads teachers to take on more autonomy oriented or more controlling styles.

In order to further understand the meaning of these correlational results, Deci *et al.* measured children's mastery motivation, perceived competence and self-esteem on day two of the school year and again eight weeks later. They reasoned that any change in these child variables occurring between the first days of school and later in the year could be accounted for by the teacher and classroom environment. The results indicated that teachers' orientations toward support versus control of children's autonomy were predictive of change on these child variables such that the more controlling the teacher, the greater the decrements in mastery motivation, perceived cognitive competence and self-esteem across the eight week interval.

The results of the above studies point to the importance of teachers' styles in facilitating children's desire to take on challenging material and their curiosity in school. Another issue, probably even more crucial for development and for adjustment in the classroom, because much of what is taught in school is not inherently interesting, concerns children's attitudes or orientations toward school and the learning process. Ryan, Connell and Deci (1985) have reasoned that children take on different orientations toward engaging in school-related activities which are not inherently interesting or fun. Some children will engage in such activities only because of external contingencies or pressures imposed by caretakers, i.e., because they will either get in trouble if they don't comply or because of imposed directives. These children tend to be externally oriented in their learning behaviour. On the other hand, some children have taken upon themselves the motivation and responsibility for their own learning. They may not always like the activities they do in school but they have identified with the value and importance of school and learning and so have internalized the regulation of their school activity. These different orientations toward regulating school behaviour can be placed along a continuum according to how self-determined children are for their school behaviour. Connell and Ryan (1985) have developed a questionnaire called the Self-Regulation Questionnaire to assess children's characteristic styles of self-regulation on this self-determination continuum. The questionnaire yields a summary score called the Self-Determination Index (SDI) which describes children's placement along the self-determination continuum.

In a recent study, Grolnick and Ryan (1986a) explored the relation of teachers' orientations toward support versus control of autonomy to children's self-regulation on the self-determination continuum. In order to do this, they performed a short-term longitudinal analysis of changes in children's self-determination for learning across the first five months of the school year. Elementary school children in grades 3–6 from 20 classrooms completed the Self-Regulation Questionnaire on day two of the school year and again in February of the same year. Teachers completed the Problems in School Questionnaire early in the school year. It was found that children who were in the classrooms of more autonomy-supportive teachers increased in their identification with the value and importance of achievement-related behaviours between the two assessments relative to children of more controlling teachers. Thus, even when activities or information taught in the classroom are not intrinsically or inherently motivating, teachers' styles can be important in helping children to move towards self-determination or autonomy for their learning.

As stated earlier, supporting autonomy, especially when activities or materials to be learned are not inherently motivating, does not mean allowing children to do whatever they want. Teachers often need to set limits or rules about what needs to be accomplished in the classroom. Supporting autonomy is not antithetical to limits; rather, it implies a particular manner in which limits are conveyed, i.e., one in which limits are stated matter-of-factly without language making salient pressure and control and in which children's feelings about the limits are acknowledged. In a relevant study Koestner, Ryan, Bernieri and Holt (1984) argued that the same limits could be communicated in a controlling or noncontrolling manner and that, whereas the former would be likely to undermine intrinsic motivation, the latter would maintain or enhance it.

In their study, Koestner *et al.* (1984) set limits on first and second grade children's neatness in a painting activity. In the controlling group, children were told that they should keep the materials and themselves neat so they would have to wear a smock, keep the paints neat and not spill them. The noncontrolling group was given the same limits and directions with two subtle differences. First, the words 'should' and 'have to' were not used. Secondly, it was acknowledged that they may not feel like doing these things but they were being asked to do them nonetheless. For example, the experimenter said, 'I know that sometimes it's fun to slop paint around, but for now, please keep it on the small center sheet.' By acknowledging the potential conflict for the child, it is reasoned that a power struggle between adult and child can be avoided and the child can accept the limit without a loss of self-esteem. These principles are central to Ginottian limit setting (Ginott, 1961; Orgel, 1983).

The results of the study revealed that children who had been given controlling limits were subsequently less intrinsically motivated to paint relative to those receiving noncontrolling limits who did not differ from a no-limit comparison group. Children did not however differ in the degree of compliance. This study demonstrated that it is possible to limit children's behaviour without undermining their sense of autonomy and so their motivation. This illustrates that autonomy support can include firmness and structure along with a willingness to support choice and independence.

Facilitating Autonomy — The Role of Parents

The previously discussed studies suggest that teacher styles can have important consequences for children's motivation and self-determination in the classroom. By allowing them autonomy and supporting their independent efforts to solve their own problems they help children to move toward taking more responsibility for their school-related behaviour and so require less external control and pressure. However, as stated earlier, children enter the classroom with widely different motivational orientations on the self-determination continuum. These may be in part a function of previous classroom experiences. It seems plausible, however, that at least part of their attitudes and orientations may be a function of the orientations of another major socializing influence, namely parents.

In a recently completed series of studies, we hypothesized that parents who tend to control children's autonomy at home should interfere with their children's movement toward self-regulation and self-responsibility in the classroom. This lack of self-regulation was expected to be manifest not only in children's descriptions of themselves as less self-determining (Connell and Ryan, 1985) on the Self-Regulation Questionnaire, but also in higher levels of adjustment difficulties in the classroom as rated by their teachers (Hightower, *et al.*, in press). Failures of self-regulation are evident to the extent that children do not behave appropriately or follow classroom procedures. In addition, children's tendencies to stay focused on tasks which they are expected to work on and to have good study and work habits are also a reflection of their ability to be self-regulating with regard to their school behaviour. We thus included teacher ratings of children's acting-out (disruptive, aggressive behaviour) and learning problems (academic motivation and performance difficulties) in the classroom. It was also expected that parental orientations on the autonomy-support to control continuum would be related to children's self-evaluations. Our reasoning was that it is only when one feels a sense of ownership or self-determination for behaviour that positive experiences and feedback will affect self-evaluation (Deci and Ryan, 1985).

In one attempt to explore these possible parental contributions to children's autonomy in school, Ryan, Deci and Grolnick (1986) developed a survey to assess children's perceptions of their mothers and fathers on the autonomy-support to control continuum. This measure, called the Parent Orientation Scale, was administered to children from three different school districts. Approximately 450 rural, 560 suburban, and 450 urban children completed the Parent Orientation Scale as well as other questionnaires tapping their self-evaluations and motivation in school. In addition, teachers rated children on rating scales tapping competence and motivation in the classroom. Children's perceptions of their parents on the autonomy-support dimension were then examined for relations with these child-related variables.

The results of this study suggested that parental autonomy support, as experienced by the child, had a number of significant school-related concomitants. Specifically, children who saw their parents as more supportive of their autonomy were higher in perceived competence in school and in general than those describing their parents as more controlling. Furthermore, perceptions of autonomy-supportive parents, especially mothers, were associated with higher levels of mastery motivation and more self-determined motivational orientations in children. Perceptions of autonomy support were also positively associated with higher teacher ratings of competence and ability in children. Relations between children's perceptions of their parents and teacher ratings were particularly strong for girls.

Thus, the above results point to the importance of perceived parental autonomy support for children's self-determination and competence in school. Also in the Ryan, Deci and Grolnick (1986) study, the relations between children's perceptions of their parents' autonomy support and their perceptions of the teacher and classroom environment were examined. It was reasoned that children who experience their parents as more controlling might tend to see their classroom environment as more controlling than those who see their home environment as supporting their autonomy. Correlational analyses confirmed this hypothesis. Thus, the perceived parental environment may set the stage not only for self-related cognitions and affects with regard to school but also the way in which the teacher is experienced. The lack of a feeling of self-determination or autonomy may then create a self-fulfilling prophecy where the child expects control and acts in such a way that the teacher must respond controllingly to get the child to do his or her work.

As was the case with studies exploring children's perceptions of the classroom environment, the fact that the environment was viewed through the child's eyes makes it impossible to confirm the hypothesis that actual parent orientations affect children's self-determination in the classroom. A more direct assessment of parental styles was thus a focus of another study conducted by Grolnick and Ryan (1986b).

Grolnick and Ryan (1986b) interviewed mothers and fathers of 48 third through sixth grade children from a rural elementary school. The focus of this interview was on the ways in which the parent motivates his or her child to engage in school and home-related activities such as doing homework as well as the way the parent responds when his or her child exhibits positive or negative behaviour with respect to the particular activity. Parents' responses to the series of interview questions were rated by two independent raters on three component scales associated with the autonomy-support to control dimension. The three component scales measured the following aspects of autonomy support: *values autonomy* was the extent to which the parent valued the child's autonomy and saw its promotion as a goal versus valued obedience and conformity first and foremost. *Autonomy-promoting techniques* reflected the extent to which the parent employed autonomy-oriented motivational and disciplinary techniques such as reasoning, encouragement and empathic limit setting (Koestner, Ryan, Bernieri and Holt, 1984) versus relying on controlling, power assertive methods such as physical punishment or controlling rewards. And *non-directiveness* was defined as the extent to which the parent includes the child in decisions and problem solving versus imposes his or her own agenda on the child. A given parent's score for autonomy support was the average of his or her ratings on the three scales. Maternal, paternal, and combined parent (defined as the average between maternal and paternal scores) ratings were then related to children's self-determination (Connell and Ryan, 1985), behavioural adjustment (Hightower *et al.*, in press), and perceived competence with respect to school.

The results of this interview study provided support for the hypothesized relations between parental autonomy support and children's autonomy in the classroom. Children whose parents were rated as more supportive of autonomy were more self-determined in the classroom than those whose parents were rated as more controlling. In addition, children of more autonomy-supportive parents were rated by their teachers as displaying less acting-out problems in the classroom and as having fewer learning difficulties than those of more controlling parents, suggesting that children of autonomy-supportive parents are more likely to internalize the rules and regulations of their classrooms. Parental autonomy support was also positively associated with various indices of children's school-related competence, including achievement scores, grades, and teacher-rated competence. In these relations, maternal autonomy support was generally more strongly related than paternal autonomy support. However, the strongest relations were usually for the overall parental environment (defined as the mean maternal/paternal autonomy support score). There was also a marginally significant positive relation between maternal autonomy support and children's perceived competence in the academic domain.

The above findings suggest that, through their support for autonomy and independence in their children, parents prepare their children for a school environment requiring self-regulation and autonomous functioning. More controlling parental styles may have the effect of forestalling the developmental movement toward autonomy and self-regulation in children making it necessary for teachers to motivate these children through prodding and pushing. It is easy to see how such a pernicious cycle of control is perpetuated.

Autonomy in Children's Learning — Quality and Quantity

In the studies we have reviewed so far, we have shown that autonomy in the classroom has important consequences for children's self-related cognitions and motivational orientation in school. We have also provided some evidence that children's positions along the developmental continuum of autonomy may be at least in part a function of the degree of autonomy support provided by significant others such as parents and teachers. Thus, facilitating self-determination in the classroom may be presumed to be an important goal for teachers. It might be argued, however, that the bottom line for educational goals must be learning outcomes *per se*. From this viewpoint, the prime argument for increased autonomy in the classroom would come from evidence that it facilitates actual learning and retention of information. Addressing this issue, we suggest that children's autonomy in the learning process may, in fact, have important consequences for learning outcomes, particularly with regard to the quality of learning (Grolnick and Ryan, in press).

The issue of 'quality' in learning is a complex one. Most of the practical assessment tools used to measure learning outcomes in educational contexts emphasize quantitative rather than qualitative dimensions, and thus ignore important aspects of what skilled facilitation of learning can impart. For our part we would define the qualitative aspects of learning not in terms of the accretion of rote facts, but rather in terms of the integration of what is learned into a long-term knowledge base; and the ability and willingness to transfer and apply that knowledge in new situations. These qualitative aspects, in other words, are reflections of the *integration* of what is learned.

The integration of learning we believe to be an active process requiring self-determination on the part of the learner (Grolnick and Ryan, in press). Benware and Deci (1984) recently made this point in a study examining learning under an active versus passive motivational set. When college students learned material expecting to teach it to another student, their conceptual understanding of the material was enhanced relative to that of students learning the material because they expected a graded test would follow.

Grolnick and Ryan (in press) recently conducted a study examining both varied learning contexts and individual differences in motivational styles in children as they related to the quality and quantity of learning in a reading comprehension task. In this study, fifth grade children were asked to read a grade level passage from a social studies book under one of three learning conditions: controlling-directed, non-controlling-directed, and non-directed. These conditions varied in the extent to which autonomy for learning was afforded. In the controlling-directed (CD) condition, children were told to read the material because they would be tested and graded for their learning. In this condition, evaluation and pressure were salient thus creating a situation where children felt externally controlled. In the non-controlling-directed (NCD) condition, children were asked to read the same passage and were told that they would be asked questions about it later. The focus, however, was on learning the material for its own sake. Evaluation and pressure were nonsalient thus creating a context where children might feel relatively more autonomous. In a third condition, the nondirected (ND) condition, children were asked to read the grade level material but were not told that they would be tested or asked questions later. It was presumed that, since there was no explicit direction to learn the material, any learning that did take place would be the result of the children's own internal proneness or tendency. Thus, the ND condition involved the highest relative degree of autonomy.

Following these experimental inductions and children's reading of the passage, children filled out questionaires assessing their emotional reactions to the reading materials. These questionnaires included items measuring their interest in the reading materials and their experience of pressure and tension while reading. Following these questions, children were asked to write down verbatim as much of the passage they read as possible, thus assessing their rote recall of the passage. This was followed by an assessment of their conceptual learning in which they were asked to tell us 'what was the main point of the passage or what the author was trying to say.' One week later a new experimenter came into the classroom groups and reassessed children's rote and conceptual learning as well as their interest/enjoyment of the previous learning session and their willingness to read similar materials.

Each of the three experimental contexts resulted in learning but of different types and was accompanied by different emotional reactions. With regard to the emotional experience of learning, children in the controlling-directed condition described the materials as less interesting and their experience of learning as more pressured relative to the children in the NCD or ND conditions. Rote recall was higher in the CD and NCD conditions relative to the ND condition. This is not surprising given that children in the ND condition did not expect a subsequent assessment and thus were not oriented to the details of the passage they read. Interestingly, however, conceptual learning was as high in the ND condition as in the NCD condition and children in these two conditions had higher conceptual learning than those in the CD condition. The argument that pressure and control undermine the active process of integration of information was thus supported by these findings.

Some of the most compelling results of this study occurred, however, at the one-week follow-up session. We were interested in how the three environments for learning would affect the retention of the information children learned. Examination of the difference between the amount of rote information recalled at the follow-up relative to the initial learning session revealed that children in the CD condition lost the most information between our sessions. We would argue that this indicates that information learned because of instrumental goals and pressure is poorly maintained because once the outcome is achieved, i.e., the test taken or the reward attained, there is no longer any reason to further process the information. We have previously referred to this as the 'core dump' phenomenon whereby information force fed into the system is dumped following completion of the program.

The fact that conceptual learning was as good in the non-controlling-directed condition as compared to the non-directed condition was surprising. It indicates, however, that children do pick up and integrate information encountered in their environments without any direction to do so. As Montessori would argue, we often fail to capitalize on this natural tendency to learn believing that children need always to be directed. What accounts for this natural learning? Ryan, *et al.* (1985) examined natural or 'spontaneous' learning in a study with college students. They found that, when spontaneous learning occurred, it was a function of the extent to which students were interested in the material and felt no pressure or 'ego-involvement' while learning. Thus, increasing spontaneous learning may involve decreasing pressure and control.

The Grolnick and Ryan (in press) study, thus, provided evidence that learning conditions relevant to autonomy can have consequences for the quality of learning and retention of information as well as for the emotional experience of learning. However, recent research has shown that the quality of learning outcomes is not solely a function of the environment but also of the motivational orientation of the learner (for example, Dweck and Elliot, 1983). In order to examine how individual differences in children's motivational stance in school affects learning, children in the Grolnick and Ryan (in press) study completed the Self-Regulation Questionnaire. Children's self-determination in school, as indexed by the SDI, was then related to emotions and learning outcomes. Because of their more active approach to learning, more self-determined learners were expected to exhibit better integration of information resulting in higher conceptual learning and retention of information relative to more externally oriented learners. Similarly, more self-determined learners were expected to find our learning materials more interesting and experience less pressure in our learning session than their less self-determined counterparts.

Analyses investigating relations between children's self-determination and learning generally supported these hypotheses. Across learning conditions, more self-determined children evidenced higher conceptual learning and the lower feelings of pressure and tension while reading. In addition, the more self-determined learners lost less information between our initial and follow-up sessions relative to those who were less self-determined. Thus, not only do immediate conditions for learning influence the chance the information will be integrated, children's orientations to learning may facilitate or undermine integrative processes as well. As we have seen in the earlier reviewed work, these orientations may be a function of long-term experience with autonomy-supportive versus controlling home and school environments.

Ryan and Grolnick (1986) in a subsequent project further explored individual differences in motivational orientations and learning outcomes in a developmental study of third through sixth graders. Children at each grade level were asked to read the fifth grade level materials used in the previous study within a spontaneous learning context. Thus, children were asked to read the materials but not told that any kind of learning assessment would follow. Their emotional reactions and rote and conceptual learning were then assessed as in Grolnick and Ryan's (in press) study. Interestingly, the results differed strongly by grade. For fifth graders, the results were virtually identical to those in the previous study, i.e., more self-determined styles in children were associated with higher conceptual learning, lower experienced pressure and better retention of information relative to lower self-determined styles. However, for third and fourth grade children the results were the opposite. Although none of the children displayed high conceptual scores or described very low levels of pressure, self-determined styles were negatively associated with these indices. These results can be interpreted in terms of the importance of optimal challenge or level of difficulty in motivation. We suggest that children are self-determined to integrate only information or regulations that are congruent with their internal structures and abilities. The material was not optimally challenging for our younger subjects and so only external orientations could push the children to learn. Thus, in providing learning contexts facilitative of autonomy or self-determination, it is crucial to be sure that information presented is at or just above the current ability level of the student. Material too difficult or too easy will undermine self-determination and motivation.

The issue of self-determination and optimal challenge for learning have also been explored in research by Danner and Lonky (1981). Using the approach of cognitive evaluation theory (Deci and Ryan, 1980) and Piaget's (1952) equilibration model, they tested the hypotheses that children would be most intrinsically motivated to assimilate material just above their current level of ability; and that extrinsic inducements would interfere with this natural propensity to seek optimal challenges. They studied an elementary school population engaged with conceptual sorting tasks and obtained results supporting these propositions. Their findings fit with those above in suggesting that motivational principles are crucial to the production of quality learning.

When considering the kinds of learning that educators value and hope to facilitate, it is clear that the issues of autonomy and optimal challenge are of great importance. In order to conceptualize this, we consider the outcomes of two contrasting models of learning: integration and accretion. Integration, a process of development, is evident when information is acted upon and transformed by the learner into a form where it can be meaningfully integrated into existing, internal structures (Deci and Ryan, 1985). It therefore requires autonomous energy on the part of the learner. Because such learning is integrated with past knowledge and skills, it is more likely to be maintained over time and transferred to new contexts (Grolnick and Ryan, in press). Accretive learning, on the other hand, can be force-fed to the child because it involves no energy on the part of the learner. In this model, the prescriptions and motivations of learning are the teacher's rather than the learner's. Accretive learning involves knowledge acquired in a passive, rote manner and is therefore less likely to be maintained or generalized. Because the ultimate goals of teaching involve learning that is integrated, maintained, and generalizable, providing a context for learning which supports autonomy must be a goal for education.

Summary

The goals of education involve more than only academic concerns. Schools and teachers also strongly influence children's self-related attitudes, adjustment, and life long motivations for learning. Our perspective suggests that learning is a developmental process involving elaboration and integration of internal structures. As a process of development, the energy for learning begins from within and so requires active participation on the part of the learner. Accordingly, quality in education involves the facilitation of children's active participation and autonomy in their learning so as to capitalize on the natural developmental tendencies in this direction.

In exploring the six propositions outlined at the beginning of the chapter, we have provided evidence to suggest that the facilitation of these developmental propensities depends heavily on the support for autonomy afforded by parents and teachers. When children feel more self-determined in school, they also feel more competent academically and in general. We have argued, and provided some data to suggest, that the extent to which children experience autonomy in their learning is at least in part a function of the orientations of significant others in their lives. More autonomy-supportive teachers can facilitate children's feeling active in the learning process and make it more likely that they will initiate further in the future. In addition, the autonomy-supportive versus controlling nature of home environments leads to the growth of more self-responsibility and regulatory capacity, i.e., to more independence and autonomy. Finally, studies of actual learning suggest that, when children are more self-determined, the quality of learning is enhanced with better integrated and maintained learning as the outcome.

The view of education espoused herein is one in which the child plays an active part. Self-determined activity we believe results in the integrated internalization of values and knowledge, phenomena which cannot be forced into one, but rather must be openly and willingly accepted and assimilated. From this view, the task of teaching is one of preparing the conditions in which openness to learning and responsibility are maximized. The artful task of teaching and parenting with respect to education is thus one of creating conditions ripe for autonomous assimilation and growth. In short, it is the art of instantiating for every child a facilitating environment.

Note

Preparation of this manuscript was facilitated by a research grant from the National Institute of Child Health and Human Development (HD 19914-01) to the Human Motivation Program in the Department of Psychology at the University of Rochester.

References

BENWARE, C. and DECI, E.L. (1984) 'Quality of learning with an active versus passive motivational set', *American Educational Research Journal*, 21, pp. 755–65.

BRUNER, J.S. (1962) *On Knowing: Essays for the Left Hand*, Cambridge, Mass., Harvard University Press.

CONNELL, J.P. (1985) 'A new multidimensional measure of children's perceptions of control', *Child Development*, 6, pp. 281–93.

CONNELL, J.P. and RYAN, R.M. (1985) 'A theory and assessment of children's self-regulation within the academic domain'. Unpublished manuscript, University of Rochester.

DANNER, F.W. and LONKY, E. (1981) 'A cognitive-developmental approach to the effects of rewards on intrinsic motivation', *Child Development*, 52, pp. 1043–52.

DECHARMS, R. (1976) *Enhancing Motivation: Change in the Classroom*, New York, Irvington.

DECI, E.L. and RYAN, R.M. (1980) 'The empirical exploration of intrinsic motivational processes', in BERKOWITZ, L. (Ed.) *Advances in Experimental Social Psychology* (Vol. 13, pp. 39–80), New York, Academic Press.

DECI, E.L. and RYAN, R.M. (1985) *Intrinsic Motivation and Self-determination in Human Behavior*, New York, Plenum.

DECI, E.L., NEZLEK, J., and SHEINMAN, L. (1981) 'Characteristics of the rewarder and intrinsic motivation of the rewardee', *Journal of Personality and Social Psychology*, 40, pp. 1–10.

DECI, E.L., SCHWARTZ, A.J., SHEINMAN, L. and RYAN, R.M. (1981) 'An instrument to assess adults' orientations toward control versus autonomy with children: Reflections on intrinsic motivation and perceived competence', *Journal of Educational Psychology*, 73, pp. 642–50.

DEWEY, J. (1938) *Experience and Education*, New York, Collier.

DWECK, C.S. and ELLIOT, E.S. (1983) 'Achievement motivation', in MUSSEN, P.H. (Ed.) *Handbook of Child Psychology* (Vol. 4, 4th ed., pp. 643–91), New York, Wiley.

GINOTT, H. (1961) *Group Psychotherapy with Children: The Theory and Practice of Play-therapy*, New York, McGraw-Hill.

GROLNICK, W.S. and RYAN, R.M. (1986a) 'Teacher and parent influences on children's self-regulation'. Unpublished manuscript, University of Rochester.

GROLNICK, W.S. and RYAN, R.M. (1986b) 'Parent styles associated with children's school-related adjustment and competence.' Unpublished manuscript, University of Rochester.

GROLNICK, W.S. and RYAN, R.M. (in press) 'Autonomy in children's learning: An experimental and individual difference investigation', *Journal of Personality and Social Psychology*.

HARTER, S. (1981) 'A new self-report scale of intrinsic versus extrinsic orientation in the classroom: Motivational and informational components', *Development Psychology*, 17, pp. 300–12.

HARTER, S. (1982) 'The perceived competence scale for children', *Child Development*, 53, pp. 87–97.

HIGHTOWER, A.D., WORK, W.C., COWEN, E.L., LOTYCZEWSKI, B.S., SPINELL, A.P., GUARE, J.C. and ROHRBECK, C.A. (in press) 'The teacher-child rating scale: A brief objective measure of elementary children's school problem behaviors and competencies', *School Psychology Review*.

KOESTNER, R., RYAN, R.M., BERNIERI, F. and HOLT, K. (1984) 'Setting limits in children's behavior: The differential effects of controlling versus informational styles on intrinsic motivation and creativity', *Journal of Personality*, 52, pp. 233–48.

ORGEL, A.R. (1983) 'Hiam Ginott's approach to discipline', in DORR, D., ZAX, M. and BONNER, J. (Eds) *Comparative Approaches to Discipline for Children and Youth*, New York, International Universities Press.

PIAGET, J. (1952) *The Origins of Intelligence in Children*, New York, International Universities Press.

PIAGET, J. (1971) *Biology and Knowledge*, Chicago, University of Chicago Press.

ROGERS, C. (1969) *Freedom to Learn*, Columbus, Ohio, Merrill.

RYAN, R.M. and GROLNICK, W.S. (1986) 'Origins and pawns in the classroom: Self-report and projective assessment of individual differences in children's perceptions', *Journal of Personality and Social Psychology*, 50, pp. 550–8.

RYAN, R.M., CONNELL, J.P. and DECI, E.L. (1985) 'A motivational analysis of self-determination and self-regulation in education', in AMES C. and AMES R.E. (Eds) *Research on Motivation in Education: The Classroom Milieu*, New York, Academic Press.

RYAN, R.M., CONNELL, J.P. and GROLNICK, W.S. (in press) 'When achievement is *not* intrinsically motivated: A theory and assessment of self-regulation in school', in BOGGIANO A.K. and PITTMAN, T.S. (Eds) *Achievement and Motivation: A Social-developmental Perspective*, Cambridge, Cambridge University Press.

RYAN, R.M., CONNELL, J.P., PLANT, R., ROBINSON, D. and EVANS, S. (1985) 'The influence of emotions on spontaneous learning'. Unpublished manuscript, University of Rochester.

RYAN, R.M., DECI, E.L. and GROLNICK, W.S. (1986) 'Children's perceptions of parental involvement and autonomy-support'. Unpublished manuscript, University of Rochester.

Self-Efficacy and Motivated Learning[1]

Dale H. Schunk
University of North Carolina

There is growing evidence that students' beliefs influence their motivation and learning (Bandura, 1986; Brophy, 1983; Corno and Mandinach, 1983; McCombs, 1984; Nicholls, 1983; Rotter, 1966; Schunk, 1985b; Thomas, 1980; Weiner, 1979). In this chapter I will examine the role of *perceived self-efficacy*, or personal beliefs about one's capabilities to organize and implement actions necessary to attain designated levels of performance (Bandura, 1982, 1986). The central idea is that self-efficacy exerts an important influence on *motivated learning*, or motivation to acquire skills and knowledge rather than merely to complete activities (Brophy, 1983). I will use the expression *self-efficacy for learning* to refer to students' beliefs about their capabilities to apply their knowledge and skills effectively in instructional contexts and thereby learn new cognitive skills.

My plan for this chapter is initially to discuss self-efficacy as it relates to a model of motivated learning. Research will be summarized that bears directly on the influence of self-efficacy on motivated learning. I will conclude by offering some implications for classroom practice.

Self-Efficacy, Motivation and Learning

Self-efficacy is hypothesized to have diverse effects in achievement settings (Bandura, 1982; Schunk, 1985b). Self-efficacy can affect choice of activities. Students who have a low sense of efficacy for learning cognitive skills may attempt to avoid tasks, whereas those who judge themselves more efficacious should participate more eagerly. Self-efficacy also is hypothesized to affect effort expenditure and persistence. Especially when facing obstacles, students who have a high sense of efficacy for learning should expend greater effort and persist longer than those who doubt their capabilities.

Students acquire information about their self-efficacy from performance accomplishments, vicarious (observational) experiences, forms of persuasion, and inferences from physiological states (Bandura, 1982). In general, successes raise self-efficacy and failures lower it, although once a strong sense of efficacy is developed an occasional failure may not have much effect. In classrooms, students acquire much information about their own capabilities through social comparison, or comparing one's performances with those of one's peers. The modeling literature supports the idea that students who are similar in important ways — age, background, perceived competence — offer the best basis for comparison (Rosenthal and Bandura, 1978; Rosenthal and Zimmerman, 1978; Zimmerman, 1977). Observing similar peers perform a task can convey to students that they, too, are capable of accomplishing the task (Berger, 1977; Levine, 1983). Information acquired vicariously ought to have a weaker influence on self-efficacy than performance-based information, because a vicarious boost in self-efficacy can be negated if one subsequently fails.

Students often receive persuasory information via suggestions or exhortations from teachers that they possess the capabilities to perform a task (for example, 'You can do this'). Although positive persuasory feedback can enhance self-efficacy, this increase is apt to be short-lived if students subsequently perform poorly. Finally, students acquire some information about their learning capabilities from physiological symptoms. For example, emotional indexes such as rapid heart rate or sweating could be interpreted by students to mean that they are not very capable of learning. When students notice that they are reacting in a less agitated fashion, they may feel more efficacious about their learning abilities.

Information acquired by students from these sources does not automatically influence self-efficacy (Bandura, 1986; Schunk, 1985b). Self-appraisal of one's capabilities is an inferential task in which students weigh and combine the contributions of such personal and situational factors as perceived ability, difficulty of the task, amount of effort expended, amount of external (teacher) aid received, task outcomes (successes or failures), pattern of successes and failures (increasing, constant, decreasing), perceived similarity to models, and persuader credibility.

Even when students assess their learning abilities primarily through their own performances, efficacy appraisals are not mere reflections of those performances. Successes do not guarantee higher efficacy, nor will failures necessarily have a negative impact. Rather, various educational practices can moderate the effects of outcomes on self-efficacy. For example, students should develop a high sense of efficacy for learning as they work at a task and experience some success. Some educational practices may validate this sense of efficacy and sustain motivation by clearly conveying to students that they are acquiring knowledge and skills. Other practices may offer less clear information about skill acquisition, or even convey to students that they are not particularly skillful. In these latter situations, motivation will suffer and students will not feel efficacious about learning.

I do not wish to imply that self-efficacy is the only influence on motivated learning. Even high self-efficacy will not produce learning when the requisite learning *skills* are lacking. *Outcome expectations*, or one's beliefs concerning the outcomes of one's actions, constitute another influence on behavior. Students are not motivated to behave in ways that they believe will result in negative outcomes, regardless of whether self-efficacy is high. In school, high self-efficacy and positive outcome expectations often are linked; students who feel capable of learning expect positive teacher feedback and good grades. Another influence on motivated learning is the *value* students place on outcomes, or how much they desire those outcomes relative to others. If peer approval is more important than good grades and the former depends on not performing well, then students may not show much motivation to learn even if they feel efficacious about learning. In short, assuming that students possess the skills to learn, believe that positive outcomes will result, and value those outcomes, self-efficacy is hypothesized to influence motivated learning.

A Model of Motivated Learning

Entry Characteristics

Students enter learning situations with different aptitudes and prior experiences. Aptitudes include general abilities, skills, strategies, interests, attitudes, and personality characteristics (Cronbach and Snow, 1977). Educational experiences derive from prior schools attended, interactions with teachers, time spent on different subjects, and so on. These two factors are related. For example, students high in reading ability ought to perform better on tasks requiring reading, which should earn teacher praise and good grades. In turn, students may develop greater interest in reading, which can further improve their ability.

Self-Efficacy for Learning

At the outset of a learning endeavour, students hold beliefs concerning their capabilities for acquiring knowledge, developing skills, mastering the material, and so on (Schunk, 1985b). Aptitudes and prior experiences affect self-efficacy for learning. Students who previously performed well in a subject ought to believe that they are capable of new learning, whereas students who have experienced difficulties may doubt their capabilities. At the same time, self-efficacy for learning is not a simple reflection of aptitudes and prior experiences. Collins (1982) identified students of high, average and low mathematical ability; within each level, she identified students with high and low mathematical self-efficacy and gave them problems to solve. Regardless of ability level, students with higher self-efficacy solved more problems correctly and chose to rework more problems they missed.

Task Engagement Variables

I use the term *task engagement* to refer to students' cognitive activities — attending, processing and integrating information, thinking, mentally solving problems — as well as their verbalizations and behaviours (Brophy, 1983; Corno and Mandinach, 1983; Winne, 1985). Associated with instructional contexts are variables that can affect students' self-efficacy and motivated learning. Some task engagement variables that I believe are important are shown in Table 1.

Table 1: Task Engagement Variables

Purpose and Content of Instruction
Instructional Presentation
Strategy Training
Performance Feedback
Attributional Feedback
Goal Setting
Rewards

I will discuss these in depth in the following section. I want to emphasize that these variables differ in the cues they make salient and which, along with performance successes and failures, students use to appraise their self-efficacy. In other words, students take into account the cues made salient by these variables and judge how well they are acquiring knowledge and skills. In turn, efficacy appraisals influence motivated learning.

Efficacy Cues

As noted earlier, *performance outcomes* are important cues used by students to appraise self-efficacy for learning. In general, students who succeed should continue to expect success, whereas those who fail may doubt their capabilities to learn.

Outcome patterns constitute a second type of cue. Early learning is often fraught with failures, but the perception of progress can promote self-efficacy (Schunk, 1985b). Self-efficacy may not be aided much if students believe that their progress is slow or that their skills have stabilized at low levels.

Attributions (perceived causes) for prior successes and failures are used to appraise self-efficacy for learning. Successes and failures in achievement settings often are attributed to ability, effort, task difficulty, and luck (Frieze, 1980; Weiner, 1979). Children view effort as the prime cause of outcomes and ability-related terms as closely associated, but with development a distinct conception of ability emerges (Nicholls, 1978). Ability attributions become increasingly important influences on perceived capabilities, whereas the role of effort declines in importance (Harari and Covington, 1981).

Students also derive cues from the learning *context*. Consider the role of help from others. Teachers who provide much assistance to students may improve their skills but do little to raise their self-efficacy; students may believe that they could not succeed on their own. Another cue is teacher praise, which can convey how the teacher views students' abilities (Weiner *et al.*, 1983). Especially when students believe that a task is easy, praise combined with effort information (for example, 'That's good. You've been working hard') signals low ability. Students who believe that the teacher does not expect much of them are apt to hold low self-efficacy for learning. Other contextual factors include students' perceptions of the working conditions and distractions from others.

Perceived *similarity to models* can affect self-efficacy. When students regard peers as similar in competence, observing peers improving their skills can vicariously boost students' beliefs about learning, whereas observed failures cast doubt on students' own capabilities to succeed (Bandura, 1986). Model similarity also can be based on personal attributes, such as age, sex, and ethnic background, even when the attributes have little bearing on the modeled behaviours (Rosenthal and Bandura, 1978).

Students' judgments of *persuader credibility* should affect self-efficacy for learning. Students may experience higher self-efficacy when they are persuaded by a trustworthy source (the teacher) that they are capable of learning, whereas they may readily discount the advice of less credible sources. Students also may discount the advice of an otherwise credible source if they believe that the source does not fully understand the nature of the task demands (for example, difficult for students to comprehend) or the effect of contextual influences, such as too many distractions.

Various *bodily symptoms* serve as physiological cues for appraising self-efficacy. Sweating and trembling may signal that students are not very capable of learning. Conversely, students who notice that they are reacting in less agitated fashion to academic tasks may feel more efficacious about continuing to learn. Included in this category are cues emanating from fatigue and physical illness.

Task Engagement Variables

Purpose and Content of Instruction

The purpose of instruction, or what uses students will make of the material to be learned (Marx, 1983), ought to affect students' self-efficacy for academic learning. When teachers announce that material will be covered on a test, students who have performed poorly on previous tests may experience anxiety, which could result in low efficacy. Conversely, students who previously earned good grades on term papers may react with high self-efficacy to the announcement that they will have to write a term paper on the topic they are studying.

Content difficulty would seem to be an especially important variable. Subject matter that is perceived as difficult to learn may lead to attributions of high task difficulty, which can negatively affect self-efficacy; material that students believe is easy to learn ought to result in high self-efficacy. For example, many children find reducing fractions to lowest common denominators difficult. Those who believe that they are competent in the component skills (multiplication, division) may feel more efficacious about learning than students who doubt their capabilities in the prerequisites.

In an important study, Salomon (1984) found that students perceived learning from television to be easier than learning from print. In turn, students held higher self-efficacy about learning from television, and consequently invested less mental effort in learning. For written materials, higher self-efficacy led to greater mental effort.

Instructional Presentation

How teachers present academic material can affect students' self-efficacy for learning. Students who readily comprehend the teacher's instruction and explanations are apt to believe that they are making progress in learning, which should enhance self-efficacy for continued learning (Schunk, 1985b). Teachers' use of instructional time also is important. Teachers who provide students with multiple opportunities for task engagement (instruction, practice, review) increase their opportunities to experience successes.

Included here are students' perceptions of how well they learn from the teacher's methods. Students who believe that they can capture the main points of a lecture and take good notes should hold higher self-efficacy for understanding a lecture than students who doubt their capabilities to perform these tasks. Shy students may experience anxiety about participating in group discussions, which may lead them to believe that they will not learn much from the experience.

Brophy (1983) has shown that an important aspect of instructional presentation is how the teacher opens the lesson. Teachers often give no introduction but rather move directly into the task. Teachers also cue positive expectations when they assert that students should enjoy the task or do well on it, or negative expectations by stating that students may not like the task or perform well. To the extent that children view the teacher as a credible judge of their abilities, negative expectation statements ought to lead to lower self-efficacy than positive statements.

Strategy Training

Much classroom learning depends on being able to apply strategies, or planned and deliberate cognitive activities leading to sequenced actions. There has been much recent interest among educational psychologists in training students to apply strategies to comprehension, mathematical, and problem solving tasks. Strategy training can foster self-efficacy for learning (Schunk, 1985b). The belief that one understands and can effectively apply a strategy leads to a greater sense of control over learning outcomes, which can raise self-efficacy. Brown and her colleagues emphasize that strategy training needs to include instruction and practice in applying the strategy, training in self-regulated implementation and monitoring of strategy use, and information on strategy value and on the range of tasks to which the strategy can be applied (Baker and Brown, 1984; Brown, Palincsar and Armbruster, 1984). Each of these aspects should have a positive influence on students' self-efficacy.

One means of teaching students a strategy involves having them verbalize aloud the steps in the strategy as they apply them to tasks. Verbalization can facilitate learning because it directs students' attention to important task features, assists strategy encoding and retention, and helps students work systematically (Schunk, 1985b). Verbalization may be most beneficial for students who typically perform in a deficient manner, such as impulsive, remedial, learning disabled, retarded or emotionally disturbed children (Borkowski and Cavanaugh, 1979; Hallahan, Kneedler and Lloyd, 1983; Licht and Kistner, 1986).

During a listening comprehension training program, Schunk and Rice (1984) had language-deficient children in grades two through four either verbalize steps in a strategy prior to applying them to questions or not verbalize steps. Strategy verbalization led to higher self-efficacy across grades, and promoted performance among third and fourth graders. Perhaps the demands of verbailization, along with those of the comprehension task, were too complex for the second graders. In a follow-up study with fourth and fifth graders, Schunk and Rice (1985) found that strategy verbalization led to higher reading comprehension, self-efficacy, and ability attributions across grades. Strategy verbalization may enhance self-efficacy for learning through its effect on ability attributions.

Schunk and Cox (1986) presented learning disabled students in grades six through eight with subtraction training over sessions. One group verbalized aloud solution steps and their application to problems (continuous verbalization), a second group verbalized aloud during the first half of training but not during the second half (discontinued verbalization), and a third group did not verbalize (no verbalization). Continuous verbalization led to higher self-efficacy and skill than the other two treatments, which did not differ in outcomes. Continuous verbalization probably made the effectiveness of the strategy highly salient to students, which should have raised their self-efficacy for continued learning. When instructed to no longer verbalize aloud, discontinued verbalization students may have had difficulty regulating their performances.

Modeling

Teachers often model the application of cognitive skills or utilize symbolic models (i.e., films, videotapes). Modeling also can raise students' learning efficacy because it implicitly conveys that they are capable of succeeding and will do so if they perform the same sequence of actions (Schunk, 1985b).

In an early study (Schunk, 1981), children deficient in division skills received either modeling or didactic instruction, after which they solved problems. Modeling children observed an adult verbalize aloud division operations while simultaneously applying them to problems; the didactic treatment consisted of children reviewing instructional pages that explained and exemplified the same operations. Although both treatments promoted self-efficacy, modeling led to higher skill development. These results suggest that didactic children were overly swayed by their modest training successes while not fully understanding the nature of the division process.

An important cue used to assess self-efficacy is perceived similarity between observer and model. Observation of a similar peer learning a task can convey to students that they, too, are capable of performing well. In school, success at many tasks depends on underlying abilities. Especially among low achievers who may doubt that they are capable of attaining the teacher's level of competence, observing peer success may be more beneficial.

To test this idea, Schunk and Hanson (1985) showed children, who had experienced difficulties learning to subtract, videotapes portraying an adult teacher and a same-sex peer (student) model. The teacher repeatedly provided instruction on subtraction with regrouping, after which the model solved problems. Other students viewed videotapes portraying only the teacher, or did not view tapes. Students assessed their self-efficacy for learning to subtract and then received training. Observing a peer model enhanced self-efficacy for learning, as well as posttest self-efficacy and skill, more than the teacher model or no model; teacher model subjects outperformed children without any model. Both the peer and teacher model led to more rapid problem solving during training (i.e., greater motivation) compared with no model children.

Another means of increasing perceived similarity is to use coping rather than mastery models. Coping models initially demonstrate the typical fears and deficiencies of observers but gradually improve their performance and gain confidence, whereas mastery models demonstrate faultless performance and high confidence from the outset (Kazdin, 1978; Kornhaber and Schroeder, 1975; Meichenbaum, 1971; Thelen *et al.*, 1979). To the extent that students view a coping model's initial difficulties and gradual progress similar to their typical performances, a coping model might better promote self-efficacy.

In the Schunk and Hanson study, subjects observed either a peer mastery or coping model. The mastery model learned readily and verbalized positive beliefs reflecting high efficacy (for example, 'I can do that one'), high ability, low difficulty, and positive attitudes. The coping model initially made errors and verbalized negative beliefs, but gradually improved and verbalized coping statements ('I'll have to work hard on this one'). Eventually, the coping model's verbalizations and behaviours matched those of the mastery model. The two types of model were equally effective. It is possible that children's prior classroom successes with subtraction, even though limited, led them to conclude that if the peer model could learn, they could as well. In a follow-up study, Schunk, Hanson, and Cox (1986) used a task (fractions) that subjects had little, if any, prior successes with. Observing a coping model raised children's perceptions of similarity in competence, self-efficacy for learning, posttest self-efficacy and skill, more than observing a mastery model.

Another influential modeling variable is number of models. Compared with a single model, multiple models increase the probability that observers will perceive themselves as similar to at least one of the models (Thelen *et al.*, 1979). In a second study, Schunk *et al.* (1986) found that observation of multiple models led to higher self-efficacy for learning than observation of a single model; however, this effect did not depend on perceived similarity in competence. Observing several peers learn either rapidly or gradually led children to believe that they, too, could learn.

Performance Feedback

The role of teacher feedback is minimal where students can derive their own information on how well they are learning. Some mathematical exercises, for example, allow students to check their answers. Many times students require teacher feedback because otherwise they do not know if they are making progress in learning. In these instances, feedback that highlights progress (for example, 'You're doing much better') ought to promote self-efficacy.

During a subtraction training program over sessions, some children recorded the number of pages of problems they completed; others had their pages recorded by a proctor[2]; children in a third condition received no feedback (Schunk, 1983c). Both forms of feedback were equally effective and led to higher self-efficacy and skillful performance compared with no feedback. The three treatments did not differ in the number of problems that children solved during training, which supports the idea that, although self-efficacy is influenced by prior performances, it is not merely a reflection of them (Bandura, 1982).

Attributional Feedback

Effort attributional feedback is a persuasive source of efficacy information. To be told that one can achieve better results through harder work can motivate one to do so and convey that one possesses the necessary capability to succeed. Much research shows that linking performance outcomes with effort enhances students' effort attributions, persistence, and achievement (Andrews and Debus, 1978; Chapin and Dyck, 1976; Dweck, 1975; Medway and Venino, 1982; Miller, Brickman and Bolen, 1975). How effort is linked to outcomes also seems important. During a subtraction training programme (Schunk, 1982), children either had their prior achievement linked with effort ('You've been working hard'), their future achievement linked with effort ('You need to work hard'), or did not receive effort feedback. Linking prior successes with effort led to higher posttest subtraction skill and self-efficacy, as well as motivation during training. These results suggest that linking effort with prior achievement conveys that children have acquired skills and are capable of further learning.

To test the presumed benefits of ability feedback, Schunk (1983a) gave children either ability feedback for prior successes ('You're good at this'), effort feedback, ability plus effort (combined) feedback, or no feedback, during a subtraction training program. Children receiving only ability feedback demonstrated the highest posttest self-efficacy and skill; the effort-only and ability plus effort conditions did not differ. Children in the latter condition may have discounted the ability information; they might have wondered how well they were learning if they had to continue to work hard to succeed.

Research shows that the sequence of attributional feedback influences achievement outcomes. During a subtraction training program over sessions, children received ability feedback, effort feedback, ability feedback during the first half of training and effort feedback during the second half, or the reverse (Schunk, 1984). Ability feedback for early successes, regardless of whether it was continued or not, led to higher ability attributions, posttest self-efficacy and skill, compared with early effort feedback. These results support the idea that early successes are a signal that one has the capability to learn (Weiner, 1974).

Schunk and Cox (1986) gave students effort feedback during the first half of training, during the second half, or did not provide effort feedback. Each type of feedback promoted posttest self-efficacy and skill better than no feedback; early effort feedback led students to place greater emphasis on effort as a cause of success. The students in this study had identified learning disabilities in mathematics, so effort feedback for early or late successes may have seemed highly credible because students had to expend effort to succeed.

Goal Setting

Goal setting involves comparing one's present performance against a standard (Bandura, 1986). When students are given or set a goal, they may experience a sense of efficacy for attaining it, which is substantiated as they work at the task and observe their goal progress. Goal properties — specificity, difficulty level, proximity — are especially important (Locke *et al.*, 1981). Goals that incorporate specific performance standards are more likely to raise learning efficacy because progress toward an explicit goal is easier to gauge (Schunk, 1985b). General goals (for example 'Do your best') do not enhance motivation. Goal difficulty, or the level of proficiency required as assessed against a standard, can raise self-efficacy. Students may initially doubt their capabilities to attain difficult goals, but these offer more information about learning capabilities than easier goals. Proximal goals, which are close at hand, result in greater motivation than distant goals. It is easy for students to judge progress toward an immediate goal, whereas progress toward a long-term goal is often difficult to assess.

Schunk (1983b) tested the effects of goal difficulty. During a division training program, children received either difficult (but attainable) or easier goals of completing a given number of problems each session. To preclude children believing that the goals were too difficult, which would have stifled motivation, half of the subjects in each goal condition were told directly by a proctor that they could attain the goal ('You can work 25 problems'), whereas the other half received social comparative information indicating that other similar children had been able to complete that many problems. Difficult goals enhanced rate of problem solving during training and led to higher posttest division skill; telling children directly that they could work the problems promoted self-efficacy.

Bandura and Schunk (1981) demonstrated the benefits of proximal goals. Children worked on a training packet consisting of seven sets of material. Children were told that they would work on the packet over seven sessions. Some students pursued a goal of completing one set each session; a second group was given a distant goal of completing the entire packet by the end of the last session; and a third group was given only a general goal of working productively. Proximal goals heightened motivation and led to the highest self-efficacy and subtraction skill. The distant goal resulted in no benefits over those obtained from receiving training.

Schunk (1985a) found benefits due to students setting their own goals. Participation in goal setting presumably heightens goal commitment, which is necessary for goals to enhance performance (Locke *et al.*, 1981). Sixth graders classified as learning disabled in mathematics received subtraction training over sessions. Some children set performance goals each session; others had comparable goals assigned; children in a third condition received training but no goals. Self-set goals led to the highest posttest self-efficacy and skill, and these children judged their expectancy of goal attainment each session higher than students who were assigned goals. Students in each goal condition completed more problems during training than no-goal students.

Rewards

Much research shows that offering rewards can promote task performance (Lepper, 1983). Rewards also constitute an important influence on students' learning efficacy. Rewards are likely to enhance self-efficacy when they are tied to students' actual accomplishments. Telling students that they can earn rewards based on what they accomplish can instill a sense of self-efficacy for learning (Schunk, 1985b). As students then work at a task and note their progress, this sense of efficacy is validated. Receipt of the reward further validates self-efficacy, because it symbolizes progress. In contrast, when rewards are offered merely for working at a task, students may not experience a comparable sense of efficacy. Such rewards actually may convey negative information: students might infer that they are not expected to learn much because they do not possess the requisite capabilities.

During a division training program (Schunk, 1983d), some children (performance-contingent reward) were told that they would earn points for each division problem solved and that they would exchange their points for prizes equal in monetary value to the points. Others (task-contingent reward) were informed that they would receive prizes for participating in the training. Children in a third condition (unexpected reward) were unexpectedly allowed to choose prizes at the end of training. Performance-contingent rewards led to the most rapid problem solving during training, as well as the highest division self-efficacy and skill. Offering rewards for participation led to no benefits compared with merely receiving training.

The classroom reward structure also can affect self-efficacy. Competitive structures reduce the possibilities for students receiving rewards when others are successful (Ames, 1984). Students who do not receive rewards may form low ability attributions, which will not raise self-efficacy. Under cooperative conditions, group members share rewards based on the collective group performance. Successful groups can enhance perceived capabilities of low performers; however, cooperative groups that fail can stifle motivation and highlight ability differences between students. In individualistic structures, students' achievements are independent of one another. This structure can highlight progress as a cue for assessing self-efficacy, unless students believe that they are not making progress (Schunk, 1985b).

Implications for Educational Practice

The preceding discussion contains some obvious implications for educational practice. Lessons ought to be introduced in a positive manner to promote students' beliefs in their capabilities for learning. Teachers need to present academic material in ways that foster student understanding. When complex material is being covered, teachers may need to break it down into smaller units and provide added opportunities for student practice and review. Feedback to students should contain information not only on the accuracy of their work but also on their progress in skill acquisition (for example, 'You're catching on'). Teachers need to ensure that students work at tasks systematically and may have to provide explicit strategy training to those students who fail to grasp cognitive skills. Wherever possible, rewards need to be linked to student progress, regardless of whether rewards are tangible (for example, stickers), symbolic (grades), or social (praise) in nature.

Other implications may not be quite as obvious. I will discuss in greater depth the role of peer models, effort feedback, and goal setting.

Peer Models

One use of peers as models is in tutoring contexts. Tutoring can result in academic and social-emotional benefits for tutors and tutees. Feldman, Devin-Sheehan and Allen (1976) suggest that a greater age differential between tutor and tutee may lead to higher tutee performance, but that the nature of the interaction may be better when tutor and tutee are peers.

Peers also serve as models when they demonstrate skills to other class members. Such demonstrations can be beneficial. For example, it is not unusual for children to experience self-doubts, and possibly anxiety, about executing gymnastic movements such as cartwheels or somersaults. Observing peers perform these movements without untoward consequences may motivate children to try the exercises themselves. As children perform the exercises, they should begin to notice that they are improving and not injuring themselves, which can sustain motivation. With skill improvement, children are apt to engage in further social comparison to determine how smooth their movements are compared with those of others.

Teachers teach students skills, but peers may be more beneficial in enhancing children's attitudes and perceived capabilities (Kornhaber and Schroeder, 1975; Schunk and Hanson, 1985), especially among children who have experienced prior difficulties, anxiety or self-doubts about their learning capabilities. Although the typical practice in choosing peer models is to use students who master skills readily, this arrangement may not have a strong impact on self-efficacy. To the extent that perceived similarity in competence is important , low achievers who have mastered skills may be excellent models.

Teachers also might want to consider using coping and multiple models, but there are qualifications. Coping models might be best with students who find tasks anxiety provoking or who typically experience difficulties learning new material. Among normal learners, observing a mastery model might better enhance perceived capabilities. Observation of a peer having difficulty learning could convey high task difficulty, which will not raise children's beliefs about performing well. Similarly, remedial students who observe many normal learners perform well may not feel very efficacious despite the multiple models. Multiple models may be most beneficial when children perceive themselves as similar to the models in the ability (for example, mathematical, reading) underlying performance of the skill.

Effort Feedback

Linking students' achievement outcomes with effort can promote effort attributions, persistence, capability self-perceptions and skills. One explanation for these results is as follows. As students work at a task, they begin to develop self-efficacy for performing well. Telling them that effort is responsible for their successes conveys that they are developing skills and that they can continue to perform well with hard work. The perception of skill improvement can raise self-efficacy and lead to greater skill development. Conversely, linking students' difficulties with low effort can lead to enhanced motivation assuming that students view the effort feedback as credible; that is, they believe that increased effort will produce better results.

A recommendation that teachers link students' successes and failures with effort fits well with teaching practice. Student effort is valued by teachers, and books on teaching recommend that teachers encourage student effort (Good and Brophy, 1984). But effort feedback for the same task over an extended period is not necessarily desirable. Even low-achieving students become more skillful as they work at a task over time. Students actually might feel less efficacious if they continually received effort feedback because they might wonder why they always have to work hard to succeed. They might doubt that they can sustain the level of effort necessary to succeed.

What effort feedback means to students stems largely from interactions with teachers. Teachers often combine effort with praise in hopes of encouraging students to persevere at tasks (for example, 'That's good. You're really working hard'). When students believe that a task is easy, praise combined with effort signals low ability. Effort feedback over an extended period can imply lower ability if students believe that their skills have improved. Although effort feedback may be credible to students in the early phases of skill development, teachers may want to switch to ability feedback (for example, 'You're good at this') as students' skills improve.

Goal Setting

Teachers continually set goals for themselves and their students in the form of lessons to be taught and skills to be learned. Much goal setting occurs in classrooms; however, little of it is student initiated. Goals will not promote achievement if students are not committed to attaining them. One potential benefit of self-set goals is that they may foster goal commitment. A second benefit is that students may learn to appraise their capabilities more accurately. Accuracy of self-appraisal is important, because misjudgments in either direction can have negative consequences. Students who overestimate their capabilities are apt to become demoralized through repeated task failures, whereas those who underestimate what they can do may shun challenging tasks and thereby preclude opportunities for skill development. Although students may require training on how to set challenging but attainable goals, goal setting can have short- and long-term benefits.

Let me give a research example of a goal-setting procedure that can be implemented in classrooms. Gaa (1973) assigned first and second graders to one of three conditions: conferences with goal setting, conferences without goal setting, no conferences. All children received the same in-class reading instruction. Goal-setting conference children met with the experimenter once a week for four weeks; children received a list of reading skills and selected those that they would attempt to master the following week. They also received feedback on their previous week's goal accomplishments. Children who participated in conferences without setting goals met with the experimenter for the same amount of time but received only general information about material covered previously and what would be covered the following week. During the last week of training, all subjects set performance goals to assess the effects of treatments on the goal-setting process.

Goal setting exerted motivational and informational effects. Compared with children in the other two groups, children who participated in goal-setting conferences attained a higher level of reading achievement. During the last week of training, they also set fewer goals and showed a smaller discrepancy between goals set and mastered. In short, participation in goal setting increased accuracy of perceived capabilities.

Conclusions

Although our understanding of self-efficacy and motivated learning in the classroom is in no sense complete, the research discussed in this chapter is beginning to shed light on the ways in which students' approaches to, and performances in, the classroom are affected by their beliefs about their efficacy. Moreover, there is clear evidence suggesting that students' beliefs about their competencies are themselves susceptible to influence by teachers.

There are various sources of information relevant to the topics in this article. College courses in motivation, learning theories, and child development routinely cover many of these topics. Inservice programmes on motivation and teaching strategies would be beneficial to teachers wanting to improve their classroom skills. More basically, I think that when teachers plan lessons they need to consider how their activities and those of the students might affect students' beliefs about their capabilities to learn. Most students want to do well in school. Teachers who strive to teach skills and enhance students' beliefs in their capabilities will enhance motivated learning in their classroom.

Notes

1 This article was prepared while the author was supported by grants from the Spencer Foundation and the National Science Foundation (BNS-8509545). Requests for reprints should be sent to Dale H. Schunk, School of Education, Peabody Hall 037A, University of North Carolina, Chapel Hill, NC 27514.

2 A proctor is a teacher drawn from outside of the school.

References

AMES, C. (1984) 'Competitive, cooperative, and individualistic goal structures: A cognitive-motivational analysis', in AMES, R. and AMES, C. (Eds) *Research on Motivation in Education: Student Motivation*, (Vol. 1, pp. 177–207) Orlando, FL, Academic Press.

ANDREWS, G.R. and DEBUS, R.L. (1978) 'Persistence and the causal perception of failure: Modifying cognitive attributions', *Journal of Educational Psychology*, 70, pp. 154–66.

BAKER, L. and BROWN, A.L. (1984) 'Metacognitive skills and reading', in PEARSON, P.D. (Ed.) *Handbook of Reading Research* (pp. 353–94), New York, Longman.

BANDURA, A. (1982) 'Self-efficacy mechanism in human agency', *American Psychologist*, 37, pp. 122–47.

BANDURA, A. (1986) *Social Foundations of Thought and Action: A Social Cognitive Theory*, Englewood Cliffs, NJ, Prentice-Hall.

BANDURA, A. and SCHUNK, D.H. (1981) 'Cultivating competence, self-efficacy, and intrinsic interest through proximal self-motivation', *Journal of Personality and Social Psychology*, 41, pp. 586–98.

BERGER, S.M. (1977) 'Social comparison, modeling, and perseverance', in SULS, J.M. and MILLER, R.L. (Eds) *Social Comparison Processes: Theoretical and Empirical Perspectives* (pp. 209–34), Washington, D.C., Hemisphere.

BORKOWSKI, J.G. and CAVANAUGH, J.C. (1979) 'Maintenance and generalization of skills and strategies by the retarded', in ELLIS, N.R. (Ed.) *Handbook of Mental Deficiency, Psychological Theory and Research* (2nd ed., pp. 569–617), Hillsdale, N.J., Erlbaum.

BROPHY, J. (1983) 'Conceptualizing student motivation,' *Educational Psychologist*, 18, pp. 200–15.

BROWN, A.L., PALINCSAR, A.S. and ARMBRUSTER, B.B. (1984) 'Instructing comprehension-fostering activities in interactive learning situations', in MANDL, H., STEIN, N.L. and TRABASSO, T. (Eds) *Learning and Comprehension of Text* (pp. 255–86), Hillsdale, NJ, Erlbaum.

CHAPIN, M. and DYCK, D.G. (1976) 'Persistence in children's reading behavior as a function of N length and attribution retraining', *Journal of Abnormal Psychology*, 85, pp. 511–15.

COLLINS, J. (1982) 'Self-efficacy and ability in achievement behavior'. Paper presented at the meeting of the American Educational Research Association, New York, March.

CORNO, L. and MANDINACH, E.B. (1983) 'The role of cognitive engagement in classroom learning and motivation', *Educational Psychologist*, 18 pp. 88–108.

CRONBACH, L.J. and SNOW, R.E. (1977) *Aptitudes and Instructional Methods*, New York, Irvington.

DWECK, C.S. (1975) 'The role of expectations and attributions in the alleviation of learned helplessness', *Journal of Personality and Social Psychology*, 31 pp. 674–85.

FELDMAN, R.S., DEVIN-SHEEHAN, L. and ALLEN, V.L. (1976) 'Children tutoring children: A critical review of research', in ALLEN, V.L. (Ed.) *Children as Teachers: Theory and Research on Tutoring* (pp. 235–52), New York, Academic Press.

FRIEZE, I.H. (1980) 'Beliefs about success and failure in the classroom', in MCMILLAN, J.H. (Ed.), *The Social Psychology of School Learning* (pp. 39–78), New York, Academic Press.

GAA, J.P. (1973) 'Effects of individual goal-setting conferences on achievement, attitudes, and goal-setting behavior', *Journal of Experimental Education*, 42, pp. 22–8.

GOOD, T.L. and BROPHY, J.E. (1984) *Looking in Classrooms* (3rd ed.), New York, Harper and Row.

HALLAHAN, D.P., KNEEDLER, R.D. and LLOYD, J.W. (1983) 'Cognitive behavior modification techniques for learning disabled children: Self-instruction and self-monitoring', in MCKINNEY, J.D. and FEAGANS, L. (Eds) *Current Topics in Learning Disabilities* (pp. 207–44), Norwood, N.J., Ablex.

HARARI, O. and COVINGTON, M.V. (1981) 'Reactions to achievement behavior from a teacher and student perspective: A developmental analysis', *American Educational Research Journal*, 18, pp. 15–28.

KAZDIN, A.E. (1978) 'Covert modeling: The therapeutic application of imagined rehearsal', in SINGER, J.L. and POPE, K.S. (Eds) *The Power of Human Imagination: New Methods in Psychotherapy* (pp. 255–78), New York, Plenum Press.

KORNHABER, R.C. and SCHROEDER, H.E. (1975) 'Importance of model similarity on extinction of avoidance behavior in children', *Journal of Consulting and Clinical Psychology*, 43, pp. 601–7.

LEPPER, M.R. (1983) 'Extrinsic reward and intrinsic motivation: Implications for the classroom', in LEVINE, J.M. and WANG, M.C. (Eds) *Teacher and Student Perceptions: Implications for Learning* (pp. 281–317), Hillsdale, N.J., Erlbaum.

LEVINE, J.M. (1983) 'Social comparison and education', in LEVINE, J.M. and WANG, M.C. (Eds) *Teacher and Student Perceptions: Implications for Learning* (pp. 29–55), Hillsdale, N.J., Erlbaum.

LICHT, B.G. and KISTNER, J.A. (1986) 'Motivational problems of learning-disabled children: Individual differences and their implications for treatment', in TORGESEN, J.K. and WONG, B.W.L. (Eds) *Psychological and Educational Perspectives on Learning Disabilities* (pp. 225–55), Orlando, F.L., Academic Press.

LOCKE, E.A., SHAW, K.N., SAARI, L.M. and LATHAM, G.P. (1981) 'Goal setting and task performance: 1969–1980', *Psychological Bulletin*, 90, pp. 125–52.

MARX, R.W. (1983) 'Student perception in classrooms', *Educational Psychologist*, 18, pp. 145–64.

MCCOMBS, B.L. (1984) 'Processes and skills underlying continuing intrinsic motivation to learn: Toward a definition of motivational skills training interventions', *Educational Psychologist*, 19, pp. 199–218.

MEDWAY, F.J. and VENINO, G.R. (1982) 'The effects of effort feedback and performance patterns on children's attributions and task persistence', *Contemporary Educational Psychology*, 7, pp. 26–34.

MEICHENBAUM, D. (1971) 'Examination of model characteristics in reducing avoidance behavior', *Journal of Personality and Social Psychology*, 17, pp. 298–307.

MILLER, R.L., BRICKMAN, P. and BOLEN, D. (1975) 'Attribution versus persuasion as a means for modifying behavior', *Journal of Personality and Social Psychology*, 31, pp. 430–41.

NICHOLLS, J.G. (1978) 'The development of the concepts of effort and ability, perception of academic attainment, and the understanding that difficult tasks require more ability', *Child Development*, 49, pp. 800–14.

NICHOLLS, J.G. (1983) 'Conceptions of ability and achievement motivation: A theory and its implications for education', in PARIS, S.G., OLSON, G.M. and STEVENSON, H.W. (Eds) *Learning and Motivation in the Classroom* (pp. 211–37), Hillsdale, N.J., Erlbaum.

NICHOLLS, J.G. (1984) 'Achievement motivation: Conceptions of ability, subjective experience, task choice, and performance', *Psychological Review*, 91, pp. 328–46.

ROSENTHAL, T.L. and BANDURA, A. (1978) 'Psychological modeling: Theory and practice', in GARFIELD, S.L. and BERGIN, A.E. (Eds) *Handbook of Psychotherapy and Behavior Change: An Empirical Analysis* (2nd ed., pp. 621–58), New York, Wiley.

ROSENTHAL, T.L. and ZIMMERMAN, B.J. (1978) *Social Learning and Cognition*, New York, Academic Press.

ROTTER, J.B. (1966) 'Generalized expectancies for internal versus external control of reinforcement', *Psychological Monographs*, 80 (Whole No. 609).

SALOMON, G. (1984) 'Television is "easy" and print is "tough": The differential investment of mental effort in learning as a function of perceptions and attributions', *Journal of Educational Psychology*, 76, pp. 647–58.

SCHUNK, D.H. (1981) 'Modeling and attributional effects on children's achievement: A self-efficacy analysis', *Journal of Educational Psychology*, 73, pp. 93–105.

SCHUNK, D.H. (1982) 'Effects of effort attributional feedback on children's perceived self-efficacy and achievement', *Journal of Educational Psychology*, 74, pp. 548–56.

SCHUNK, D.H. (1983a) 'Ability versus effort attributional feedback: Differential effects on self-efficacy and achievement', *Journal of Educational Psychology*, 75, pp. 848–56.

SCHUNK, D.H. (1983b) 'Goal difficulty and attainment information: Effects on children's achievement behaviors', *Human Learning*, 2, pp. 107–17.

SCHUNK, D.H. (1983c) 'Progress self-monitoring: Effects on children's self-efficacy and achievement', *Journal of Experimental Education*, 51, pp. 89–93.

SCHUNK, D.H. (1983d) 'Reward contingencies and the development of children's skills and self-efficacy', *Journal of Educational Psychology*, 75, pp. 511–18.

SCHUNK, D.H. (1984) 'Sequential attributional feedback and children's achievement behaviors', *Journal of Educational Psychology*, 76, pp. 1159–69.

SCHUNK, D.H. (1985a) 'Participation in goal setting: Effects on self-efficacy and skills of learning disabled children', *Journal of Special Education*, 19, pp. 307–17.

SCHUNK, D.H. (1985b) 'Self-efficacy and classroom learning', *Psychology in the Schools*, 22, pp. 208–23.

SCHUNK, D.H. and COX, P.D. (1986) 'Strategy training and attributional feedback with learning disabled students', *Journal of Educational Psychology*, 78, pp. 201–9.

SCHUNK, D.H. and HANSON, A.R. (1985) 'Peer models: Influence on children's self-efficacy and achievement', *Journal of Educational Psychology*, 77, pp. 313–22.

SCHUNK, D.H. and RICE, J.M. (1984) 'Strategy self-verbalization during remedial listening comprehension instruction', *Journal of Experimental Education*, 53, pp. 49–54.

SCHUNK, D.H. and RICE, J.M. (1985) 'Verbalization of comprehension strategies: Effects on children's achievement outcomes', *Human Learning*, 4, pp. 1–10.

SCHUNK, D.H., HANSON, A.R. and COX, P.D. (1986) 'Peer models: Effects on children's achievement behaviors'. Unpublished manuscript, University of North Carolina.

THELEN, M.H., FRY, R.A., FEHRENBACH, P.A. and FRAUTSCHI, N.M. (1979) 'Therapeutic videotape and film modeling: A review', *Psychological Bulletin*, 86, pp. 701–20.

THOMAS, J.W. (1980) 'Agency and achievement: Self-management and self-regard', *Review of Educational Research*, 50, pp. 213–40.

WEINER, B. (1974) 'An attributional interpretation of expectancy-value theory', in WEINER, B. (Ed.) *Congitive Views of Human Motivation* (pp. 51–69), New York, Academic Press.

WEINER, B. (1979) 'A theory of motivation for some classroom experiences', *Journal of Educational Psychology*, 71, pp. 3–25.

WEINER, B., GRAHAM, S., TAYLOR, S.E. and MEYER, W. (1983) 'Social cognition in the classroom', *Educational Psychologist*, 18, pp. 109–24.

WINNE, P.H. (1985) 'Cognitive processing in the classroom', in HUSEN, T., and POSTLETHWAITE, T.N. (Eds) *The International Encyclopedia of Education* (Vol. 2, pp. 795–808), Oxford, England, Pergamon Press.

ZIMMERMAN, B.J. (1977) 'Modeling', in HOM, H. and ROBINSON, P. (Eds) *Psychological Processes in Children's Early Education* (pp. 37–70), New York, Academic Press.

Contexts for Independent Learning★

Ted Glynn
University of Otago

One major world view that dominates the field of developmental psychology is the organismic world view. This world view depicts individuals, including children, as active agents who know the world in terms of their own operations upon it. Individuals are seen as being in control of their own learning. This control is exercised by individuals initiating and maintaining their own learning opportunities within a responsive social context.

The responsive social context is increasingly seen by developmental psychologists (Bronfenbrenner, 1979; Wood, 1982) as of fundamental importance for the acquisition of intellectual skills. It is within responsive social contexts that individuals acquire not only specific skills but also generic knowledge about how to learn. It is this generic knowledge that allows individuals a measure of control over, and hence independence in, these social contexts.

Educational policy statements, school prospectuses and, more recently, the 'core curriculum', abound with aims and objectives to do with achieving individual autonomy and independence as a learner. Yet there is growing evidence that in many contemporary classrooms at primary, secondary and tertiary levels, we may be providing precisely the wrong contexts for students to become autonomous and independent learners. Too many classroom learning environments simply do not qualify as responsive social contexts. Individual learners have minimal control over learning interactions and hence are excessively dependent on external control by teachers.

Theoretical explanations for differences between unskilled and skilled performance are being sought increasingly in terms of characteristics of the specific contexts in which performance occurs and less in terms of qualitative differences in global capacities or in thinking processes between

★ Inaugural Lecture, University of Otago, 12 September 1984. This chapter was published in *Educational Psychology*, (1985), 5, 1, pp. 5–15

individuals (Wood, 1982). For example, differences in complexity of oral language between three-year-old children might be explained by differences in the amount and quality of language exchange with caregivers. They might also be explained by differences in caregiver skills in interpreting and responding to needs signalled by an individual child's use of language in a particular context.

If we are genuinely concerned about aims of autonomy and independence in learning, then we need to discover and analyze those characteristics of responsive environments which support and promote independent learning. On the basis of existing research it is possible to specify four such characteristics of responsive learning contexts.

Initiations by the Learner

The first characteristic of a responsive learning context is that it should promote initiations by the learner. Whether the context is that of infants learning to speak, children learning to handle a paintbrush, adolescents learning social skills or adults learning creative writing, if these learners are to take control of their learning, they must be able to initiate interaction with materials or people.

However, many learning environments are arranged so that the learner can only respond to questions or stimuli under the control of someone else. For example, a classroom teacher may ask a child to draw a picture of her house and then ask a series of direct questions to elicit specific information, thereby retaining total control of the interaction. A more responsive teacher might set up the classroom with a range of engaging materials, wait until a child has selected an object or activity and then respond to that initiation, perhaps by means of a procedure known as Incidental Teaching.

Hart and Risley (1968, 1974, 1975, 1980) have systematically studied this procedure, especially in the context of young children's learning of language. Essentials of the procedure are first the teacher or staff member immediately selects an appropriate response to the child's initiation, be it supplying information to a question, handing over an object or item of material or providing access to a required activity or new task. Next, the provision of the requested item, information or activity, is made contingent on the child engaging in a further brief language exchange on the topic initiated. The child not only controls the initiation, but also identifies for the adult the most powerful reinforcer with which to respond at that moment. Hart and Risley (1980) demonstrated that disadvantaged children exposed to Incidental Teaching of language in a day care environment, improved in frequency of language use and elaboration of language to levels approaching those of a middle-class control group. The procedure has also been employed in modified form for teaching receptive language to an autistic youth (McGee *et al.*, 1983), and for teaching polite language as part of a programme for children with behaviour problems (Glynn *et al.*, 1984).

Incidental Teaching is a powerful procedure, because it results not only in children obtaining specific information to questions which are highly salient to them at a particular time, but also, because children learn the general strategy of engaging and maintaining adult attention. Further, in the case of language learning, new words learned through Incidental Teaching are readily generalizable beyond the original context. This is because the future use of those words can be occasioned by several different factors, such as the child's desire for the same or similar information or access to the same or similar materials in new contexts, even with different adults. In contrast, language learned from direct responses occasioned by teacher-initiated formal instruction is far less likely to be generalized to new contexts. This is particularly true of those where the specific adult is no longer present.

In tightly controlled learning contexts, as provided by many 'efficient' teachers, there may be little opportunity for child initiation and so little chance for Incidental Teaching. Almost all teacher behaviour in such contexts consists of giving instructions, presenting materials, monitoring that everyone is following instructions and performing the set task and in providing corrective feedback (usually contingent on accuracy). Charles, Glynn and McNaughton (1984) compared the use of Incidental Teaching and Talking Up, an adult-initiated procedure designed to prompt child language through direct questions and comments from caregivers. The Talking Up procedure was found to be counter-productive. Increased use of Talking Up resulted in a reduction in child-initiated language. This was partly because caregiver time was diverted from responding to child initiations and partly because children had fewer opportunities to initiate since they were busy answering questions.

If many teachers did not see themselves as needing to be so constantly in control, things might be different. Several studies of children's oral reading in a one-to-one context established that if teachers or parents will delay by only a few seconds their corrective responses to children's errors, children will initiate their own error correction strategies (McNaughton and Glynn, 1981; Singh and Singh, 1984[1]). Self-correction of errors is a strong predictor of children becoming independent readers (Clay, 1979) since it provides evidence that children have perceived a mismatch between what they have said and the context of the words read.

Similarly, studies of language use by retarded children demonstrate that delay of prompting by teachers resulted in increased language initiations by children (Halle, Marshall and Spradlin, 1979; Halle, Baer and Spradlin, 1981). Baker *et al.* (1983) report a study of pre-schoolers' language at mealtimes. In this study when caregivers sat with children, interacted with them and allowed self-service of food, children's total language as well as their self-initiated language was much higher than when caregivers supervised the meal from a distance and pre-served the children's food. VanBiervliet, Spangler and Marschall (1981) showed that language interaction at mealtimes among retarded males was greater when a family-style rather than an institutional-style meal procedure was adopted. Family-style seating and serving provided more opportunities for talking about food as well as less dependence upon staff for assistance.

These various studies suggest that a key factor in promoting child initiations is for adults to relinquish direct control over child behaviour. This will allow opportunities both for children to initiate and for adults to be able to respond. These studies suggest that if adults were to shift from an essentially supervisory/custodial role to a more responsive/interactive one, children will utilize available opportunities to initiate interactions. The important qualification is of course that the learning context should contain a variety of engaging materials, to provide worthwhile content and focus for these initiations.

Activities Shared Between Less Skilled and More Skilled Performers

A second characteristic of a responsive learning context is shared activity. More specifically, a responsive learning context should provide opportunity for the learner to engage in a shared activity with a more skilled performer, with whom there is a positive social relationship. This of course is part of Bronfenbrenner's specification of a 'primary developmental context' in which children acquire important intellectual and social skills (Bronfenbrenner, 1979). This concept of shared activity is interesting. It implies that particular learning tasks be functional for both the less skilled and the more skilled performer. Thus a parent teaching a child to speak is also acquiring skills. The parent is learning to interpret tentative and imprecise child utterances in terms of the specific contexts in which they occur and in terms of detailed knowledge of that individual child. Growth in the child's skill at using language is paralleled by growth in the parent's skill in interpreting and responding to child language. It is the parent's precise and unique knowledge of the individual that allows her to respond with a new language challenge which is of just the right content focus and level of complexity for the child. The conversational task is truly a shared one and is motivating and functional to both parties. Mutual improvement in skill is likely to enhance still further the positive relationship between parent and child.

An interesting example of shared activity in a more formal educational context is in the 'paired reading' technique devised by Morgan and Lyon (1979). This procedure begins with the child and parent simultaneously reading from a familiar text, selected by the child. When the child feels ready to read independently he or she can knock on the table to signal that the adult should stop reading. The adult remains silent until the child makes an error, whereupon simultaneous reading is resumed. This is a procedure where the pace and degree of tutor assistance provided in a learning session is directly under the control of the learner.

An interesting thing about classroom lessons in basic subjects is that children seldom get the opportunity to share an academic task with a more skilled performer. It is extremely rare for children at school to see adults enjoying doing expressive writing, working at a maths problem or doing recreational reading. Paradoxically they may be more likely to see these at home. At school, teacher time is frequently spent entirely in issuing instructions, presenting set tasks, monitoring on-task behaviour and giving evaluative feedback on children's performance. One recent study introduced into a programme of recreational reading a component where the teacher concurrently modelled silent reading for enjoyment (Pluck *et al.*, 1984). Children's observed engagement with books was markedly higher when the teacher concurrently modelled reading than when she did not. The effect was even stronger among the poorer readers in the class. By sharing the task with the children, this teacher provided not only an effective model of skilled performance but also avoided engaging in more controlling or directive behaviours such as monitoring and commenting on children's performance.

Fortunately, the sharing of tasks between less skilled and more skilled performers does occur in some tertiary education settings. Often university staff and senior students work together on a specific research question, which is highly motivating and functional to both parties. As shared work is accomplished, positive interpersonal relationships are enhanced and the learning interaction acquires a distinctly social characteristic. A responsive learning context develops. As was the case with the parent of the child learning to speak, some university staff working with senior students have profitably adopted a responsive/interacting role rather than more traditional controlling/supervisory role towards students doing research. This approach to sharing research tasks between less skilled and more skilled performers is captured very clearly in the 'Colleague Model' of the Department of Human Development of the University of Kansas[2]. The approach is also embodied very strongly in the programme of study undertaken by students at Te Wananga o Raukawa, a new tertiary institution (Raukawa Trustees, 1984). Major academic tasks for students include researching whakapapa (genealogies), land transactions, health and literature for the local communities by interviewing kaumatua (elders) in each community. Students must undertake these discussions in Maori. By sharing these tasks, which are clearly functional for both parties, kaumatua and students stand to gain in knowledge and information.

Reciprocity and Mutual Influence

A third characteristic of a responsive learning context is reciprocity or mutual influence. Each party in the interaction not only shares the learning task but also modifies the behaviour of the other. Reciprocity and mutual influence are beautifully illustrated in Roger Hall's Multiple Choice[3]. Roberto and Paul, adolescents who have dropped out of school, exchange roles as the less skilled and the more skilled performer. Over time, and in the context of a growing positive relationship, Roberto teaches Paul to repair cars and Paul teaches Roberto to read. Paul's relationship with his mother also deepens as they come to exchange roles, so that in some contexts (such as managing accounts) Paul becomes the more skilled performer.

Reciprocity and mutual influence are well documented in research on peer tutoring. Limbrick, McNaughton and Glynn (1985) employed low-achieving, older readers to tutor low-achieving, younger readers. Over time there were substantial gains in reading accuracy and in reading comprehension for both tutees and tutors. There was also anecdotal evidence of developing positive interaction on the playground between tutees and tutors. Although exact details of the learning interaction were not recorded, it is thought that tutors' behaviour was modified in response to tutee gains in skill and not just in response to programme requirements.

Dineen, Clark and Risley (1977) introduced a peer tutoring programme for spelling. Children served both as tutors and tutees on different lists of words. Learning gains were just as impressive on lists children taught to someone else as on lists they learned themselves as tutees. The task was highly motivating since it allowed children to reciprocate by exchanging roles as teacher and learner. This procedure has been replicated with foreign language vocabulary learning in a New Zealand secondary school[4]. Entirely similar results were obtained in this study. Children gained as much on lists taught to someone else as on lists they learned themselves. They also requested additional sessions when the study was complete.

Sanders and Glynn (1977) conducted a study in which peer managers were employed to monitor on-task behaviour of target children in a junior classroom. This study reported changes not only in the appropriate behaviour of target children but also unprogrammed changes in the managers' provoking and reacting to inappropriate behaviour in the target children. In addition, target subjects who had been paired with peer managers for whom they had expressed low preference increased their preference for and liking of those peers by the end of the study.

Within a research project in which parents were trained to provide remedial reading tutoring for their own children, anecdotal evidence of concurrent changes in the social relationship between parent and child is also reported (McNaughton, Glynn and Robinson, 1982). The particular tutoring procedures employed stressed the need for parents to delay their response to errors, to respond with the minimal prompt required to cue children to correct their own errors and to reinforce children's self-corrections or corrections which followed the provision of prompts. As parents successfully implemented these procedures, children's reading became increasingly accurate and independent of parent control. These claims are substantiated by data which showed marked gains in children's oral reading accuracy and level, along with parents' increased use of delay in responding to errors and parents' decreased supplying of correct words. In the project, as children began to make progress in reading after the parent tutoring programme was in place, parents reported feeling more positive towards their children and enjoyed spending more time with them. Previously, interaction with their children around academic learning tasks had been aversive or even painful.

Taken together these studies offer some suggestive but post hoc evidence for increased positive social outcomes arising from the experience of reciprocity and mutual influence around shared learning tasks. In these studies the degree of control over the less skilled party by the more skilled party has been something well short of total, because of the operation of reciprocity and mutual influence. In contrast, it is important to note that in contexts where reciprocity and mutual influence are minimized the interaction may be counter-productive. The less skilled performer may be maintained in a state of 'instructional dependence' (McNaughton, 1981). Some traditional remedial teaching strategies can be seen in this light. There is a reciprocal effect of reinforcing the teacher for providing more and more help, thus assuming even greater control over the learning interaction. This can be seen in extreme form when a child encounters a new and unknown world while reading to a remedial reading tutor. Instead of attempting to solve that word, from the resources within the reading text, the child looks away from the text, into the tutor's eyes and cues the tutor to supply the correct answer.

Given this concern about instructional dependence in tightly controlled contexts, it would appear worthwhile to enhance reciprocity and mutual influence within classroom learning contexts. Where this can be achieved through the use of peer tutoring around shared learning tasks, there might well be a reduction in the degree of teacher control over learning and an opportunity for independent initiations to occur. Also there might well be more teacher time for responding to these initiations.

Amount and Type of Feedback

A fourth characteristic of a responsive learning context is the amount and type of feedback provided for learners' initiations. Descriptive studies of teacher verbal response to child behaviour in New Zealand and United

States classrooms suggest that the ratio of teacher response to appropriate versus inappropriate response to child behaviour is of the order 1:3 (Thomas *et al.*, 1978). Clearly this ratio is counter-productive, if appropriate behaviour is expected. There is also a group of studies which demonstrate the advantage of reinforcing academic task completion rather than 'pre-requisite' attending behaviours (Marholin and Steinmann, 1977; Henderson, 1976). It is argued that reinforcement for task completion rather than for attention to task has the advantage of avoiding unnecessary dependence on task-irrelevant social reinforcement from the teacher. This may be a form of behaviour control that interferes with independent learning.

Underachievement in written tasks in some secondary schools may be in part a function of feedback which is excessively delayed and infrequent. Scriven and Glynn (1983) found that merely increasing the consistency and frequency of feedback to fourth formers on the rate and accuracy of their task completion yielded dramatic gains in work completed and minor gains in accuracy (which was already quite high). Interestingly, there were coincidental changes over time in teacher behaviour with this class. As students completed more and more work, the teacher made fewer and fewer controlling comments. These changes support the view that with a higher rate of task completion, student performance had become less dependent on teacher control.

Elsewhere it has been argued that teachers may be responding to accuracy in children's academic work at the expense of fluency (Glynn, 1982). This may be particularly true of written expression. In providing excessive feedback on accuracy of letter formation, spelling, syntax, many teachers may have been extinguishing fluency. Certainly such feedback offers the child minimal opportunity for reciprocity and mutual influence. Vargas (1978) argued that expressive writing should allow the beginning writer to exert some control over the reader. For young children she recommended a procedure in which a responsive reader performs tasks or actions specified by the writer. The beginning writer can thus 'see' the functional outcome of writing in terms of its observed effects. For example, one young writer might have enjoyed telling the reader to go and jump off a chair. With older children such overt control over the reader may not be needed. Instead, the reader might respond in writing. But the response would not take the form of corrective feedback. Rather, it would take the form of a personal comment or reaction to the content of what is written. In this way, as in an extended oral language exchange, the writing task becomes a shared reciprocal one which allows the writer to obtain some control over the responsive reader.

Jerram[5] has carried out a study in which a teacher of eight year-olds established her writing programme so that only content feedback, and no corrective feedback, was provided for the class. This teacher wrote a personal response to each child's writing after every session. Under conditions of content feedback, children markedly increased their rate of writing. More importantly, writing produced under conditions of content feedback was rated as more interesting and imaginative by separate groups of parents, peers and educators. During writing time in this class, children were free to write, or not, as they wished. The teacher had little need to control these children during writing, since they came to regard writing as a very positive and enjoyable experience. Incidentally, although there was no corrective feedback from the teacher, children's spelling of words at their current level remained highly accurate over time. In addition, children introduced more and more difficult words which were beyond their initial spelling list.

Under the heading of responsive feedback, recent exploratory studies on the use of microcomputers as learning tools rather than as teaching machines are important. Recent papers by Boswell[6], Mackrell[7], Nolan[8] and Ryba[9] have made quite an exciting case for the microcomputer providing young learners and handicapped learners with a measure of real control over their learning, by putting them in a context which allows them to initiate interactions, to experience reciprocation and mutual influence and to escape total instructional control by teachers. These authors provide educational psychology with an interesting challenge to generate data on the characteristics of both problem-solving and interpersonal processes which result when, for example, two or more learners interact at the keyboard. Some writers view the microcomputer as a radical tool for deschooling society. For example, Linowes[10] notes that demands for radical changes in learning made possible by microcomputer are being initiated not by teachers or educational institutions but by the computer industry, students and parents. The rapidly growing incidence of homes with computers certainly greatly extends the potential of the home context rather than the school context as a setting for the development of intellectual skills. We may be approaching an interesting situation in which, for many children, the learning of important numeracy and literacy skills might be better accomplished at home, while the learning of social skills might be better accomplished at school. Again this is an important theme confronting Paul and his mother in Multiple Choice.

If we value educational goals such as autonomy and independence in the learner, we need to establish contexts in which learners can have access to learning tasks free from excessive control by teachers or instructors. This in itself presents the task of engineering substantial behaviour change on the part of teachers and instructors.

Allowing Learners to Take Control

Another form of feedback from a responsive learning context is feedback on a special type of initiation by the learner, namely formulating plans to change one's own behaviour. This type of feedback derives from the

Correspondence Training paradigm of Risley (1977). Applied more widely, this paradigm suggests an important strategy for teaching people ways of changing their own behaviour. For example, individuals may make statements about changing their behaviour before a supportive and responsive audience (friends, peers or colleagues). Continued regular contact with members of this audience provides opportunities for feedback about one's intended behaviour change and actual behaviour change. However, the critical feature was stating an intention or plan in the first place, before a responsive audience. In the context of residential staff training, for example, one study reported that while staff had learned to implement correctly several child behaviour management procedures in a training context, they were not applying these procedures outside of the training context (Glynn *et al.*, 1984). Next a component was introduced in which staff identified to an audience specific procedures they would practise at specific times when performance feedback would be available. Under this condition staff increased their use of targeted procedures well above the levels achieved as a result of traditional training components (such as modelling and feedback alone). The gains in implementation were seen at least in part as attributable to the advance planning procedure putting staff members more clearly in control of their own learning. The feedback procedure also became more of a reciprocal exchange between staff and trainer than it had been when feedback was contingent on whatever the trainer observed. A similar procedure in another study (Sanders and Glynn, 1981) resulted in better generalization of trained parenting procedures into new settings outside the home, where the initial training took place.

If we wish teachers and instructors to implement major changes in the way in which they devise and manage responsive social contexts for learning, we need to devise and manage a responsive social context in which they can do this. Our role as trainers would also need to be a responsive/interactive one, and not a custodial/supervisory one.

Conclusion

In summary, research reviewed identifies a number of specific teaching behaviours consistent with following an interacting/responsive role in a learning context. These behaviours include providing interesting materials to promote engagement by the learner; reducing and delaying direct teacher intervention to allow opportunities for learners to initiate; maximizing opportunities for shared activity between skilled and unskilled learners; responding to learner initiations so as to encourage reciprocity and mutual influence; providing regular responsive feedback only on form and accuracy; and making explicit plans to modify one's own teaching behaviour before a supportive audience.

Performing all of these behaviours would shift teachers a long way from the model of tight instructional control displayed in many educational settings. Teachers displaying these behaviours would be providing 'loose' training (Stokes and Baer, 1977) in that they relinquish direct control over the precise timing and sequence or specific context of all the learning interactions. But in handing over much greater control to the learner they would be providing for strong generalization of what is learned into new contexts, particularly to contexts where the learner must perform independently of teacher control.

In educational terms, teachers would be shifting away from reliance on tightly packaged and presented skills training programmes and towards something like the earlier child-centred 'developmental' lesson. This shift would require a great deal more, not less, professional competence on the part of teachers. The challenge for educational psychologists is to produce research designs and to generate hard data which demonstrates that such child-centred, or rather child-controlled, learning contexts result in generalizable gains in literacy skills and social skills. The next challenge will be to convince teachers and instructors that the more they relinquish control, the more their learners will utilize opportunities for independent learning.

Notes

1 SINGH, N.N. and SINGH, J. (1984) 'A behavioural remediation package for oral reading: Effects on error rate and comprehension', paper presented at New Zealand Psychological Society Annual Conference, Massey University, Palmerston North, New Zealand.
2 HOROWITZ, F.D. (1977) 'A graduate training program: Junior colleagues in developmental and child psychology', unpublished paper, Department of Human Development, University of Kansas.
3 HALL, R.V. (1983) 'Multiple choice', unpublished manuscript, Department of English, University of Otago.
4 MIDDLEMISS, J. and GLYNN, T. (1983) 'Peer tutoring in foreign language vocabulary learning', unpublished term paper, Department of Education, University of Auckland.
5 JERRAM, H. (1984) 'Content feedback for children's expressive writing', MA thesis in Education, University of Auckland.
6 BOSWELL, C. (1983) 'Learning frontiers in the computer age', paper presented to New Zealand Educational Adiminstration Society, Learning in the Computer Age Exhibition, Wellington.
7 MACKRELL, T.F. (1984) 'Computers in education: Problems and issues with instructional design', paper presented at New Zealand Psychological Society Annual Conference, Massey University, Palmerston North, New Zealand.
8 NOLAN, C.P.J. (1984) 'The microcomputer as a learning system', paper presented at New Zealand Psychological Society Annual Conference, Massey University, Palmerston North, New Zealand.
9 RYBA, K.A. (1984) 'Video games and rehabilitation: Computer aided training of cognitive processing strategies', paper presented at New Zealand Psychological Society Annual Conference, Massey University, Palmerston North, New Zealand.
10 LINOWES, D.F. (1983) 'Computers and the learning environment: Tasks for

teachers, parents and industry', reprinted from Vital Speeches of the Day (City of News Publishing Co., American Library, United States Information Service, American Embassy, Wellington).

References

BAKER, M., FOLEY, M., GLYNN, T. and McNAUGHTON, S. (1983) 'The effect of adult proximity and serving style on pre-schoolers' language and eating behaviour', *Education of Psychology*, 3, pp. 137–48.

BRONFENBRENNER, U. (1979) 'Contexts of child rearing, problems and prospects', *American Psychologist*, 34, pp. 844–50.

CHARLES, H., GLYNN, T. and McNAUGHTON, S. (1984) 'Childcare workers' use of Talking Up and Incidental Teaching procedures under standard and self-management staff training packages', *Educational Psychology*, 4, pp. 233–48.

CLAY, M.M. (1979) *Reading: The Patterning of Complex Behaviour*, Auckland, Heinemann

DINEEN, J.P., CLARK, A.B. and RISLEY, T.R. (1977) 'Peer tutoring among elementary students: Educational benefits to the tutor', *Journal of Applied Behaviour Analysis*, 10, pp. 231–8.

GLYNN, T. (1982) 'Building an effective teaching environment', in WHELDALL, K. and RIDING, R. (Eds) *Psychological Aspects of Learning and Teaching*, London, Croom Helm.

GLYNN, T., CLARK, B., VAIGRO, W. and LAWLESS, S. (1984) 'A self-management strategy for increasing implementation of behavioural procedures by residential staff', *The Exceptional Child*, 31, pp. 19–24.

HALLE, J.W., BAER, D.M. and SPRADLIN, J.E. (1981) 'Teachers' generalized use of delay as stimulus control procedure to increase language use in handicapped children', *Journal of Applied Behaviour Analysis*, 14, pp. 389–409.

HALLE, J.W., MARSHALL, A.M. and SPRADLIN, J.E. (1979) 'Time delay: A technique to increase facilitate generalization in retarded children', *Journal of Applied Behaviour Analysis*, 12, pp. 431–9.

HART, B. and RISLEY, T. (1968) 'Establishing use of descriptive adjectives in the spontaneous speech of disadvantaged preschool children', *Journal of Applied Behaviour Analysis*, 1, pp. 109–20.

HART, B. and RISLEY, T. (1974) 'Using preschool materials to modify the language of disadvantaged children', *Journal of Applied Behaviour Analysis*, 7, pp. 243–56.

HART, B. and RISLEY, T.R. (1975) 'Incidental teaching of language in the preschool', *Journal of Applied Behaviour Analysis*, 8, pp. 411–20.

HART, B. and RISLEY, T.R. (1980) 'In vivo language intervention: Unanticipated general effects', *Journal of Applied Behaviour Analysis*, 13, pp. 407–32.

HENDERSON, M. (1976) 'Increasing appropriate classroom behaviour and academic performance by reinforcing correct work alone', *Psychology in Schools*, 12, pp. 195–200.

LIMBRICK, E., McNAUGHTON, S. and GLYNN, T. (1985) 'Reading gains for under-achieving tutors and tutees in a cross age peer tutoring programme', *Journal of Child Psychology and Psychiatry* (in press).

McGEE, G.G., KRANTZ, P.J. MASON, D. and McCLANNAHAN, L.E. (1983) 'A modified incidental-teaching procedure for autistic youth: Acquisition and generalization of receptive object labels', *Journal of Applied Behaviour Analysis*, 16, pp. 329–38.

McNAUGHTON, S.S. (1981) 'Low progress readers and teacher instructional behaviour during oral reading: The risk of maintaining instructional dependence', *The Exceptional Child*, 28, pp. 167–75.

McNaughton, S.S. and Glynn, T. (1981) 'Delayed versus immediate attention to oral reading errors: Effects on accuracy and self-correction', *Educational Psychology*, 1. pp. 57–65.

McNaughton, S., Glynn, T. and Robinson, V.M. (1982) *Parents as Remedial Reading Tutors: Issues for Home and School*, Wellington, New Zealand Council for Educational Research.

Marholin, D.I. and Steinmann, W.M. (1977) 'Stimulus control in the classroom as a function of the behaviour reinforced', *Journal of Applied Behaviour Analysis*, 10, pp. 465–78.

Morgan, R. and Lyon, E. (1979) '"Paired reading": A preliminary report on a technique for parental tuition of reading retarded children', *Journal of Child Psychology and Psychiatry*, 20, pp. 151–60.

Pluck, M., Ghafari, E., Glynn, T. and McNaughton, S. (1984) 'Teacher and parent modelling of recreational reading', *New Zealand Journal of Educational Studies*, 19, pp. 114–23.

Raukawa Trustees (1984) *Te Wananga o Raukawa Calendar*, Wellington, New Zealand.

Risley, T. (1977) 'The social context of self control', in Stuart, R.B. (Ed.) *Behavioural Self-management: Strategies, Techniques and Outcomes*, New York, Bruner Mazel.

Sanders, M.R. and Glynn, E.L. (1977) 'Functional analysis of a programme for training high and low preference peers to modify disruptive classroom behaviour', *Journal of Applied Behaviour Analysis*, 10, p. 503.

Sanders, M.R. and Glynn, T. (1981) 'Training parents in behavioural self-management: An analysis of generalization and maintenance', *Journal of Applied Behaviour Analysis*, 14, pp. 223–7.

Scriven, J. and Glynn, T. (1983) 'Performance feedback on written tasks for low-achieving secondary students', *New Zealand Journal of Educational Studies*, 18, pp. 134–45.

Stokes, T.F. and Baer, D.M. (1977) 'An implicit technology of generalization', *Journal of Applied Behaviour Analysis*, 10, pp. 349–67.

Thomas, J., Presland, I.V., Grant, D. and Glynn, E.L. (1978) 'Natural rates of teacher approval and disapproval in Grade 7 and 8 classrooms', *Journal of Applied Behaviour Analysis*, 11, pp. 91–4.

Vanbiervliet, A., Spangler, P.F. and Marshall, A.M. (1981) 'An ecobehavioural examination of a simple strategy for increasing language in residential facilities', *Journal of Applied Behaviour Analysis*, 14, 299–305.

Vargas, J. (1978) 'A behavioural approach to the teaching of composition', *Behaviour Analyst*, pp. 16–24, Spring.

Williams, J. and Williams, R. (Eds) (1973) *D.H. Lawrence on Education*, Harmondsworth, Penguin.

Wood, D.J. (1982) 'Models of childhood', in Chapman, A.J. and Jones, D.M. (Eds) *Models of Man*, Leicester, British Psychological Society.

Notes on Contributors

Cathy Carter Associate Professor, Division of Teaching and Teacher Education, College of Education, University of Arizona, USA.

Ron Dawson General Inspector for Special Needs, Staffordshire, UK.

Walter Doyle Professor, Division of Teaching and Teacher Education, College of Education, University of Arizona, USA.

P.S. Fry Professor of Educational Psychology, University of Calgary, Alberta, Canada.

Wendy S. Grolnick Human Motivation Program, Department of Psychology, University of Rochester, New York, USA.

Ted Glynn Professor of Education, University of Otago, Dunedin, New Zealand.

Nigel Hastings Principal Lecturer, Faculty of Social Science and Teaching Studies, Bulmershe College of Higher Education, Reading, UK.

Ramon Lewis Senior Lecturer, School of Education, La Trobe University, Victoria, Austalia.

Malcolm Lovegrove Reader, School of Education, La Trobe University, Victoria, Austalia.

Frank Merrett Honarary Research Fellow, Centre for Child Study, University of Birmingham, UK.

Colin G. Rogers Lecturer, Department of Educational Research, University of Lancaster, UK.

Richard M. Ryan	Associate Professor, Human Motivation Program, Department of Psychology, University of Rochester, New York, USA.
Dale H. Schunk	Associate Professor, School of Education, University of North Carolina at Chapel Hill, North Carolina, USA.
Josh Schwieso	Senior Lecturer, Faculty of Social Science and Teaching Studies, Bulmershe College of Higher Education, Reading, UK.
Keith Topping	Educational Psychologist, Kirklees Psychological Service, Huddersfield, UK.
S.A.M. Veenman	Lecturer, Institute of Education, Catholic University of Nijmegen, The Netherlands.
Kevin Wheldall	Director, Centre for Child Study, University of Birmingham, UK.

Index

Note: For citations and references, only the first-named author is indexed. Within a chapter no citations to authors' own works are indexed.

Index